FAITH AND VICTORY
Prayer Strategies and Decrees

Volume One
Updated & Revised

Written prayers for you to speak out loud!
Designed for breakthrough!

FAMILY - MARRIAGE - HOME - LAND - FINANCES

And more!

Written By: Annamarie Strawhand

Edited By: Gynti Pinon

© Copyright 2023 Annamarie Strawhand (Author)
and Faith Lane Media, LLC (Publisher)

All rights reserved. No part of this publication may be reproduced, redistributed, or transmitted in any form or by any means, including photocopying, recording, or other electronic or mechanical methods, without the prior written permission of the author and publisher, except in the case of brief quotations embodied in reviews and certain other noncommercial uses permitted by copyright law. For permission requests, please write to the publisher, Faith Lane Media, LLC
P.O. Box 7068 Virginia Beach, Virginia USA 23457

Dedication

This prayer strategy book is dedicated to Father God in faith that He already knows the very moment we will come to Him and speak these prayers. He is waiting for us to come to Him so He can bless us according to His promises. I thank the Lord Jesus Christ for making everything of the Kingdom of God directly accessible for us through His finished work on the Cross. Thank You, Holy Spirit, for being our helper, counselor, and prayer partner.

Introduction

Hello, my faithful friend!

I am so excited to finally have this book of prayers organized for you! As you read through this book, I encourage you to pray these prayers with faith. Believe God is doing miracles as you pray them. I can give you the words here to speak, but the most important thing is that you *believe* what you are speaking and you *see it done* by faith. You don't have to yell or scream or get worked up. The key is to speak these words confidently and boldly and know God is doing it!

When prayed with faith, we have witnessed these prayers and strategies bring incredible breakthroughs and miracles to many families and individuals over the last five years of our ministry. I personally have received breakthroughs and miracles with these prayers. The strategies and prayers in this book were always (and always will be) freely accessible on our website. I received many requests to take all these prayers from our website and collect them all into a book, arranged by subject, giving easy access to these as needed for you all to have as a reference and tools for your spiritual toolbox!

Understand you should keep praying these prayers in faith consistently, pressing deeply to Father God until you see a breakthrough. Do not do them just to repeat them like a robot or like a ritual. These prayers were written with the direct help of the Holy Spirit. Invite the Holy Spirit to be with you as you pray. He can also bring revelation to you, directing you to the next steps while you are in prayer. Many of the next steps can be other prayers right here in this book. Just know that as soon as you begin to pray, Heaven is activated on your behalf by the Authority and Name of Jesus Christ in whom you pray and by the move of the Holy Spirit in whom you partner with in prayer.

Father God is faithful to His Word, and all of our prayers confirm with scripture. Many of them include declarations of scripture. The greatest form of praise you can give Father God is thanking Him in advance for your answered prayer and speaking His Words of promise back to Him. Angels of the Lord harken to the Word of God and are activated when you speak the Word of God to be sent on assignments on your behalf. So speak the scriptures with the prayers. We must SEE IT by faith, SPEAK IT by faith, and humbly remind our Father God of His word of promise to perform what we see and speak according to Jeremiah 1:11.

Here is your first declaration - speak this right now:

> ☐ *"Heavenly Father, Your word says in Jeremiah 1:11-12 that You are asking me to see by faith, and that when I speak what I SEE, you will perform it quickly. So I see now by faith _____. I believe, Father, that You are faithful to your word. That You will now hasten this, accelerate this to me in the natural even right now. You say, Father, in Jeremiah 1:11-12, that you are waiting on Your word to perform it, and I am in faithful expectation to see this word come to pass quickly for your glory, in Jesus' name! Thank You, Father, for the promises in Your word. I stand on this today! Amen."*

When you pray and believe in FAITH - God is not *delaying* things - He's *arranging* things! You keep praying and you will see VICTORY! God is waiting for us to step up in faith so He can bring it all together for us! This is how He shows His glory in our lives.

This collection of our written prayers is Volume One. As we keep getting more prayers as the Holy Spirit gives them to us, we will soon add a Volume Two! Most of the prayers here in Volume One come with teachings. As you read through, I encourage you to take in the teaching with each prayer to give you more biblical understanding surrounding the prayer. Your faith will grow and your relationship with the Lord and His faithfulness! Many of the teachings and prayers give you action steps to take. We must pray the prayers, but it's just as important that we take the action steps in faith suggested along with the prayers. These are crucial strategies. Faith without works is dead.

I have taught you all about Abraham's Key. Abraham was a friend of God and his faith and works pleased God, and God prospered Abraham. Jesus said this about us doing the works of Abraham to His disciples in John 8:39 - "Abraham is our father," they replied. "If you were children of Abraham," said Jesus, "you would do the works of Abraham."

Works are important when they are paired with prayer and faith. These are faith action steps that *complete* a prayer. When you take the action steps in these prayers that are instructed, you are directly showing obedience to God by putting your feet to your faith. Don't be afraid to take the steps. Jesus is also praying for you with the Father all the way through this process. The Bible says that Jesus is interceding for you in Heaven so that your faith will not fail and you will do what He taught us to do — to do the works of Abraham!

FAITH + OBEDIENCE + WORKS = Abraham's Key!

James 2:22 "You see, his faith and his actions worked together. His actions made his faith complete. 23 And so it happened just as the Scriptures say: "Abraham believed God, and God counted him as righteous because of his faith. He was even called the friend of God. 24 So you see, we are shown to be right with God by what we do, not by faith alone."

So, my faithful friend, this is not just a prayer book, it's an action book. It's also designed to activate you as a powerful intercessor for the kingdom of God. Once you begin praying, know that a great cloud of witnesses in Heaven begins to cheer you on to the victory. You have the keys in your hands right here, now step into the driver's seat, be encouraged, and know that NOTHING is impossible with God!

All of Heaven is cheering you on, and I am too!

Much Love,

Annamarie Strawhand

Tips
- When you see a blank line _____ in the written prayer, that is where you speak the person's name you are praying for. If you are praying over yourself, just say "me" or "I."

- Take time to pray and decree as you read through the book. I suggest doing all the prayers in order if you don't have a specific need. Because you are being thorough by praying through the entire book, you will break down all strongholds that could unknowingly be holding back your current need!

- Make time to do these prayers in a quiet place. If other family members are not ready to pray these with you, then wait until they are not home or go to a private room or outside since these need to be prayed out loud.

- Before praying any of the prayers listed, always do the Suit Up and Seat of Authority Prayer FIRST.

Table Of Contents

Part I — Daily Suit Up And Authority in Christ Prayers
- Updated: Daily Suit Up Prayer (Armor of God - Seat of Authority)
- Wielding The Scepter Of Righteousness

Part 2 — Anointing and Home Blessings
- How To Pray Over And Apply Anointing Oil
- Spiritual House Cleaning Strategies With Prayer
- Breaking Unholy Soul Ties Connected To Items
- Room By Room Prayer For House Dedication And Anointing
- Updated: Cleanse And Claim The Atmosphere For God's Glory
- Prayers And Decrees For Sounding The Shofar For Your Home And Property
- Speak The Priestly Blessing In Your Home
- Anoint Your Entire Home And Dedicate It To God
- Prayer for Groceries and Purchases Coming Into Home

Part 3 — Dream Interpretation Prayers
- Dream Interpretation and Prayer To Cancel A Bad Or Demonic Dream

Part 4 — Courts of Heaven & Land Assignments
- How To Appear and Pray In The Courts of Heaven
- Gatekeepers Prayer Guide And Decrees
- Updated: How To Do A Land Assignment For Blessing And Cleansing Your Land
- Schools And US Dept Of Education Prayer
- US Judicial System Prayer
- USPS - Post Office Prayer

Part 5 — Faith Activation
- Prayer Activation Strategy: "Marvelous" Faith
- Prayer for Discernment
- Prayer for Grace

Part 6 — Family And Relationships
- Five Strategies For Praying Your Prodigals Home (And Back To God)
- Prayer For Family - How To Pray Protection Over Your Spouse And Children
- Prayer For The Fruit Of The Womb And The Fruit Of The Loins (Our Children)
- Prayer To Remove Ungodly Relationships And Influences (Axe Of God's judgment)
- Prayer To Send The Holy Spirit To Loved Ones

Part 7 — Financial Breakthrough
- How To Pray Over Your Offerings To The Lord - Kingdom Finance Prayers And Declarations
- Opening The Gates And Doors Of Blessing Into Your Household

Part 8 — Healing & Soul Cleansing
- Healing Prayer For Yourself and Loved Ones
- Updated: Prayers For Mouth Issues and Other Gates of Your Body

- Prayer To Be Delivered And Healed From Rejection
- Updated: Soul Cleansing And Healing Prayer

Part 9 — Repentance & Salvation
- Power Of Repentance - How To Pray A Prayer Of Repentance To Remove Any Consequences Against You
- Salvation Prayers - Give Your Life To Jesus And Invite The Holy Spirit Baptism

Part 10 — Spiritual Warfare
- Cancel Any "Soulish" Prayers, Negative Words, And Curses Off Your Life
- Discerning, Removing, And Avoiding The Spirit Of Divination/Python Spirit
- Discerning The Spirit Of Discord And Removing It: Revelation And Prayers
- Fourth Watch Prayer For Deliverance
- Prayers And Decrees Against Witchcraft
- Prayers For Calming The Storm In Your Mind
- Decrees For A New Clean Heart - Healed Heart To Know God
- Updated: Prayers To Remove Spiritual Arrows and Daggers
- Prayer To Renounce And Break Unholy Covenants
- Steps And Prayers To Remove Demonic Frequencies From Your Home
- How To Pray The Prayer of Jabez Over Yourself and Your Loved Ones

Part 1
Daily Suit Up and Authority In Christ Prayers

Updated: Daily Suit Up Prayers For Your Kingdom Purpose For God
(Armor of God - Seat of Authority)

Daily Suit Up Steps

This must be done each day out loud so it is heard in the spirit realm. We go about the Father's business each day with His divine protection and blessing. I do this in the morning, but you can do this before bed each night to decree over the night and the next day. Hebrew days actually begin at sundown, so either way, you are covering your next 24 hours by speaking these decrees based on Ephesians 6:10-20.

Declare Out Loud And Do The Motions Of Putting On Each Piece Of The Armor Of God

- ☐ **Belt Of Truth:** *"I put on the belt of truth. I am girded in the truth of God. My core is strengthened. I will not double over. I stand tall and strong in the Lord. My belt of truth has a compass on it and always points me to the truth of God and His word on my kingdom path!"*

- ☐ **Breastplate Of Righteousness:** *"I put on the breastplate of righteousness that the Lord Jesus Christ made for me Himself. My heart is guarded. My soul is guarded. My spirit is guarded. Nothing can come against me, in the name of Jesus. I move forward powerfully for the Lord. The Lord God Himself is my rear guard. I walk in the righteousness of the Lord Jesus Christ."*

- ☐ **Shoes Of The Gospel Of Peace:** *"I put on my shoes of the Gospel of peace. I will not lose my peace today. I will go forward powerfully and spread the Gospel and the glory of the Lord Jesus Christ."*

- ☐ **Shield Of Faith:** *"I take the shield of faith, and I quench all the fiery darts of the wicked. No one can curse whom the Lord has blessed, and the Lord has blessed me! No weapon formed against me shall prosper. Every tongue that rises against me, I condemn right now, in the name of Jesus. I speak to every curse of witchcraft and every single demonic word and word of negativity that's ever been spoken against me, be quenched and canceled now in the name of Jesus!"*

- ☐ **Helmet Of Salvation:** *"I put on the helmet of salvation. I have the mind of Christ. I command every thought in my mind to come under the obedience of Jesus Christ. Nothing demonic can come against my mind today, in the name of Jesus."*

- ☐ **Sword Of the Spirit:** *"I take my sword of the Spirit, which is the word of God — my two-edged sword. Holy Spirit, give me remembrance of the word of God today as I need it. I hang onto and hold up my sword of the Spirit all day and all night. I stand on the word of God, in Jesus' name. In the name of Jesus, I chop off the head of every lying, deceiving serpent right now, and I cast it out to the dry place, and, Father, I ask You to bring Your holy fire and destroy it, in Jesus' name."*

- ☐ **Kingdom Ambassador/Spokesperson:** *"Holy Spirit, give me utterance that I will speak boldly as I ought to speak, and I shall stand and speak boldly as an ambassador for the kingdom of God."*

TAKE YOUR SEAT OF AUTHORITY

Sit In A Chair; Turn To Your Left, And Say Out Loud

- ☐ *"Father God, I accept Your gracious word that You have given me according to Ephesians Chapter 2. In humble faith, I now take my Seat of Authority at Your right hand, in Christ Jesus. I now rule and reign in Christ Jesus through Christ Jesus. I proclaim Jesus Christ is the name above all names — King of kings and Lord of lords. I put everything of the kingdom of darkness under my feet because it is all under the feet of King Jesus. I command by Jesus Christ's Authority right now that everything I encounter today must bow the knee to the lordship of Jesus Christ! I enforce the authority of Jesus Christ over everything in my life, household, and family today, in Jesus' name!"*

Out loud, cover yourself, your family, your house, your vehicles, your work, and your ministry with the blood of Jesus. Commit your day and night to the Lord, and apply the blood daily to whatever you want protected.

- ☐ *"In Jesus' name, I place _____ in the blood of Jesus Christ today. I cover everywhere my good name is and the names of my loved ones are in the blood of Jesus. Lord Jesus, release the power of Your blood over _____. Lord, let Your blood speak today over _____. Lord, Your blood speaks life now into _____. Lord Jesus, Your blood exposes and destroys all darkness operating in and around _____. Thank you, Jesus, for Your precious blood! I proclaim the blood of Jesus speaks a better word over all words today, in Jesus' name! I enforce the blood of Jesus over everything in my life today, in Jesus' name!"*

Send the Hosts of Heaven (The Angel Armies of God) to take you and your household and family OFF the frequency of the demonic and invite the Holy Spirit.

Decree

- *"In the name and authority of Jesus Christ, in whom I am seated, I ask You now, Father God, for the hosts of Heaven, the angel armies of the Lord, to assist me today as one of my mighty spiritual weapons. Thank You, Father, for sending Your angels to keep me in all my ways according to Your word in Psalm 91. I now invite the hosts of Heaven, God's army angels — by faith, now assigned to me — to come now, in Jesus' name, and take me and my household, my work, ministry, family, and children OFF the frequency of the demonic! I declare that the demonic cannot see, hear, or perceive us today! O God, arise and scatter Your enemies far, far away from me and my household, in Jesus' name! I declare that the only frequency that my house, my family, and I operate on today is the frequency of the HOLY SPIRIT, in Jesus' name! Holy Spirit, YOU are welcome here! Come surround and fill us with Your presence! Thank You, Father God! Amen!"*

Decree

- *"Almighty God, I proclaim Your glory is my covering today, and Your favor surrounds me as a shield! I am in expectation of signs, wonders, and miracles in my life and in my family! I go forward on this day in faith and boldness for YOUR kingdom and glory, in Jesus' name! Amen."*

NOW YOU ARE SUITED UP AND READY TO GET IT DONE FOR THE LORD!

Amen and Whoo hooo!!! Have an amazing and blessed day!

Prayer Of Protection For Families

If you want to pray a prayer of protection over your spouse/children for the day, here is mine that I pray over my husband and daughter: "Prayer For Family – How To Pray Protection Over Your Spouse And Children." It's here in the book.

Extended Version Of Daily Suit Up Steps

This must be done out loud each day so it is heard in the spirit realm. We go about the Father's business each day with His divine protection and blessing.
I do this in the morning, but you can do this before bed each night to decree over the night and the next day. Hebrew days actually begin at sundown. So either way, you are covering your next 24 hours by decreeing these scriptures.

Put On The Full Armor Of God – Ephesians 6:10-20

Stand up and decree out loud as you physically put on each piece of armor. DO THE MOTIONS. You can also decree that you are standing in for your loved ones as an intercessor, and you can put the armor of God pieces on them in the spirit. Make sure you say this in its entirety, especially taking the oath of boldness and ambassadorship for the kingdom of God at the end.

Decree

- ☐ *"I am strong in the Lord and in the power of his might. I put on the whole armor of God, that I may be able to stand against the wiles of the devil. For we wrestle not against flesh and blood, but against principalities, against powers, against the rulers of the darkness of this world, against spiritual wickedness in high places. Wherefore, take unto me the whole armor of God, that I may be able to withstand in the evil day, and having done all, to stand. I stand, therefore, having my loins girt about with truth, and I have on the breastplate of righteousness. My feet are shod with the preparation of the Gospel of peace. Above all, I take the shield of faith, wherewith I shall be able to quench all the fiery darts of the wicked. And I put on the helmet of salvation, and I take the sword of the Spirit, which is the word of God! I pray always with all prayer and supplication in the Spirit, and watching thereunto with all perseverance and supplication for all saints; And for me, that utterance may be given unto me, that I may open my mouth boldly, to make known the mystery of the Gospel, For which I am an ambassador in bonds: that therein I may speak boldly, as I ought to speak."*

I put on my armor daily! I can tell the difference if I skip a day! Don't leave yourself vulnerable to attacks of the enemy.

TAKE YOUR SEAT OF AUTHORITY AT THE RIGHT HAND OF GOD IN CHRIST JESUS DAILY

Decree Ephesians Chapter 1:17 all the way to Ephesians Chapter 2:4-7

Suggested book: *The Authority of the Believer and How To Use It*, by Dr. Billye Brim

Take your seat, look to your left because Father God puts you at His right hand in His Son, Jesus Christ, and pray this out loud:

- ☐ *"Lord, I believe that Your word is for me, and I accept it as such. I am seated now at Jesus' right hand in heavenly places. I ask You to teach me daily how to walk in the authority that You have given to me so that I can be all that You have called me to be for Your kingdom so that Your will, plans, and purposes will be fulfilled, in Jesus' name. Amen."*

Proclaim

- ☐ *"I believe and decree that God 'hath quickened us together with Christ and hath raised us up together, and made us sit together in heavenly places in Christ Jesus,' according to Ephesians 2:5-6."*

Out loud, cover yourself, your family, your house, your vehicles, your work, and your ministry with the blood of Jesus. Commit your day and night to the Lord, and apply the blood of Jesus daily to whatever you want to be protected.

- ☐ *"In Jesus' name, I place _____ in the blood of Jesus Christ today. I cover everywhere my good name is and the names of my loved ones are in the blood of Jesus. Lord Jesus, release the power of Your blood over _____. Lord, let Your blood speak today over _____. Lord, Your blood speaks life now into _____. Lord Jesus, Your blood exposes and destroys all darkness operating in and around _____. Thank You, Jesus, for Your precious blood!"*

Then from your Seat of Authority, you speak to the kingdom of darkness and tell them you have authority over them, that you put them under your feet, and they are not allowed to touch you or your loved ones today because the blood of Jesus is against them, and they are helpless against the blood of Jesus Christ!

MEAN WHAT YOU SAY! DEMONS ONLY RESPOND TO THE AUTHORITY OF JESUS CHRIST, NOT SCREAMING AND YELLING. USE CALM AUTHORITY AND MEAN IT!

YOU CAN DO THE ABOVE DAILY FOR THE SHORT VERSION, BUT IF YOU ARE GETTING A LOT OF WARFARE YOU CAN KEEP GOING WITH THESE REMAINING STEPS BELOW

- Pray the Lord's Prayer out loud. Then decree: "Father, Your glory is my covering, in Jesus' name!"
- Repent for any sins. Ask for forgiveness, grace, and mercy, and ask Jesus to wash you clean with His blood. Ask the Lord to create in you a clean heart, and invite the Holy Spirit to fill you. Command your mind, body, soul, heart, and spirit to yield to the power of the Holy Spirit that day and night.
- Psalm 23 – Decree over you and your household for the leading of the Lord and anointing. You can also apply oil to your head and the soles of your feet. I get my anointing oil here: Judaica Webstore
- Psalm 24 – Decree an open heaven over you and your household and that the King of glory shall come in!
- Psalm 91 – Pray this prayer of protection over you and your household as you walk in your kingdom assignment.
- 1 Chronicles 4:10 - Decree the prayer of Jabez over yourself/family for God to expand your territory and advance your divine purpose. I do this weekly.
- Numbers 6:22-27 - Decree the Aaronic Blessing or play the recording in Hebrew in your home. I do this weekly. Here is a recording in both Hebrew and English On Youtube "The Aaronic Blessing"
- Play the recording of the shofar in your home. This is the sound of the trumpet in Zion to take out any spiritual enemies and call forth the hosts of Heaven to fight for you, according to Nehemiah 4:20. Each morning, I put a recording of the shofar on loop while I work during the day. While playing the shofar in your home, you can also ask Father God to send the hosts of Heaven — Heaven's armies — to fight for you in a specific situation. This is the one I play: "12min Of Non-Stop Shofar" on YouTube.
- Ask Father God to send the hosts of Heaven to take you and your household and family OFF the frequency of the demonic that day. Decree: "In the name and authority of Jesus Christ in whom I am seated, I ask You, Father God, to send the hosts of Heaven, the angel armies of Almighty God, to assist me today as one of my mighty spiritual weapons. I ask for the hosts of Heaven, God's army angels, to go now, in Jesus' name, and take me and my household, my family, and my children OFF the frequency of the demonic! I declare that the demonic cannot see, hear or perceive us today! O God, arise and scatter Your enemies far, far away from me and my household, in Jesus' name! I declare that the only frequency that my house, my family, and I operate on today is the frequency of the HOLY SPIRIT, in Jesus' name! Thank You, Father, for sending Your angels to keep me in All of my ways!"
- Household Decree: "As for me and my house, we shall serve the Lord God of Israel, the God of Abraham, Isaac, and Jacob and his only Son, Jesus Christ of Nazareth — Yeshua HaMashiach — King of kings, the Name above all names! Every knee shall bow to the Lord Jesus Christ who goes before me!"
- You can also decree over your land and property from your Seat of Authority In Christ Jesus.

Decree

- ☐ *"I decree from my Seat of Authority in Jesus Christ, I am a king and a priest of the order of Melchizedek! I have the Scepter of Righteousness in my hand and I hold it up over my land, my home, and all of my property! I decree that the Scepter of Righteousness of Jesus Christ rules and reigns over this land, home, and property at _____ (address), and so it is written in that the scepter of wickedness cannot touch the land allotted to the righteous! I beat down the scepter of wickedness and smash it to pieces with the Scepter of Righteousness and sweep the pieces into the dry places to be burned up by the fire of God, never to come near this property again! Therefore, this land, home, and all of the property here of my household is consecrated and dedicated to the kingdom of Almighty God, Jesus Christ, the King of glory, the Righteous One, and the Scepter of Righteousness rules here! I decree Psalm 45:6-7, 'Your throne, O God, is forever and ever; a scepter of righteousness is the scepter of Your kingdom. You love righteousness and hate wickedness; therefore God, Your God, has anointed You with the oil of gladness more than Your companions.' Thank You, Father God, for my authority in Jesus Christ and the right to rule and reign through Him and with Him! Your kingdom and glory forever and ever on earth as it is in Heaven! Amen."*

This is a powerful way to take your place of authority in Christ Jesus and operate in the covering and protection of the kingdom of God each day as we carry out what the Lord has called us to do.

Wielding The Scepter Of Righteousness

Taking Your Daily Seat Of Authority And Wielding The Scepter Of Righteousness

This is the definition of scepter - scep·ter/septər/or sceptre noun 1. an ornamented staff carried by rulers on ceremonial occasions as a symbol of sovereignty.

Believers in Christ, it is time to start truly using your authority that Jesus died and rose to give to us. Each day as you take your Seat of Authority in Christ Jesus, go a step further and take the Scepter of Righteousness of KING JESUS in your hand in the spirit, and use it! Hold it up each day and beat down the scepter of wickedness! Do this over your city and region in the spirit. It is those who are in Christ Jesus who have dominion over the land!

Sit In A Chair, Turn To Your Left and Face Forward, And Say Out Loud

- ☐ *"Father God, I accept Thy gracious word I believe that Thou hast thus wrought for me according to Ephesians Chapter 2. In humble faith, I do now take my Seat of Authority in the heavenly places in Christ Jesus at Thy right hand where I now rule and reign in Christ Jesus, King of kings, and through Christ Jesus of the priestly kingly order of Melchizedek over all the land, the waters, the mountains, and over every area of influence in the earth, in Jesus' name! I put the kingdom of darkness under my feet! I walk in the righteousness of Jesus Christ, and I now take the Scepter of Righteousness in my hand. It is written in Psalm 125:3 that the scepter of wickedness will not remain over the land allotted to the righteous. I declare this land of _____ has been allotted to the righteous. Therefore, the scepter of wickedness can no longer remain here over _____. I hold up the scepter of righteousness by the authority of Jesus Christ, and I beat down the scepter of wickedness and smash it to pieces! I scrape the pieces into the fire of Almighty God to be burned to ashes! It is written that the scepter of wickedness cannot remain, so it shall be!! In the name of Jesus Christ, I decree and declare this land of _____ is the land allotted to the righteous, and the Scepter of Righteousness rules and reigns over _____ forever! I decree that the scepter of wickedness is now destroyed and can never come near _____ again, in Jesus' name!! By the authority of Jesus Christ in whom I am seated, I take dominion over _____, in the name of Jesus Christ, and claim it for Almighty God! I call forth the angel armies of Almighty God to come and blow the victory trumpets of the Lord over this land! Let the plans and purposes of Almighty God and the Lord Jesus Christ come forth upon this land right now and prosper it, in Jesus' name! Let the righteous people of this land now receive their rightful inheritance from the Lord!! Hallelujah!!"*

Part 2
Anointing and Home Blessings

How To Pray Over and Apply Anointing Oil

I love anointing oils. I have been using them for the last five years or so since the Holy Spirit began teaching me the importance of anointing ourselves, our children, and our homes with oil that has been specifically dedicated to God.

As Christians, we must understand that anointing a person, home, or something in your house with oil is not a "religious ritual." The anointing with oil is a prophetic act of faith.

When you accept Jesus Christ as your Lord and Savior, you become part of His priesthood. You have been made a king and a priest through Christ Jesus.

Revelation 1:6: "And hath made us kings and priests unto God and his Father; to him be glory and dominion forever and ever. Amen."

The book of Hebrews Chapter 7 refers to Jesus as a king and a priest of the order of Melchizedek. In the book of Genesis, Melchizedek was the king of Salem. Abraham brought his tithes to Melchizedek. Then Melchizedek brought out bread and wine and did both priestly and kingly duties for his people and Abraham. Melchizedek had authority in both ministry and marketplace and even more. This is who we are in God's kingdom.

This is what Jesus did for us — gave us this authority. Priests were called to anoint the sick, anoint a home or livestock, and, most of all, anoint a king or leader that God had chosen and set aside for a special purpose for God's plans, such as young David, the shepherd boy, who went on to become King David. So when you anoint something by faith, you are performing your priestly duty according to the word of God.

When you apply and speak over the anointing oil as you apply it, the anointed person, home, or item is then set aside and dedicated for the plans and purposes of God. It then comes under the authority and dominion of God's kingdom, which includes the favor and protection of God. His Holy Spirit is now upon it. This is the purpose of the anointing.

I have spoken these prayers that I have for you below to pray over your oil and consecrate it to God, as well as the declaration to speak when you apply the oil.

Prayer To Dedicate Your Anointing Oil To God - (Do This Before Anointing Anything)

1. Take your oil out of the box, and before taking off the cap, lift the oil and bottle up to God.
2. Pray out loud over the oil and the bottle:

- ☐ *"Father God, thank You for this oil to be used for anointing. In Jesus' name, I lift up this oil and the bottle that it is in and dedicate it and consecrate it to You, Almighty God, and to Your kingdom. Lord Jesus, I place this oil and the bottle in Your precious blood. Lord Jesus, I ask You to release the power of Your blood over this oil and sanctify it. Your blood, Lord, breaks all curses and demonic assignments now off this oil and cleanses and destroys all darkness. Through the blood of Jesus, I declare this anointing oil is now redeemed out of the hand of the devil and into the hand of God and is set aside for the plans and purposes of God all for the glory of God by the blood of Jesus! Thank You, Jesus, for the power of Your blood now activated on this oil. This bottle is now made pure and holy for anointing purposes by the blood of Jesus Christ.*

- ☐ *"Father God, I ask You to bless this oil and pour Your Holy Spirit upon and into this oil. Holy Spirit, I invite You to take over this oil, in Jesus' name. Everywhere this oil touches from this day forward, it will release Your dunamis power, protection, and healing. The divine presence of Your Holy Spirit is fully and divinely activated upon this oil. Father God, Your word says in Zechariah 4:6, "This [continuous supply of oil] is the word of the Lord to Zerubbabel [prince of Judah], saying, 'Not by might, nor by power, but by My Spirit [of whom the oil is a symbol],' says the Lord of hosts." Therefore, by faith and by my own authority in Jesus Christ given to me according to the word of God and the finished work of the Cross and resurrection of Jesus Christ, I proclaim that Your Holy Spirit, Father God, is now activated upon this oil, and every place it is poured, applied, and everywhere it touches and passes near shall release the power of Your Holy Spirit. In Jesus' name, I call this oil blessed, holy, sanctified, and set aside to be used only for the plans and purposes of God and of the kingdom and the glory of God, in Jesus' name. Amen!"*

3. Now, plan where you are going to apply the oil. It's a good idea to get "suited up" before you begin your priestly duties of anointing. This involves taking your Seat of Authority in Christ and putting on your armor of God. (See my "Daily Suit Up Prayer.")

4. Do the prophetic act of anointing now by faith and by your priestly authority in Jesus Christ.

Anointing A Person

Decree out loud when anointing a person - (apply oil to the forehead, back of neck, hands, and feet; insert the name of the person that you are praying for in the blanks).

- ☐ *"Father God, in the name of Jesus Christ, I anoint _____ with this holy anointing oil. I dedicate and consecrate _____'s soul, spirit, mind, and body to You, Father God! I place _____ in the blood of Jesus Christ. Lord Jesus, release the power of Your blood over _____. Your blood, Lord, destroys all darkness and brings Your glory light! I invite the power of the Holy Spirit to come now and be activated in and on _____, in Jesus' name.*

- ☐ *"I decree Your word, Father God, that says the anointing breaks the yoke over _____ now. (anoint back of neck) In Jesus' name, I command every yoke of bondage, slavery, infirmity, and discord to shatter off of _____ right now! I declare that _____ is only yoked to Jesus Christ from this day forward and His burden is easy and light. Father God, by faith, we believe that with this anointing over _____, Your Holy Spirit, kingdom, and glory are now activated over them. _____ is now dedicated and set aside for the plans and purposes of Almighty God, in Jesus' name! Your kingdom come, and Your will be done, in _____ and in _____'s life on earth as it is in Heaven, in Jesus' name. Thank You, Father God. Thank You, Lord Jesus. Thank You, Holy Spirit. We are in faithful expectation to see the glory of God come now upon _____. Amen!"*

Now, praise and thank God, and if the person you are anointing is able, have them come into agreement with this prayer and praise God with you.

Note: When anointing the sick, you can anoint the specific affected areas and invite the Holy Spirit to take over those areas and restore them to their divine order, in Jesus' name.

Anointing Children

When you anoint your children and dedicate them to God, it is good to do it right before bedtime. I would anoint my child's head and feet at night to help her sleep. I dedicated her sleep and dreams to God and spoke scripture over her. I would anoint her forehead and declare that she had the mind of Christ and that all her thoughts were good, pleasing, and in the will of God, and that the peace of the Lord Jesus Christ was upon her. I would anoint over her heart and feet.

Decree Out Loud As You Anoint Your Child

> ☐ *"Father God, according to your word in Jeremiah 24:7, You are giving my child a heart to know You." I would anoint her feet and decree, "These are the beautiful feet that stand upon the mountain and proclaim the good news of the Gospel of Jesus Christ."*

Children love to be anointed and prayed over, and soon, they will be asking you to do this every night because they feel the presence of God! I have had so many moms and dads that I have mentored do this over their children and have made it a special bedtime blessing.

You can teach them how Jesus was anointed and how he loved it (John 11:2). You can teach your children about the anointing, and they will someday do this for their own children. You can also anoint a baby and speak these same words. The power of the Holy Spirit will be released upon your children and their lives.

When you buy the anointing oils, pick out a scent the children would enjoy that is soothing and that will help them sleep. Frankincense and myrrh are good ones.

Anointing A Home/Land

Apply the prayed-over oil to the ground of the corners of your property, your gates, the end of your driveway, your mailbox, and even any outbuildings. I also apply it to the corners of my garden and around any fruit-bearing trees. You should always take Communion on your land first before you do the anointing, and repent for any sins on the land. It's the blood (Communion) that will cleanse the land of any curses. After taking Communion on the land, then you can dedicate the land to God by anointing with the oil. Learn how to take Communion on the land in this teaching: "How To Do A Land Assignment For Blessing And Cleaning The Land."

Decree For Anointing The Land

Pray this prayer as you pour oil on the borders (on the soil) and gate areas of the property (all four corners) and over the main doors of all buildings on the land. While applying the oil, you can prophesy over the land, saying what you want to build and grow there. Some landowners like to add wood stakes with scripture to the corners of the property anointed with oil and placed in the soil.

> ☐ *"Father God, thank You for this land. I dedicate and consecrate this land to you, Father God! I claim this land and all this property and all its gates and buildings here _____ (say the address of the land or the name of the land here) for Your plans and purposes, Father God, in Jesus' name. Father, I ask You to bless this land and all who live and work here that they shall be fruitful and prosperous. I invite You, Holy Spirit, to come upon this land and dwell here! Holy Spirit, come hover over this land, pour out Your breath of life on this land, and do creative miracles. Restore this land to its divine order,*

In Jesus' name! I bless this land and all who dwell here! I decree let it be on earth as it is in Heaven for this land, in Jesus' name! Father God, I ask You to station sentry angels to keep watch over and protect this land and property at its gates and borders with their fiery swords and shields! Let the anointing of Your Holy Spirit come upon this land, and let the fruit of the Holy Spirit come forth now in abundance from this land from this day forward, in Jesus' name! Father God, let Your kingdom and glory be the covering of this land forevermore, in Jesus' mighty name. Amen!"

Decree For Anointing Your Home

The anointing oil is to be applied over every door and window inside your home, or at least every main doorway. For doorways, I do inside and outside, and I also do the window sills and the sides of the door frames.

Pour some anointing oil on your fingertips. As you apply with a swiping motion to the tops and corners of the doors and windows, decree out loud:

- ☐ *"Father God, In the name and authority of Jesus Christ and by the power of Your Holy Spirit, with this oil, I dedicate and consecrate this home to You! I thank You for this home, Father God, and I ask You to bless this home. I decree that this home is now set aside for YOUR plans and purposes, Almighty God. I place this house and every door and window in the blood of Jesus Christ. Lord Jesus, release the power of Your blood over this house. Your blood, Lord, destroys all darkness and brings Your light and purity. I invite You, Lord Jesus, to take over every room in this house. I invite You, Holy Spirit, to come now and fill every room and every inch of this home, in Jesus' name! Father God, bless this home and everyone in it. Bless it from the very bottom to the very top, in Jesus' name. Your kingdom come, Father God, in this home as it is in Heaven. Let the anointing of the Holy Spirit be activated in this home and stay here forever. Holy Spirit, You are welcome here! Come, Holy Spirit, and dwell with us here, in Jesus' name!*

- ☐ *"Let every yoke of slavery, bondage, strife, infirmity, and discord be destroyed forever off this place, in Jesus' name! The anointing breaks the yoke! This home and this family is only yoked to Jesus Christ, and His burden is easy and light! Father God, I decree Your blessing over this home and all who dwell here as You spoke over Your people in Israel, according to Numbers 6:24-26, "The Lord bless thee, and keep thee: The Lord make his face shine upon thee, and be gracious unto thee: The Lord lift up his countenance upon thee and give thee peace." I declare Your glory, God, is now the covering of this home from this day forward, in Jesus' name. Amen!"*

Decree When Anointing An Item

We buy things and bring them into our homes without realizing where they could have been before. We should anoint the main things in our home — our beds (all four corners), our furniture, mirrors, TVs, and computers. I even anoint my internet modem and my phone (communications coming into your home). I especially anoint anything the Holy Spirit points out to me that's questionable like antiques or anything second-hand. Now, take your oil and dab some with your fingertips/hands on the top and bottom corners of the item as you pray the following prayer:

- ☐ *"Father God, I thank You for this _____. In the name of Jesus Christ, I dedicate and consecrate this _____ to You, Father God, and declare that it is designated and set aside for Your plans and purposes from this day forward. I place this _____ in the blood of Jesus Christ. Lord Jesus, release the power of Your blood over this _____. Your blood, Lord Jesus, destroys all darkness and breaks all curses and demonic assignments. By the blood of Jesus, this _____ is now sanctified. I anoint this _____ in the name of Jesus, and I invite You, Holy Spirit, to come upon this _____ with Your power, protection, and presence. Father God, bless this _____, and let it be used only for Your glory, in Jesus' name. Amen."*

Decree When Anointing Pets And Livestock

I have anointed my pets and our horse, Pongo — that took a full bottle! I have also anointed their pet beds and our horse's barn doors, stall, and pasture gates!

You might be thinking, "Wow, that might be extreme to anoint your animals." Actually, in the Hebrew culture, God's Chosen People BEGAN the anointing of the oil by pouring oil mixed with spices and herbs on the lambs and sheep to keep the fleas and parasites off of them. A good shepherd anointed his sheep.

This is why God does everything He does so His people — an agricultural people — can understand the meaning behind things!

When God told Moses the recipe for His holy anointing oil, they would have already understood the meaning behind that and had many of these spices and oils readily available. "Christ" means "anointed one." Jesus is also the Lamb of God. It's amazingly prophetic how God connects all these meanings of things. It's not by mistake.

I went into prayer about anointing my animals and that very next day God showed me about the Hebrew shepherds pouring oil on their sheep to confirm that I must do this too!

Pray this over your pet or animal while anointing their head, their feet, and their tail or back.

- ☐ *"Father God, thank You for this pet/animal _____ that You have brought to my household. They are Your beautiful creation. Father God, as I set this pet/animal aside for Your glory, God, in the name of Jesus Christ, I anoint _____ now and dedicate and consecrate _____ to You, Almighty God, for Your plans and purposes. I ask for Your Holy Spirit, who created _____, to now come upon _____ and do creative miracles (healing if needed) and make them healthy and whole in mind, body, and spirit. Bless _____ and give _____ Your protection, favor, peace, joy, and glory covering, in Jesus' name. Amen."*

I anointed my dog, Junior, when he was afraid of thunderstorms and asked for the presence and peace of the Holy Spirit to come upon him.

As for our rescue horse, Pongo, we don't know much of his past before we saved him from the auction pens, but we know by some of his fears and some of the scars on his back end that he may have had something traumatic happen to him. I anointed him on his head, back, and over his scars and commanded all those fears and memories to leave him, in Jesus' name, and for the Holy Spirit to come upon him and do creative miracles in his mind, body, and spirit and to restore him to divine wholeness that he will be a blessing for the kingdom of God.

Animals do not have souls as we do, but they have a spirit. And, yes, they do go to Heaven and wait for us if we have accepted salvation from Jesus Christ. These animals are part of our household. We are promised in the word of God that "you and your household shall be saved." That is why when you anoint your pets and livestock, proclaim them as part of your household, and dedicate your household to God. I take God at His word.

I have seen amazing changes in my pets since anointing them. Our horse, Pongo, is so much calmer and more trusting now. Thank You, Holy Spirit!

Remember, the Holy Spirit with the Word — Jesus Christ — brings creative power. This is how God created life on the earth! In the Book of Genesis, the Holy Spirit hovered and God spoke creation into the Spirit! By the authority of Jesus Christ that has been given to us (Ephesians Chapter 1-2), we speak these decrees in faith while inviting the Holy Spirit to come. That's when the glory is activated and we see miracles, signs, and wonders! I feel God's love for His creation when I anoint my animals. I feel God's love for my child when I anoint her.

Decree When Anointing A Gift For Another Person

I love to pray over and anoint a gift before I give or send it out to a person. I also pray and anoint every book that I autograph and send out as an author and ask the presence of the Holy Spirit to come upon that book to bless the reader. Again, by anointing that gift, you are doing a prophetic act of faith, and the power of the Holy Spirit comes upon that item and sets it aside for God to do a wonderful work through that anointing.

The Apostle Paul prayed and anointed "handkerchiefs." They were sent to the sick, and they got healed. (Acts 19:12) The anointing (the Holy Spirit) was on Paul so powerfully because he had dedicated and consecrated his life to God. If a person is anointed and set aside for God, the power of the Holy Spirit is on them. Even when an item touched Paul, the anointing was released. It's not the oil, it's the power of the Holy Spirit that touches the oil. When another touches it, that power is released. You are giving the gift of the Spirit!

Pray this over your gift before you give it to the person or mail it. I just dab a little oil around the corners of the gift and make sure my hands are anointed as I hold it up to God.

- ☐ *"Father God, thank You for this gift that I am about to give to _____. I dedicate and consecrate this gift to You, Father God. I place this gift in the blood of Jesus Christ. Lord Jesus, release the power of Your blood over this gift. Your blood, Lord, destroys all darkness and brings your glory light. Let the light of the Lord Jesus Christ be upon this gift and bring joy, peace, prosperity, favor, and blessing to the person who receives it. I anoint this gift and ask for the power of the Holy Spirit to come upon it. I bless the gift, and I bless the gift giver. You are the gift giver, Father God, and your word says that every good gift comes from You. I decree that because of the anointing that is now upon this gift, it is a good gift that comes from You, Father God. The recipient, _____, will feel and receive Your presence, love, and care for them with this gift by the power of Your Holy Spirit that is now upon this gift through the anointing, in Jesus' name. Amen."*

Decree When Anointing Yourself - (Long Version)

- ☐ *"Father God, I thank You for creating me and for your plans and purposes for my life. In the name of Jesus Christ, I anoint myself from the top of my head to the soles of my feet with this holy anointing oil. (rub oil on forehead/temples) I dedicate and consecrate my soul, spirit, mind, and body to You, Father God! I place myself in the blood of Jesus Christ. Lord Jesus, release the power of Your blood over me. Your blood, Lord, destroys all darkness and brings Your glory light! I invite the power of the Holy Spirit to come and be activated upon me now, in Jesus' name. I command my soul, mind, body, and spirit to come into alignment with the Holy Spirit now, in Jesus' name! I decree Your word, Father God, that says the anointing breaks the yoke over myself now. (rub oil on back of neck/shoulders). In Jesus' name, I command every yoke of bondage, slavery, infirmity, and discord to shatter off me right now! I declare that I am only yoked to Jesus Christ from this day forward and His burden is easy and light. Father God, by faith, I believe that the anointing of Your Holy Spirit, kingdom, and glory is now activated upon me and my life. (dab oil on bottoms of feet) I declare that I am fully dedicated, consecrated, and set aside for the plans and purposes of Almighty God, in Jesus' name! Father God, let Your kingdom come and Your will be done in me and in my life on earth as it is in heaven, in Jesus' name. Thank You, Father God. Thank You, Lord Jesus. Thank You, Holy Spirit. I am in faithful expectation to see the glory of God come upon me now, in Jesus' name. Amen!"*

Daily Refreshing Anointing - (Short Version)

- ☐ *"Father God, thank You for the blessing of another day! In Jesus' name, I anoint myself from the top of my head (anoint forehead or temples) to the soles of my feet (anoint top of feet and center of the bottom), and I dedicate and consecrate myself, my life, and all that I do today to You, Father God, for Your kingdom! Holy Spirit, I invite You to come upon me and fill me up with Your Spirit. Refresh me, and activate Your Glory covering over me and in me! Release the anointing of Your Spirit upon everything I do and encounter today. I decree that the joy, peace, presence, favor, and protection of the Lord surround me and goes before me today, in Jesus' name. Amen."*

- ☐ *"Father God, it is written in Your word that the Anointing breaks the yoke. Therefore I anoint my neck and shoulders (anoint back of neck and shoulders) and I command every yoke of bondage, slavery, lack, infirmity, fear, grief, false responsibility, and offense to be shattered off me now in the mighty name of Jesus Christ! I proclaim I am only yoked to Jesus Christ and His burden is easy, light, and joyful!"*

Traveling With The Anointing Oil

Many times when I travel, I anoint my vehicle (front and back bumpers and over each door). When I go on land prayer assignments, I anoint the tires on my vehicle so that the oil/anointing is released on the roads on the way there! It's like when the oxen and the camels were anointed by God's people coming to the Promised Land, so we should do the same by faith. I have peace that my vehicles and belongings are dedicated to God. The Holy Spirit has been invited to activate His Spirit, and where the presence of God is, so are the angels of the Lord! You will see protection and favor in your life from doing this.

When I travel by airplane, I anoint my luggage and carry-ons. I also have some anointing oil on my hands, and I touch the entry door to the plane and my seat when I sit down. I pray quietly, dedicating the plane to God for a safe trip. Remember, those who are in Christ Jesus carry the glory EVERYWHERE you go!

The Anointing (Holy Spirit's Presence) Loves Adventure And Surprises!

I have a funny story about anointing my luggage on a flight trip from Virginia to New York. I anointed my carry-on bag and wheels with my prayed-over anointing oil. I declared that the anointing of the Holy Spirit would be released everywhere the wheels touched and onto anyone who had contact with my bag. I asked the Holy Spirit to release His anointing and His Spirit on contact.

I had a long layover at the Washington, D.C., airport, so I went to the busy coffee shop in the airport to get a coffee with my bag in tow. I ordered my coffee and a breakfast sandwich. They messed up my sandwich, so I had to go over to the side of the counter and wait while they made me a new one. They called a number for a coffee order, and a man came rushing up to get his order and bumped his rolling bag into mine. I looked up, and the man was CNN reporter, Jim Acosta! I gave him eye contact, and he started apologizing for bumping into me. I said, "Oh, that's okay," and I smiled.

Well, I will tell you, I am not a fan of his reporting, but I felt the Holy Spirit strong, and as Jim walked away with his coffee, I heard the Holy Spirit say to pray for him right now. So I did. I knew the anointing had been transferred onto his bag because I had asked God to do that before the trip! So now I can keep asking God to activate His Holy Spirit to do a work in Jim's life. Once the anointing is applied, it's there forever — activated in the spirit realm.

God is amazing! The Holy Spirit loves to go on adventures with you, especially when you travel, so when you get your anointing oils, make sure you also get a travel size!

In my "Holy Spirit-anointing adventures," I have prayed over and anointed homes, land, cars, wedding rings, new babies, and even the beds of those who have hosted me at their homes. I love to do it. We have had so many wonderful breakthroughs and blessings that have come from this!

When you do a prophetic act of faith like this, it pleases God. Faith pleases God. It's also an act of obedience. Obedience brings breakthrough. One of my favorite verses to decree when anointing myself or another person is Isaiah 61. This is the passage that Jesus spoke over Himself at the start of His ministry. I encourage those going into ministry to also do this. It's very powerful.

Where To Buy Your Anointing Oil

Olive oil from your grocery store is sufficient for anointing purposes because it is the prayer and decree that you speak in faith, in Jesus' name and authority, that activates the anointing of the Holy Spirit over the oil and where it's applied. The oil does not have the power. The Spirit of the living God has the power, by the authority of Jesus Christ, spoken by faith. The Holy Spirit is activated in the oil and the place it is applied because of what you speak over it in faith in the name of Jesus Christ.

These are some oils that I like. I love that they are from Israel from olive trees grown where our Savior walked and ministered and did miracles and where His blood was poured into the ground. To me, that is very special and sacred.

We know that Jesus first bled into the ground in an olive grove — the Garden of Gethsemane near Jerusalem. The word "Gethsemane" actually means "olive press." Jesus was being pressed when praying before his arrest and going to the Cross. To me, that is very prophetic, confirming He was and is forever the Anointed One.

So, yes, pure olive oils from Israel are the best to do anointing with if you want to pray over them giving glory and honor to Jesus for what He suffered in the Garden. Jesus will also return on the Mount of Olives facing the King's Gate in Jerusalem, very near that same olive grove that is still there today!

I like to use different oils to do different things in my ministry. When purchasing oils, I look for Judeo-Christian/Messianic Hebrew companies that pray over their oils and also offer teachings on the oils on their websites. I especially love anointing oil companies that are reverent to these important meanings of the olive oil surrounding "Yeshua" (Jesus Christ), that get the oil from Israel and pray over every part of it in the preparation process. That is very meaningful and gives the oil so much purity and sanctity.

RESOURCES FOR ANOINTING OILS

My personal favorite oil to anoint myself with — my head and feet — before bed and in the morning, is The New Jerusalem Holy Anointing Oil in the cobalt blue bottle with the gold top. It has a very soothing scent.

The New Jerusalem Holy Anointing Oil:
www.thenewjerusalem.co/anointing-oils/holy-anointing-oil

Covenant and Intercession Oils - Abba Oils: www.abbaoil.com

Glorious Creations Healing and Dedication Oils with Jeanette Strauss:
www.GloriousCreations.net

My Jerusalem has a variety of anointing oils for different personal uses from Israel: www.myjerusalemstore.com

How To Remove Demons From Your Home - Spiritual House Cleaning Strategies With Prayers

Accelerate Holy Spirit Flow In Your Home And Family And Remove Demonic Clutter

Spiritual House Cleaning Checklist And Prayer Strategies For Christians

The Bible is CLEAR about bringing and having items in your home that do not honor God. The Bible calls them "detestable" to God! I want to honor God in my home and life, and I know you do too. This is a tactic of the enemy to use these items as a legal right to come against you and have entry into your home! We must remove things from our homes that are giving the legal right to the demonic. I have come to realize that the more I do spiritual house cleaning, the more breakthroughs and blessings come immediately behind it. Acceleration of blessing happens almost overnight!

Spiritual house cleaning is not a religious ritual. It's to make your home a place that honors God because you love Him and you want to obey His word!

Bible References To Spiritual Housecleaning

Deuteronomy 7:25-26: "You must burn up the images of their gods; do not covet the silver and gold that is on them or take it for yourselves, or you will be ensnared by it; for it is detestable to the LORD your God. (26) And you must not bring any detestable thing into your house, or you, like it, will be set apart for destruction. You are to utterly detest and abhor it because it is set apart for destruction."

Deuteronomy 7:26 (KJV): "Neither shall you bring an abomination into your house, lest you be a cursed thing like it: but you shall utterly detest it, and you shall utterly abhor it; for it is a cursed thing."

Isaiah 30:22 (KJV): "Ye shall defile also the covering of thy graven images of silver, and the ornament of thy molten images of gold: thou shalt cast them away as a menstruous cloth; thou shalt say unto it, Get thee hence."

Ezekiel 11:18 (KJV): "And they shall come thither, and they shall take away all the detestable things thereof and all the abominations thereof from thence."

Joshua 6:18 (KJV): "And ye, in any wise keep yourselves from the accursed thing, lest ye make yourselves accursed, when ye take off the accursed thing, and make the camp of Israel a curse, and trouble it."

Joshua 7:13: "Get up and consecrate the people, saying, 'Consecrate yourselves for tomorrow, for this is what the LORD, the God of Israel, says: Among you, O Israel, there are things devoted to destruction. You cannot stand against your enemies until you remove them."

These "detestable" items can cause demonic attachments that open doors to the kingdom of darkness in your home of curses, demons, and familiar spirits (that people think are ghosts). This is not to be played with and must be taken very seriously. Allowing this evil to be in your home can come against your life, marriage, family, finances, health, and more! Let's identify, remove, trash, and burn these things up ASAP!

Acts 19:19: "And a number of those who had practiced magic arts brought their books together and burned them in the sight of all. And they counted the value of them and found it came to fifty thousand pieces of silver."

They did not care about the value of those items. They burned them anyway because they had devoted their lives to Jesus Christ and wanted to show God and everyone that they put Jesus Christ first and foremost above all!

Scriptures About Honoring God With Your Home And Your Things

Romans 12:9 (KJV): "Let love be without dissimulation. Abhor that which is evil; cleave to that which is good."

2 Corinthians 6:17 (KJV): "Wherefore come out from among them, and be ye separate, saith the Lord, and touch not the unclean thing; and I will receive you."

Ephesians 5:11(KJV): "And have no fellowship with the unfruitful works of darkness, but rather reprove them."

Important Note Before You Begin Your Spiritual Housecleaning:

When you pray the prayers out loud, do them for yourself in a private place. Then do your own items that belong personally to you BEFORE you work on the family members! Do this calmly! Then when it comes to your family, DO NOT just go in and start grabbing things away! I specifically tell you NOT to do this in my teaching if you read through it.

You are to wait and pray and send the Holy Spirit to work on them for them to come to the conclusion to throw it away. This needs to be handled gently and calmly, and they have to want to do it! This has to be done a step at a time and with patience and understanding. Your kids/husband/wife may not understand this and it will take time.

You could cause more turmoil and discord in your home by just barging in and taking their stuff, so you need to sit back, calm down, and rely on the Holy Spirit to help you. Have sit-down talks and teachings with them, and lead and guide them gently so they can come to their own understanding.

You can cover them and their stuff in the blood of Jesus. Ask God to give them grace, mercy, and protection as He works on them and brings them to understanding to remove these items too. This MUST be done in steps and with love and patience. I say this from love and experience.

You Start Your Spiritual House Cleaning With A Commitment And Partnership With The Holy Spirit - (Pray Out Loud)

> ☐ *"Holy Spirit, thank You for being my life helper in everything. I want to make my life and home a place that honors God. I want Your Holy Spirit to flow powerfully and freely in my home and in my life and family! I partner with you now, Holy Spirit, to help me with my spiritual house cleaning, in Jesus' name. Show me, Holy Spirit, the things and items that need to be removed that have ungodly soul ties. Reveal to me, Holy Spirit, any items that have demonic attachments or are cursed. Reveal to me, Holy Spirit, if there is anything in my life or my home that is giving the kingdom of darkness a legal right to come against me, causing problems or coming against my blessings. Thank You, Holy Spirit. I also ask the Father to send His angels of protection, heavenly hosts, and breakthrough angels to assist in pulling down any demonic strongholds! Holy Spirit, give me sharp discernment to carry this out with You boldly and decisively with no fear or hesitation, in Jesus' name! Let's begin!"*

Remember to do your "Suit Up Prayer" every day to be ready to take on anything that day, and take your Seat of Authority in Christ Jesus next to the Father. In your Seat of Authority, you have dominion. You fight from Heaven to earth, not earth to Heaven!

See my "Daily Suit Up Prayer" here in the book.

CLAIM THE ATMOSPHERE FOR GOD'S GLORY!

You need to understand that any words of negativity, word curses, gossip, or even profanity (demonic - these words empower evil in the spirit) that have ever been spoken by anyone in your home, even past residents/owners, are still hanging in the atmosphere.

God has given us the authority in Christ to command these words and word curses to leave!

Ephesians 2:6: "For he raised us from the dead along with Christ and seated us with him in the heavenly realms because we are united with Christ Jesus."

Revelation 5:10: "And you have caused them to become a Kingdom of priests for our God. And they will reign on the earth."

Go To Each Room Of Your House and Building On Your Property And Declare Out Loud

- ☐ *"Father, because of the blood of Jesus and His FINISHED work on the cross, the devil has been defeated. I take ahold of this right now as my restraining order against all evil. According to Ephesians 2, I am seated next to You, Father, in Christ. I thank You, Father God, for my new authority in Christ given to me. Because of this authority, I now rule and reign in Christ Jesus and put everything of the kingdom of darkness under my feet because it is all under the feet of King Jesus. Therefore, I enforce the blood of Jesus and the finished work of the cross by the authority of Jesus Christ over the atmosphere in every room in my home and around my property today, in Jesus' name!*

- ☐ *"In Jesus' name, I renounce every wicked, negative, lying, gossipy, profane word or word curse, incantation, or spell that has ever been spoken in this _____ (room) in my house and the property itself at _____ (address) to leave now, in Jesus' name! I put them all in the blood of Jesus and dismantle and cancel all these demonic words and count them null and void, in Jesus' name! I place everything below this house, in this house, and above this house in the blood of Jesus! Lord Jesus, release the power of your blood! Your blood, Jesus, destroys all curses and demonic assignments right now, in Jesus' name! I proclaim this house — every room, every item, every space, every molecule of air — everything in the atmosphere of this house is now cleansed and sanctified by the blood of Jesus!*

- ☐ *"Holy Spirit, I ask You now to come in and breathe Your fresh breath of life into the atmosphere of every room in my home and the surrounding property at _____ (address). Fill every space with Your love, joy, happiness, peace, and truth, in Jesus' name. Thank You, Holy Spirit, that the atmosphere of my home and property is now filled with Your holy presence from this day forward! Amen."*

Invite The Holy Spirit OUT LOUD And Anoint Your Home

See my "How To Pray Over And Apply Anointing Oil Prayer" here in the book.

You can also anoint your home with oil over all the doors and windows. Make sure you have prayed over the oil and dedicated it to God in Jesus' name.

Decree Over The Oil As You Prepare To Touch It To Areas

- ☐ *"Everything that this oil touches will release the power of the Holy Spirit and everything anointed by this oil will be sanctified and set apart for the plans and purposes of Almighty God, in Jesus' name!"*

Declare Out Loud (as you apply the oil to your doors and windows inside and out and anything else you are led to anoint in your house)

- ☐ *"I dedicate and consecrate this home to You, Father God. Bless this home, and sanctify this home by the blood of Jesus Christ and the anointing of Your Holy Spirit. I invite You, Holy Spirit, into this home. Come fill every room and stay forever. You are welcome here, Holy Spirit, You are welcome here, King Jesus! Come and dwell with us, Lord Jesus. You are Lord and King of every room here in this home, in Your Name, Jesus. Forever and ever, amen. So Be It!"*

THE ONLY GHOST IN YOUR HOME SHOULD BE THE HOLY GHOST! The true name of the Holy Ghost in Hebrew is "Ruach," Ruach Ha Kodesh, meaning Holy Spirit, the spirit of the LIVING GOD. GOD IS NOT DEAD. HIS SPIRIT IS ALIVE AND HOLY!

Do You Think You May Have "Ghosts" Or Demonic Spirits In Your House?

Let's be clear, there is no such thing as ghosts. There are only demonic entities that take on the appearance of humans. These are familiar spirits. They get attached to families and are hard to get rid of. They also can jump into pets. You need to SUIT UP, anoint your home, then dedicate every room and every person and pet in your home to God and invite the Holy Spirit to come and fill your home.

Take Your Seat of Authority In Christ And Say Out Loud To Familiar Spirits (Demons)

- ☐ *"You vile familiar unclean spirit, you of the kingdom of darkness, listen to me! You are not welcome here! This is not your family! This is not your house! In the name of Jesus Christ, I take authority over you and command you to leave this house now and go to the uninhabited dry place and stay there! Get out and never come back, in Jesus' name! This house and this family is cleansed and covered by the Blood of Jesus! I now ask the Holy Spirit to come and fill every place that unclean spirit vacated and stand hold there. I close any and all doors to the kingdom of darkness and seal them with the blood of Jesus!!"*

Now, Let's Close Those Doors To Anything Ungodly, Unholy, Or Demonic Forever!

Close any and all doors/connections to soul ties!! You must break ungodly soul ties from your past. This will start the Holy Spirit flow that you need for the rest of the stuff!

Soul Tie Items

A soul tie happens when you have had a sexual or very close relationship with someone other than your spouse. A soul tie is also connected to a promise, agreement, or covenant you may have had with an organization, club, or person. Such as fraternities or sororities. It stays on you until you break it off and remove any gifts, clothing, jewelry, letters, pictures, or keepsakes, etc. It can affect your current marriage, family, and even business negatively if you never removed your old soul ties to past relationships. You are showing the enemy you are still in covenant with that other person or organization. You should ONLY be in covenant with God through Jesus Christ and your own spouse.

Soul ties can also come from close friendships that did not end well. You can also be stuck in a "blood covenant" with someone if you did a "blood sisters/brothers" ritual as a kid, If you pricked your thumb and pressed your blood with another person's as a gimmick, that is not good. God looks at that as a covenant and so does the enemy. You can break that off with a simple prayer. You can also ask Jesus to apply His blood over anything that is out there that you gave to the other person and break the soul tie off that.

Soul tie covenants can also be connected to people you were employed by and any kind of agreement you signed to do at that job or project. You need to break all agreements and your signature off of any documents (such as a non-compete document). Erase it with the blood of Jesus in Heaven and on earth. This could be holding back financial and other blessings toward your purpose.

Ungodly soul ties and items from any sinful relationships can also open door to the kingdom of darkness in your home and marriage. You need to remove, trash, or burn them ASAP.

Note: Spiritual housecleaning includes removing toxic relationships and also friendships that cause you to sin or with those who try to drag you down or pull you backward in your faith walk. Do not throw your pearls to the swine anymore. It's time to walk away. I have done this with many relationships. I even wrote them goodbye letters. Some I had to block on social media. That was my old life, and I will not allow anyone to try to pull me back or discourage me or mock my faith. I forgive them, bless them, and block them.

RE: JEWELRY, FURNITURE, AND VALUABLE ITEMS CONNECTED TO THAT SOUL TIE

What If The Soul Tie Item Is An Expensive Item?

The word of God says to actually burn these items even if they are of value. However, we do have the powerful blood of Jesus. You can repent for keeping them all this time, cut and sever all soul ties to that person with the sword of the Spirit of God, and lift the items up to God. Give them to God, consecrate them to God, and cover your sin and the items in the blood of Jesus. Ask the Lord to cleanse and sanctify them with His blood and to remove all curses and demonic assignments off them, in Jesus' name.

If you have anointing oil you can also anoint them and bless them for the next person who will buy it. Take the money you make, and make an offering of the first part of it to the Lord as gratitude for His forgiveness, grace, and mercy. God did tell Joshua to give HIM the silver and gold plunder from the FIRST victory at Jericho, but He did not want the idols. He told them to heap them up and burn them!! I would only sell items that don't have any occult symbols on them! Trash or burn anything with the occult and repent, repent, repent! See my repentance prayers in this book and renouncing unholy covenants prayer in this book.

Idols Or Demonic Decor

If the item is an idol or has a demonic/occult design, do not sell these! Burn them or smash and trash them! Repent for having them, and break their demonic power off of your home and life with the blood of Jesus. See the list below for these types of objects.

Hidden Demonic Attachments

Furniture that had idol worship on it, items used in violent or criminal acts, mirrors used in witchcraft or that had curses spoken over it, jewelry used in a robbery, family jewelry with bloodline curses, SOUVENIRS from foreign lands where witch doctors and Voodoo is still practiced. (These souvenirs may look harmless, but these witch doctors put curses on them and tourists buy them and unknowingly bring curses into their homes!)

Also, check stuff bought at antique or consignment stores and yard sales. You must ask the Holy Spirit to reveal if there are curses attached. Hold it up to God and ask for revelation and confirmation. I used to love to shop at yard sales, thrift shops, and consignment stores, BUT now that I know what I know, I try to never buy anything from those places anymore, especially furniture or jewelry!

Years ago, I had a consignment shop I used to go to all the time. I loved the shabby chic look in my home design, so I wanted to create a sink for my bathroom made out of an antique dresser. I found the one I wanted and waited for weeks for it to go on sale. I went back there one day with a wonderful Christian girl who used to work for me. I bought it, and she helped me load it in my van and bring it home. I did not know the dresser was cursed. I put it in my bathroom ready to convert it to a vanity sink. Immediately I had a huge, ugly fallout with this wonderful girl who worked for me. It was terrible. We had never had a problem before. She was so sweet, and I had loved her and her work. She left in tears. Then all kinds of strife began in my home with my family. My cats were even creeped out by it and would hiss when they walked by the dresser sometimes. This went on for years and something kept happening to where financially we could not finish the bathroom.

I then moved the dresser to my teen daughter's room. She needed the drawer space. Almost immediately, I saw a change in her. She started getting rid of her cute clothes and started wanting to buy dark-type clothes with skulls and stuff like that on them and began filling those dresser drawers up with that stuff!

One day I was reading Jeanette Strauss' book, *Redeem Your Home*. She talked about demonic attachments on furniture. I heard the Holy Spirit tell me to go look at that dresser and stare at it. So I did, and my spiritual eyes were opened! I saw that there had been Idol worship on top of that dresser before I got it! I was shocked! It all made sense!

I went to my daughter's room, and I calmly told her I would be buying her new furniture. I did not tell her why. I made a fun shopping trip with her, and we got all brand new stuff for her room. I removed the cursed one and did the prayers of repentance!! We saw a change and shift for the better almost immediately when it was gone. I reached out to that Christian girl who used to work with me, and we reconciled in forgiveness. Thank You, Holy Spirit!

Belongings Of Other People That Live With You

If the cursed or demonic item belongs to another person, such as your child or spouse, ask the Lord for grace and mercy for them and you, cover your home and everything in it in the blood of Jesus, and ask the Holy Spirit to go and show that person to remove the items. Your children, if small, will be better about the stuff being removed. Have a gentle talk with them. Teens and other adults can be difficult, so you need my Holy Spirit prayer (see below).

Kid Safety From Demons

The "virtual games," such as anime and anything where they set up an online house or hotel are demonic portals for kids and your house. You can repent for allowing them to play them and command any familiar spirits or demons to leave!

First, cut them off of your kids with your sword of the Spirit, bind them and command them to leave now, and ask your Angels of The Lord that are assigned to you or Almighty God to arrest and chain up these demons and familiar spirits and take them to the dry place! Cleanse and seal your kids and your house and computers in the blood of Jesus, and close up any place they came in with the fire of the Holy Spirit and forbid them from ever returning, in Jesus' name. Make sure no games or stuff from them are around or left.

I am asking the Holy Spirit to reveal and remove with angelic help. The deal with video games and virtual reality has to do with if they "become" a character. That's what God was showing me.

This is a quenching of their identity in Christ. Make sure you invite the Holy Spirit to come and take over that place forever! By your authority in Christ speak over your children in prayer and command every "character identity" that your children play-act in online games be canceled removed and erased by the Blood of Jesus. Ask the Holy Spirit to then go to your child and reveal to them their true identity in Christ and their true calling for the Kingdom of God.

Violent Or Demonic Video Games Played By Teens Or Spouses

Place them and the game in the blood of Jesus. Send the Holy Spirit to hover over them and begin a work in them to guide them to the truth. Ask the Father for grace and mercy over you, your loved one, and your home, and ask for angelic protection while the Holy Spirit does a work in them to see the truth.

I want to be clear, If you live in a house with other people, you cannot remove their ungodly or cursed things from the house unless they agree to it, and you cannot "push" or "convince" them. They must be led by the Holy Spirit. You go ahead and remove your own things — what you have control over in your home. Even with your kids, this is a process, and you need to send the Holy Spirit ahead of you to work on opening their eyes first. They can witness you doing it with your own stuff, and it will get them to thinking.

You can say to your kids and spouse, "I am getting rid of this stuff because I really love Jesus, and I don't want anything that would not honor Him around me and in my space. I also don't want anything in my space that has anything evil attached to it because that could be holding back my blessing!"

Then when your blessings and breakthroughs come, you make a big deal of it right in front of everyone, "Praise God! My blessing is here. I knew if I got rid of that stuff miracles would come!" Do you get what I am saying here? They need to WITNESS the glory of God operating in what you are doing. It makes them think, and you can keep sending the Holy Spirit to work on them.

DO NOT GET RELIGIOUS, JUDGMENTAL, OR FORCEFUL ABOUT OTHER PEOPLE'S STUFF! JUST BE THE EXAMPLE IN KINDNESS AND LOVE!!

Mom Tip

When they are not around, you can pray over and anoint the kids' computers where they play the games, their phones, the internet modem, etc. See the end of this teaching on how to anoint the objects and your home.

SEND THE HOLY SPIRIT TO YOUR LOVED ONES TO HELP THEM REMOVE UNHOLY ITEMS. HE WILL HELP YOU!

Pray This To Send The Holy Spirit To A Loved One To Help Them Remove Evil Items In Their Lives

- ☐ *"Holy Spirit, my helper in all things, I send You to my loved one, _____, to do a work in them. Hover over them and do creative miracles in them. I ask You, Holy Spirit, to reveal to them the activities, things, and items in their lives that do not honor God. Convict them in their heart to remove these unholy and ungodly activities and items from their life forever and reveal the love, grace, and mercy of Father God. Fill those places where those items and activities were with Your Holy Spirit. I place the blood of Jesus on every portal, gate, or door where those demonic assignments were operating around my loved one. I close those demonic portals, gates, and doors forever and seal them with the blood of Jesus! Holy Spirit, I ask You now to point _____ to Jesus Christ so that they will desire Him and want to lead a life that reveals life, light, and truth in Christ Jesus. I declare Jeremiah 24:7 over my loved one, _____, that God is giving them a heart to know Him right now! I am in faithful expectation to see Your miracle-working power, Holy Spirit, in my loved one. Help me to work with You, Holy Spirit, to be an example to them. Give me the words to speak to them that will stir their heart to love all things that magnify our Father God and to remove all things in their life that do not honor Father God, in Jesus' mighty name. Amen."*

HOUSE CLEANING CHECKLIST - REPENT, REMOVE, AND TRASH THESE ITEMS ASAP

- Horror, murder, and crime movies/DVDs
- Vampire movies/vampire romance novels
- Harry Potter Books/DVDs (or anything with sorcery or magic)
- Yoga Books/DVDs (yoga is based on occultic worship)
- Pornographic movies, DVDs, magazines, books - *Fifty Shades of Grey* (sexual fantasy), etc.
- Tribal decor - dream catchers, Voodoo, totems, Indian wedding vases, Kachina dolls, African masks
- Wooden carved items with tribal faces or animal spirit gods (souvenirs from vacations)
- Mexican sun god decor (Mayan or Aztec)
- Anything New Age or occultic/witchcraft (crystals, books, decor or clothing with symbols, upside down stars, Hindu elephants or, ying/yang symbol, etc.)
- Occultic decor - Buddhas, etc.- incense holders that burned incense to false gods
- Statues and pictures of Catholic saints, rosary or prayer beads, candles to saints
- Demonic video games - *Dungeons and Dragons*, etc.
- Demonic music/CDs/records (rock bands such as Black Sabbath, AC/DC, etc.)
- Personal items from a former owner of the house (possible curse or negative attachment), such as finding old whiskey bottles (alcoholism), etc.
- Good luck charms, rabbits' feet, clovers, horseshoes on the wall for luck, anything you wear/display for luck - repent and throw away

- Soul tie items from former lovers or former close relationships - jewelry, rings, gifts, love letters, emails, texts (remove/delete)
- Furniture that may have had idol worship on it or was in a house before you that was cursed (ask the Holy Spirit to reveal)
- Guns or knives/weapons that may have been used in a murder or blood sacrifice (ask the Holy Spirit to reveal)
- Death-related decor/items - skulls, etc.
- Masonic (freemasons) cult items - this will have to go through the Courts of Heaven Repentance to break bloodline curses if you were a Freemason or had someone in your bloodline that was a Mason. See my "Breaking Unholy Covenants Prayer"
- Water witching rods, energy-related pendulums, ouji boards, mood rings, magic 8 balls that are used to answer questions (witchcraft, magic, or sorcery)
- Collections/decor that include occultic characters or symbols, fairies, dragons, smurfs, goblins, elves, mermaids, witches, monsters, vampires, peace signs (upside-down cross), etc.
- Angel decor items that are female (no angel in the Bible is female. Female angels represent familiar spirits, so remove them)
- DELETE old social media posts, files on computers, and apps on phones that are sexual, profane, ungodly, dark, New Age, magical, or occultic. Remove any subscriptions to pages or channels that are New Age or occultic - energy healing, chakras, the law of attraction, hypnosis, past lives, reincarnation, psychics, angel numerology, etc.
- Remove anything related to Halloween
- Remove Starbucks Coffee and anything to do with it (demonic water spirit - mermaid goddess symbol - very evil)

STEP-BY-STEP PRAYERS OVER ITEMS IN YOUR HOME

1. Repentance - (Pray Out Loud)

☐ *"Father God, I come before You now to repent for my sin of allowing this cursed and detestable thing, _____, to be in my home and in my life. I am sorry, Father, for sinning against You and Your word. I want to honor You, Father God, with everything in my life. I am asking You, Father, for forgiveness, grace, and mercy. I am grateful for the finished work on the Cross of Your Son, Jesus Christ, and for His shed blood that redeems me and is my only defense and covering for my sins. Lord Jesus, please cover my sins with Your blood. Wash them clean off of me and off of my soul. Thank You, Jesus, for Your blood. Father, according to Your word in Hebrews 8:12 that says You will forgive my iniquities and will remember my sins no more and that You will do this for Your sake, Father God, I ask that the sins that I have repented of here today be remembered no more, and wiped from the record books of Heaven by the blood of*

Jesus. Thank You, Father, for Your grace, mercy, and forgiveness, in Jesus' name. Amen."

2. Remove And Renounce - (Pray Out Loud)

☐ "Father God, In the name of Jesus, I am removing this sinful, cursed, and detestable thing, _____, from my home and life forever. I renounce, nullify, and cancel any words, agreements, money transactions, and soul ties connected with it. I place this _____ in the blood of Jesus! Lord Jesus, release the power of Your blood! Your blood, Lord, destroys all darkness! I cleanse myself and every person, place, or thing that touched this _____ with Your blood, Jesus! The enemy is helpless against your blood, Lord, and must leave. I now take my sword of the Spirit that You have given me according to Your word in Ephesians 6:17, and I cut and sever all soul ties, curses, witchcraft, demons, and demonic assignments attached to this _____ OFF of me, my family, my home, and my life right now in the name of Jesus (make a cutting motion in the spirit with your sword). I now command all UNGODLY soul ties, curses, witchcraft, demons, familiar spirits, and demonic assignments to leave my house and family NOW, in Jesus' name! I take my authority in Jesus Christ, in whom I am seated, and I renounce anything from the kingdom of darkness that has been operating in my home. I nullify all demonic assignments and break all of your power. I bind you and command ALL these things from the kingdom of darkness to leave now. GET OUT, and go to the uninhabited dry place in the name and authority of Jesus Christ and by the power of His blood!! I thank my LORD Jesus Christ, the ONLY Lord I serve, and I ask you, Lord JESUS, to send Your heavenly hosts and warrior angels to arrest, shackle, and chain up these demons, their assignments, and their curses, to pull down all demonic strongholds and platforms, and to release the fire of God against them! I close the door forever to all ungodly soul ties, curses, witchcraft, demons, and demonic assignments and seal this door in the blood of Jesus Christ. Father, raise up a hedge of Your holy fire of protection around me and my home. Let Your Holy Ghost fire come now into my home and around my family to burn up any remnant of the kingdom of darkness in the spirit realm. Holy Spirit, fill every empty place these soul ties, curses, witchcraft, demons, and demonic assignments vacated and stand hold there, in Jesus' name!

- ☐ *"THE ONLY SPIRIT IN MY HOME IS THE HOLY SPIRIT FROM THIS DAY FORWARD IN JESUS' MIGHTY NAME!"*

WHAT YOU SHOULD TRASH AND BURN

Any item connected with witchcraft, sorcery, freemasonry or the occult should be trashed or burned.

WHAT YOU CAN PRAY OVER AND ANOINT

If the item is something you can sell or give away, you can ask God to sanctify it. Cover it in the blood of Jesus, and bless it and anoint it for the next person.

If you purchased something recently and problems started happening around you and your home and family when you brought the item into your home it could have a curse attached to it, so do the prayer below. I do this anyway over all new items I bring in my home, especially furniture and decor, and any gifts I decide to keep. You do not have to keep every gift that is given to you, especially if it makes you have a check in your spirit and uncomfortable in any way!

Sanctification And Anointing Of An Item - (Pray Out Loud)

- ☐ *"Father God, I lift up this item, _____, and I offer it up to You, Almighty God, creator of the universe in whom all things were made! I surrender this item to You, Father, and into Your kingdom. I consecrate and dedicate this item, _____, to You, Father, and ask You to bless it and sanctify it. I cover this _____ in the blood of Jesus. Lord Jesus, release the power of Your blood, destroy all darkness on this item, and wash it clean. Restore it, Lord, to You. I take the anointing oil that I have also dedicated to You, Lord, and I anoint this _____ with the oil of the Holy Spirit and the blood of Jesus Christ. I bless this _____, in the name of Jesus. I decree that this item is now blessed by God and will now be used for the plans and purposes of Almighty God and for Your glory, Father God. Let the next person who has this item be blessed and highly favored, Father, and let this item now carry the anointing of Your Holy Spirit, in Jesus' mighty name. Amen."*

Breaking Unholy Covenants and Soul Ties Connected To Items

Each Individual In Your Family Should Pray This Out Loud If Willing

- ☐ *"Father God, I come before You to confirm by faith that I stand on and now fully agree with YOUR word, according to Galatians 2:20, that "I am crucified with Christ: nevertheless I live; yet not I, but Christ liveth in me: and the life which I now live in the flesh I live by the faith of the Son of God, who loved me and gave himself for me." Therefore, Father God, my testimony is this: Through the blood of Jesus Christ, I am redeemed out of the hand of the devil — spirit, soul, and body. I belong to Jesus Christ and am sanctified and set apart to You, Father God, by the blood of Jesus. Thank You, Jesus, that Your blood speaks for me before our Father God night and day on the Mercy Seat! Thank You, Father, for YOUR grace, forgiveness, and mercy! Father God, I come before You and I renounce, rebuke, revoke, and cancel all unholy covenants and soul ties I have ever made in my life with any person or entity, and that my ancestors ever made in their lives going all the way back to Adam and Eve, in Jesus' name! I repent, Father God, for these unholy covenants and soul ties in my life and my ancestors' lives, and I ask for Your grace, mercy, and forgiveness! Lord Jesus, wash away my sins with Your blood, and wash my ancestral bloodline clean with Your precious blood, Lord Jesus! Father God, I ask that you release me and my ancestors and my descendants from any consequences and entanglements of these sins and covenants! I ask that I, my family, my marriage, my children, my bloodline, and household be fully released of any curses or demonic assignments that were connected to these unholy ungodly covenants, soul ties, or items that were connected to them. I renounce any items or gifts or paperwork or promises connected to any unholy ungodly covenants or soul ties! I decree today that the only covenant I am in and my family from this day forward is one HOLY covenant with Almighty God through the blood of Jesus Christ! My soul belongs to Jesus Christ! I also decree this over my bloodline, in Jesus' name!*

- ☐ *"Father God, I ask that all records of unholy covenants and soul ties be wiped, expunged, and erased off my record books and the record books of my ancestors in the Courts of Heaven by the blood of Jesus and remembered no more in the heavens and the earth for Your sake, Father, and my sake, in Jesus' name! I ask that the NEW HOLY COVENANT that I have with You, Father God, through Jesus Christ is written and decreed in my record books in Heaven, and this record of repentance is made available for all my future repentances and applied to all my generations thereof Father God, from this day forward, in Jesus' name. AMEN!"*

It's time for you to get FREE of all unholy entanglements that would try to hold back your divine destiny! It's time for great blessings and breakthroughs to come forth in your life, family, household, finances, ministry, and business! Whooo hooooo!!!

Room By Room Prayer For House Cleansing Dedication And Anointing

Also See my teaching, "How To Pray Over And Apply Anointing Oil," to learn how to anoint your home as you pray the prayer below.

Pray This Out Loud In Every Room Of Your Home

- ☐ *"Father, because of the blood of Jesus and His FINISHED work on the cross, the devil has been defeated. I take ahold of this right now as my restraining order against all evil. According to Ephesians 2, I am seated next to You, Father, in Christ. I thank You, Father God, for my new authority in Christ given to me. Because of this authority, I now rule and reign in Christ Jesus and put everything of the kingdom of darkness under my feet because it is all under the feet of King Jesus. Therefore, I enforce the blood of Jesus and the finished work of the cross over and in every room of my home. I invite you, King Jesus, to be Lord over every room and every space in this home. I declare, through the blood of Jesus, that my home has now been redeemed out of the hand of the devil and back in the hand of Almighty God! Now, each room is set aside for the plans and purposes of God. I consecrate and dedicate this home and everything in it to You, Almighty God! King Jesus, I invite You to stay with us here in our home! Let the blessings and protection of the kingdom of God come forth in and through every room of my home, in Jesus' name!*

- ☐ *"According to Psalm 91:1, I declare that this _____ (room), Father God, has been transformed in the spirit into Your secret place and that it abides now under Your shadow. I repent for and renounce every sin that was ever committed in this _____ (room) of my house, including but not limited to all sins listed in I Corinthians 6:9-10 — indulgence of sexual sins, idolatry, adultery, prostitution, homosexuality, theft, greed, drunkenness, abuse of any kind, and cheating or extortion of any kind.*

Updated: Cleanse and Claim The Atmosphere Of Every Room In Your Home and Property

You need to understand that any words of negativity, word curses, gossip, or even profanity (demonic - these words empower evil in the spirit) that have ever been spoken by anyone in your home, even past residents/owners, are still hanging in the atmosphere.

God has given us the authority in Christ to command these words and word curses to leave!

Ephesians 2:6: "For he raised us from the dead along with Christ and seated us with him in the heavenly realms because we are united with Christ Jesus."

Revelation 5:10: "And you have caused them to become a Kingdom of priests for our God. And they will reign on the earth."

Go To Each Room Of Your House And Around Your Property, Barns, Sheds, Garages etc And Declare Out Loud

- [ ] *"Father, because of the blood of Jesus and His FINISHED work on the cross, the devil has been defeated. I take ahold of this right now as my restraining order against all evil. According to Ephesians 2, I am seated next to You, Father, in Christ. I thank You, Father God, for my new authority in Christ given to me. Because of this authority, I now rule and reign in Christ Jesus and put everything of the kingdom of darkness under my feet because it is all under the feet of King Jesus. Therefore, I enforce the blood of Jesus and the finished work of the cross by the authority of Jesus Christ over the atmosphere in every room in my home and around my property today, in Jesus' name! In Jesus' name, I renounce every wicked, negative, lying, gossipy, profane word or word curse, incantation, or spell that has ever been spoken in this _____ (room) in my house and the property itself at _____ (address) to leave now, in Jesus' name! I put them all in the blood of Jesus and dismantle and cancel all these demonic words and count them null and void, in Jesus' name! I place everything below this house, in this house, and above this house in the blood of Jesus! Lord Jesus, release the power of your blood! Your blood, Jesus, destroys all curses and demonic assignments right now, in Jesus' name! I proclaim this house — every room, every item, every space, every molecule of air — everything in the atmosphere of this house is now cleansed and sanctified by the blood of Jesus! Holy Spirit, I ask You now to come in and breathe Your fresh breath of life into the atmosphere of every room in my home and the surrounding property at _____ (address). Fill every space with Your love, joy, happiness, peace, and truth, in Jesus' name. Thank You, Holy Spirit, that the atmosphere of my home and property is now filled with Your holy presence from this day forward! Amen."*

Go To The Center Of Your Home And Pray This Out Loud Over Your Entire Home

- [ ] *"Father God, I place this home and all of its residents in the mighty blood of Jesus. In the name of Jesus Christ, I take authority over every evil spirit, evil influence, discord, and even hidden evil things, that have inhabited this home or affected it in any way and command them all to leave this house now and go to the uninhabited dry place and stay there! Get out and never come back, in Jesus' name! I now ask the Holy Spirit to come and fill every place those evil spirits and influences vacated and stand hold there. I close any and all doors to the kingdom of darkness and seal them with the blood of Jesus!! I place everything below this house, in this house, and above this house in the blood of Jesus! Lord Jesus, release the power of your blood! Your blood, Jesus, destroys all curses and demonic assignments right now, in Jesus' name! I proclaim this house — every room, every item, every space, every molecule of air — everything in this house is now cleansed and sanctified by the blood of Jesus! Father God, in the name of Jesus Christ, I ask for You to post Your sentry angels to all of the gateway areas of my home — natural, spiritual, and digital — to keep watch and guard around the clock and protect these gates from all evil! I ask for the sentry angels of Almighty God to stop and destroy any evil or demonic assignments that would attempt to go in or out through any and all gateways of my home with their supernatural fiery swords and shields from this day forward, in Jesus' name! Holy Spirit, I ask and invite You now to come in and breathe Your fresh breath of life into every room in my home and the surrounding property at _____ (address). Fill every space with Your love, joy, happiness, peace, and truth, in Jesus' name. Thank You, Holy Spirit, that my home and property is now filled with Your holy presence from this day forward! Amen."*

Finishing Up Spiritual House Cleaning and Maintenance

After you pray over and anoint every room of your home (I do all the doorways and windows), stand in the middle of your home and play the recording of the shofar (loud) in your home. This is the sound of the trumpet in Zion to take out any spiritual enemies and call forth the hosts of Heaven to fight for you, according to Nehemiah 4:20.

Update: Cleanse The Atmosphere Everywhere Around Your Home Or Land

If you have an older house, words are still there from previous owners.

Pray Out Loud

☐ *"Father God, I come to You in the name of Jesus Christ, for it is written that we have dominion and authority in HIM in the earth and over our land and home! So, RIGHT NOW, IN THE NAME AND AUTHORITY OF JESUS CHRIST IN WHOM I AM SEATED, I evict every wicked, profane, unclean, defiled, LYING, CURSING word that has been spoken and released into the atmosphere since the beginning of time up to today at (address) _____, and I command them all off this place (room/porch/yard/etc)! I kick them out right NOW in Jesus' Mighty Name! Lord Jesus, I invite You here and give you permission to cleanse this place with Your blood. Sanctify this atmosphere and everything in it! Make it all holy back to God! WASH AWAY ANY REMNANT OF ANY UNHOLY, UNGODLY WORDS! I invite you, Holy Spirit, to come in here now and give you permission to release your dunamis resurrection power into this place and pour a cleansing fresh anointing! Father God, I invite Your holy beautiful presence of love, peace, joy, and happiness, and Your TRUTH to the atmosphere of (address) _____, in Jesus' Mighty Name! Amen!"*

Prayers and Decrees For Sounding The Shofar For Your Home and Property

(Scatters the demonic and calls in the Angels of the Lord)

- Play a shofar recording on loop in home on low all day. A recording I that I use: 12min Of Non-Stop Shofar on YouTube (great for pets in the home all day too)

- Purchase a shofar to blow daily out your front door and back door gate areas to your property daily or weekly or use the LOUD WARFARE SHOFAR recording on Youtube

The sound of the shofar is the trumpeting voice of God, and demons hate it. It's like bug repellant. It's God's frequency and sends the demonic realm into confusion and they scatter and attack themselves. Look to the teaching and prayers in this book to remove demonic frequencies out of your home and bring in God's frequency.

Decrees For Sounding The Shofar

Sound The Shofar Loud As You Speak Psalm 24 (KJV)

☐ *"The earth is the Lord's, and the fulness thereof; the world, and they that dwell therein.*

For he hath founded it upon the seas, and established it upon the floods. Who shall ascend into the hill of the Lord? Or who shall stand in his holy place? He that hath clean hands, and a pure heart; who hath not lifted up his soul unto vanity, nor sworn deceitfully. He shall receive the blessing from the Lord, and righteousness from the God of his salvation. This is the generation of them that seek him, that seek thy face, O Jacob. Selah. Lift up your heads, O ye gates; and be ye lift up, ye everlasting doors; and the King of glory shall come in. Who is this King of glory? The Lord strong and mighty, the Lord mighty in battle. Lift up your heads, O ye gates; even lift them up, ye everlasting doors; and the King of glory shall come in. Who is this King of glory? The Lord of hosts, he is the King of glory. Selah."

Declare Out Loud

☐ *"Yahweh is fighting for us! Lord, scatter my enemies and drive them out just like You did for Gideon, in Jesus' name! I decree the battle is the Lord's and the King of glory, Lord of hosts is here! Jesus Christ is VICTOR! Every knee must BOW to the lordship of Jesus*

Christ! I decree that the frequency of the VOICE of Almighty God is the only frequency allowed in this house, in Jesus' name!"

Declare Out Loud

- *"Jehovah Nissi! The Lord Is My Banner! Jehovah Jireh! The Lord Is My Provider! Jehovah Rapha! The Lord Is My Healer! Jehovah Shalom! The Lord Is My Peace!*

Declare Psalm 44:4-5

- *"You, O Lord, are my King and my God who decrees victories for _____. Through you, we push back our enemies; through your name, we trample our foes. But you give us victory over our enemies. You put our adversaries to shame! Hallelujah !!*

Finally, Declare Out Loud

- *"As for me and my house, we shall serve the Lord God of Israel, God of Abraham, Isaac, and Jacob, Father of our Lord and Savior, Jesus Christ, of Nazareth!"*

Speak The Priestly Blessing In Your Home

The blessing from the Lord to His people according to Numbers 6:24-26.

Home Blessing (Aaronic Priestly Blessing): Play a recording out loud in your home first in Hebrew then in English by a Rabbi. (I find these on Youtube.)

Speak This Blessing At Your Front Door (Or In The Middle Of Your Home)

☐ *"The Lord bless us and keep us: The Lord make his face shine upon us and be gracious unto us. The Lord lift up his countenance upon us, and give us peace."*

Anoint Your Entire Home And Dedicate It To God

Dedicate, Bless, And Anoint Your Home, Yourself, Children, Animals, And Possessions With Oil

You can use olive oil or anointing oil from the biblical recipe given by God. The important thing is that the oil has been prayed over and dedicated to God.

I have also used this oil from Jerusalem, called the Light of Jerusalem anointing oil. You can order it from the Judaica Webstore.

More Teachings On Anointing Your Home And Family

Go to my "How to Pray Over and Apply Anointing Oil" prayer here in my book for more information.

How To Pray Over Your Groceries And Any Purchase Coming Into Your Home

What Is Defiling Your Temple?

I had a teaching when we were at Nisan 10 and Nisan 11 (Palm Sunday). We are in the moment when Jesus walked into the temple after coming in on a donkey, and He inspected the temple. (Mark 11:1-11) This was the night before Jesus came back into the temple and overturned the tables and drove the money changers out with a whip because they were selling and exchanging "foreign" money and taking what should belong to God and what should be blessing His dwelling place for their own greedy gain.

We are the temple now — our bodies (and our homes when we invite the Holy Spirit in). We invite the Lord Jesus Christ into our heart and life when we receive salvation. Our spirit man is renewed — Christ who lives within us. Then the sanctification process just begins. When you receive Jesus Christ as your Lord and Savior, the sanctification process just starts, and it's time to start cleaning out the temple, folks. What's in your temple that's defiling it?

You can only do that with the help of the Holy Spirit. So after you ask Jesus Christ to be your Lord and Savior and come into your heart, your spirit man is renewed, and the sanctification process needs to start as we grow in the Lord. We have to then invite the Holy Spirit in — the presence of the Lord.

If you're not sure if you have invited Jesus Christ into your heart, and if you're not sure that you have invited the Holy Spirit to come and dwell within you, then you need to go to my website, annamariestrawhand.com, to my Salvation prayers, and do it again because we go all the way. Recommit your life to Christ today, and pray that prayer again. Invite the Lord Jesus Christ in you, and invite the Holy Spirit in you.

Then you can really start the clean-up. You can say, "Holy Spirit," and just know by faith that He's there, and you will begin to hear Him. You will begin to get stirrings in your spirit. He will begin to point out things to you that's junk in your trunk. He'll begin to say to you, "Listen, sister, there's some stuff that's defiling your temple that's going in your eye-gate. Yeah, you know those horror movies you've been watching? Time to stop doing them. They're going in your eye-gate. They're defiling your temple. Hey, you know that rap music you've been listening to with bad language or rap music you've been listening to on an unholy, ungodly frequency coming in your ear-gates? That's defiling your temple. Need to clean that stuff out. You know that junk food filled with chemicals that you've been putting in your mouth-gate? That's defiling your temple. Better stop doing that stuff."

You see, when you start realizing that within you is the Holy of Holies, the place where Jesus dwells, the place where the presence of the Lord dwells within you, Christ who lives within you, the Holy Spirit who dwells within you, you are a walking temple of the Lord, and you do not want defilement in there. And it's time to clean up. Jesus is in there overturning the tables in you. He's going, "Get this stuff up out of you right now. Come on, no more of that stuff. No more of that stuff coming in your gates."

Are you eating foods that you don't pray over that were offered up to idols? Hmm? That's why you've got to pray over everything before it goes in your mouth-gate. Paul made very clear of that, especially when he was in the Greek countries and the lower Asian and upper Asian countries and setting up churches because they were still eating foods and bringing foods into the churches that had been dedicated to idols and eating it. And he kept telling them, "You're defiling your temple," and they were like, "Whaaat?"

Are there stores that you buy food from that are run by Muslims? They offer up their meats and everything to Allah. They don't worship the Father of our Lord Jesus Christ, you see. They believe Jesus was just a prophet. So those foods need to be prayed over.

We can eat whatever we want. It's not like we can't eat pork or we can't eat shrimp. We can still eat those things because God told Peter, "Kill and eat, Peter," and He said, "Whatever I've made clean is clean." What does that mean? Pray over your food and dedicate it to God, and ask Jesus to wash it with His blood.

So I have this cup of coffee and I say, "Father, in the name of Jesus, I dedicate and consecrate this cup of coffee to You. I ask You to bless it, and I bless it in the name of Jesus. Lord Jesus, cleanse this coffee with Your blood and sanctify it, in Jesus' name." And then I drink it.

I dedicate my food to God. I ask Jesus to cleanse it with His blood, and I bless it and ask God to bless it. That means it's changed realms. The tables have been flipped on your food before it's put into your mouth-gate. It has changed realms. Amen?

I love to buy kosher foods because I know they've been dedicated to the Lord God of Israel — God of Abraham, Isaac, and Jacob — but because God told Peter as a disciple — and I'm a disciple of the Lord, and I might have to travel places, or I might have to go into places where food is not kosher, I know by what God instructed Peter — to kill and eat — and He said, "What I have made clean is clean."

Just pray over your food. Rededicate it to God. Just dedicate anything that goes into your gates to God. I don't care if you're using eye drops, makeup, anything that goes on your temple, just lift it up to God, dedicate it to Him, and ask Him to bless it.

And this is what I do; I make it easy. When I have a whole car full of groceries, I pull into the driveway with my groceries, and I say,

> ☐ *"Father God, thank You for these groceries today. I dedicate and consecrate all of the groceries in this car to You, Father God. I ask You to bless them. I wash all of these*

> *groceries and even the containers that they're in in the blood of Jesus. Let everything that comes into my home be washed in the blood of Jesus Christ right now and blessed by You, God."*

I just do it all at once with my groceries, so that when my groceries come in the house, they've all been dedicated to God even before they hit the refrigerator and the cabinets. So when you pull in your driveway with the groceries, just say this prayer: "Father God, I thank You for all of these groceries. I thank You for Your provision. I dedicate and consecrate all of these groceries to You, Father God, and I ask You to bless them. I place all of these groceries in the blood of Jesus. Let them be cleansed by the blood of Jesus so that everything that goes into my home is washed in the blood of Jesus and sanctified. I call these groceries blessed, in Jesus' name."

You can even do that as part of your suit up every morning. Say you order something online, maybe you order foods online, maybe you do online shopping, and here comes the UPS truck or the FedEx truck, "beep, beep, beep, beep, beep," backing up to your driveway, and dropping stuff off. In the morning, just say, "Anything that comes into my home, any delivery that comes into my home, I dedicate to You, Father God, and I ask You, Jesus, to wash it in Your blood. So anything coming in my home today, I dedicate to Almighty God. Let it be washed in the blood of Jesus Christ."

That includes your mail coming in from the mailbox and deliveries. Maybe somebody's coming into your house to do some service or something. You know, work on your heat or your air conditioning or your plumbing or whatever. Just say, "Let everything that comes into this home today be dedicated to Almighty God and washed in the blood of Jesus."

You don't want to get obsessive-compulsive about it. Just do it as part of your daily routine, like your suit up. You know, don't start going through your cabinets and freaking out because your husband and kids will start going, "Wait a minute. She's gone a little bit off her rocker."

Just stand in the middle of the house, and keep it really simple. Say, "Father, in the name of Jesus, I dedicate all the possessions in this house right now — all the supplies, all the possessions in this home right now to You. You know where everything is God."

I'm not telling you to go into your bathroom and take everything out of the cabinets and every stick of lipstick and every shampoo, and be like [Sound effect]. Calm down. Just say, "Father, in the name of Jesus, I dedicate all of my possessions in this home, everything in this home, all of our supplies, to You, Father God. I ask You to bless everything in this home. I ask You to wash all the possessions that are in this home right now, right down to the tubes of lipstick, right down to the Q-tips, right down to the dog food, wash it all in Your blood. Cleanse it. Sanctify it. Make it holy, and I bless it too, in Jesus' name."

And you're done. You're done. Your home is like a temple too, right? Anywhere where there's gateways, and that's why I taught you all with Jeanette Strauss how to anoint your home. When you anoint the doors and windows, as it passes through, it's changing realms. It's coming into a place that's dedicated to God. Just make it simple.

Mike knows when we come home from our grocery shopping, right before he's ready to jump out of the car, I say that quick prayer over the groceries. Done.

And so just be reverent of what comes into your gateways, whether it be your home gateway or your body gateway because Jesus is doing an inspection right now. We're in a time and a season where Jesus is looking around, and He's saying, "You don't need that anymore, and I'm going to flip the tables and throw it out of here. It's defiling your temple."

Part 3
Dream Interpretation Prayers

Dream Interpretation From A Biblical Perspective – How To Cancel A Bad Or Demonic Dream

Here Are Some Things To Understand With Dreams

When you sleep, your soul and your spirit are always awake. You have three types of dreams.

1. Soulish Dreams

These come from stuff in your soul that is either from wounds or trauma from your past that gets stirred up, along with cell memories in your body that bring these things to the surface that the Holy Spirit wants you to deal with. The Holy Spirit may be bringing you to repentance and even prompting you to get these wounds healed in your soul because He loves you and wants you healed and whole. You prosper as your soul prospers. (See my Soul Cleansing Prayer.)

2. Demonic Dreams

These come from demons and demonic assignments that are working against you. These demons only have access if you allow it and agree with it. Demonic dreams must be canceled in the name of Jesus as soon as you wake up unless you destroyed the demon in your dream; then praise God. The more you suit up and take your authority in Christ every day, the more authority you will have over anything demonic in your dreams! If you had a demonic dream years ago, you can cancel it right now, in Jesus' name.

DEMONIC DREAM INTERPRETATION

If the dream had any negativity, fear, strife, angry people, confusion, or you were lost, wandering, losing things, looking for stolen things, getting into strange vehicles, stranger driving you, strange people force-feeding you, being chased, attacked or held captive, car accidents, death, or sexual perversion, it was demonic and needs to be canceled as soon as you wake up. Use discernment. If it caused you any fear or upset feeling in your spirit, listen to that feeling. Fear, strife, and strange stuff that causes confusion are not from God!!

Pray This To Cancel A Bad Or Demonic Dream

> ☐ *"Father God, in the name of Jesus, I cancel that dream I had about _____. I renounce everything in that dream, in Jesus' name, and I enforce the blood of Jesus over that dream and mark that dream and everything that happened in that dream null and void, in Jesus' name! By the authority of Jesus Christ and by the power of the blood of Jesus, I send all curses and witchcraft sent to harm me in that dream back to the place from where it was sent, and I close the doors to all curses and witchcraft and seal them with*

the blood of Jesus Christ! Father God, in Jesus' name, I ask You to release Your holy fire against any demons or demonic assignments in that dream and burn them to ashes! Henceforth, nothing from that dream will ever be able to bother me again!

- [ ] *"Father God, I ask You to send angelic protection over my dreams and sleep. I receive Your angels, Father God. Thank You for sending them to keep me in all my ways, according to your word in Psalm 91. I declare that every night from this day forward, I shall have sweet sleep and Holy Spirit-filled dreams! I now invite the Holy Spirit to come into my dreams tonight! I declare my dreams are covered and protected by the blood of Jesus Christ! Thank You, Father God, for Your love, promises, and protection over my dreams and sleep! Father God, I believe You are doing all things for my good, even speaking to me in my dreams, and I want to hear Your voice, Father God! I now dedicate and consecrate my dreams and sleep to You, Father God, all the days of my life for Your glory, in Jesus' name!"*

Confess This Out Loud Today

- [ ] *"I hear from God. I am led by His Holy Spirit. I know my Father's voice, and the voice of a stranger, I will not follow. I am guided by the Holy Spirit, and God will guide me all the days of my life. His HOLY SPIRIT will guide me and give me the answers that I need. I renounce all unholy, ungodly voices! Therefore, I invite the HOLY SPIRIT right now to come inside me and guide me. I command my mind, body, soul, and spirit to yield to the voice of the Holy Spirit, in Jesus' name!"*

For Children, Put Your Hands On Your Child's Forehead And Simply Pray

- [ ] *" I cancel the bad dream, and I ask You, Jesus, to send your angels to protect _____ while she/he sleeps. We invite You, Holy Spirit and Lord Jesus, to come into his/her dreams to bring sweet and happy messages and restful sleep, in Jesus' name. Amen."*

Children's Bedtime Note

It is helpful to anoint your children before bed to soothe them. I invite the Holy Spirit and declare scripture over them before they sleep. See my anointing prayers. Anoint the corners of their bed and over the doors and windows and dedicate it all to God in the name of Jesus.

Make sure there's nothing in your child's bedroom that could be an open door to the enemy. Remove anything of the occult! Understand that "dream catchers," though a native american practice, are not of God.

3. Holy Spirit Dreams

These dreams are messages, instructions, and confirmations from God for your life and for others' lives. All dreams from the Holy Spirit must be written down and dated. Then ask the Holy Spirit to give you guidance on the meaning of that dream and how to apply it. It can take days, weeks, or even months before you have the full revelation.

Holy Spirit dreams can include special things being handed to you in a dream for you to get a breakthrough — a key, a sword, a scroll, a lantern, etc. These items can all lead you to your next steps and, of course, take you to the word of God.

Having a baby in a dream means you are about to birth something ordained for your life's purpose. If you are actually trying to conceive a child in the natural, you may also dream about your baby or child to come.

If you see a certain prophet or teacher in a dream it means you are to seek the teachings of that person for the next step in your life right now.

Please Understand

Your dream meanings can include colors or numbers being shown to you — even other signs. YOU MUST FOCUS ONLY ON BIBLICAL MEANINGS of these things. The Holy Spirit's job is to guide you to the Word of God and deeper revelation of the kingdom. Stick with BIBLICAL sources.

For color meanings, look up the meanings of the colors of WORSHIP FLAGS. These colors have been deeply studied from the Bible before these flags are made. This is the source the Holy Spirit led me to, and He has confirmed it over and over again.

For number meanings, I suggest the teachings of Troy Brewer, *Numbers That Preach/PropheticNumbers,* for a good biblical resource.

Driving a vehicle in your dream means your divine purpose or ministry. Being in houses that need cleaning or restoration means your "soul needs a cleanup." (See my Soul Cleansing Prayer.) Being in the homes of your family members means your family bloodline may need repentance and to pray for your family's salvation. It can also mean focusing on praying for your family to receive their blessings and inheritance and to go into the Courts of Heaven to remove any curses. Being in a bathroom or going to the bathroom means you must repent of your sins and focus on soul cleansing and cleaning up your life. These are common things. I do my best to help you.

Seeing certain animals in dreams should only be studied from biblical meanings or the nature of how God made that animal. If the animal attacks you, that is demonic and must be canceled. DO NOT LOOK UP these things randomly online because it could lead you to New Age and occultic meanings that are NOT of God. Understand that "spirit animals" are NOT of God!

We only have the HOLY SPIRIT, period, and HE is the creator of all living things. His Spirit — the Spirit of the living God — is alive on the earth speaking through all creation right now to us.

For example, if you see a dragonfly or a butterfly repeatedly in the natural or in your dreams, the Holy Spirit is giving you a message. Look up the nature of these — how do they grow or transform? What is their nature? God put a message for us in the nature of His creation that could apply to our life at that moment.

If You Are Not Sure If A Dream Is From God, Pray This Prayer When You Wake Up

- ☐ *"Holy Spirit, if that dream was not of You, I do not receive it, in Jesus' name. But, Holy Spirit, if that dream was of You, I receive it and ask for the interpretation, understanding, application, and how to pray and proceed, in Jesus' name."*

Before you go to sleep, cover your dreams and sleep with the blood of Jesus. Cancel any demonic assignments and any demons that were assigned to you that night and tell them to leave and forbid them from touching your dreams and sleep, in Jesus' name. The blood of Jesus is against them! Decree that you have sweet sleep as written in the Bible and that your dreams and sleep belong to God. Invite Jesus and the Holy Spirit to visit you in your dreams and give you divine strategies for your life from the throne room of God in your sleep! Ask Father God, in Jesus' name, to post His sentry angels to surround your bed and stand guard over you with their fiery swords and shields as you sleep and to protect you from all evil day and night. Anoint your bed on all four corners and your head and feet with anointing oil. Decree your bed is holy and belongs to God! (See my anointing prayers)

Be blessed! The Holy Spirit will guide you through your dreams, and He always points to the word of God to confirm things, so stay in the word and He will reveal so much to you on your next steps in your life and purpose!

Sweet and restful dreams and sleep is God's promise to you!

Proverbs 3:24 (KJV), "When thou liest down, thou shalt not be afraid: yea, thou shalt lie down, and thy sleep shall be sweet."

Much love to you. Enjoy your sleep. It's the best time to get revelation from the Holy Spirit! He WANTS to speak to you in your dreams! He loves to meet you there and help you with your life and purpose!

Part 4
Courts of Heaven & Land Assignments

How To Appear and Pray In The Courts Of Heaven

UNDERSTAND that we do not have to go into the Courts of Heaven for every need or situation. It's just like in the natural realm of life you don't have to go to court in your city or county to solve every problem. When you go into the Courts of Heaven, it's for something that you have been dealing with for a while and the basic solutions are not working. For example, when you need to see a breakthrough and no matter what you have been doing it does not seem to be coming. This is a sure sign that there is a legal right of the accuser (the devil) to hold back your breakthrough! Discern that it is time to take your case into the Courts of Heaven. What gives the accuser a legal right to hold back your breakthrough? SIN — your own sin and the sins of your bloodline.

As a faith and victory coach and mentor, I have experienced great breakthroughs in my own life and in the lives of my clients and students by going into the Courts of Heaven with our cases. We have the right to do this as the redeemed of Jesus Christ. You must be a born again believer in Christ to access the Courts of Heaven and to be able to ask for the blood of Jesus to speak on your behalf. I want you to get good at this, for your own lives, for your family, and to help others. (See my "Salvation Prayer" here in the book.

It is time for the Body of Christ to go boldly to the Throne of Grace and Mercy and enforce the finished work of the Cross and the blood of Jesus against any legal rights of the enemy and get these demonic accusations and curses removed so they are never allowed to come back and have any effect ever again! Let's get this taken care of once and for all!

Teaching Note

In the Courts of Heaven, forgive those who have hurt you or your children, and release/renounce all bitterness and negative words against them onto the Cross of Jesus. Forgiveness strips the enemy of any legal right he is using in your relationships. When you repent for holding bitterness and unforgiveness of those who hurt you or hurt your kids, it breaks any strongholds the enemy had. Don't blame your ex husbands/wives, family members, or their friends or teachers for causing your kids to rebel. It's the legal right of the accuser to operate through these people. Once you forgive and release all bitterness and blame, those influences will leave you and your children, and within weeks you will see breakthrough. Trust me on this, I had to do this with my own child and forgive and release all bitterness against a horrible friend she had in her life that I was doing warfare against for years. It was not until I forgave, loosed all bitterness, and prayed for their salvation that my daughter was finally released from that ungodly influence!

The enemy uses our own bitterness, blame, and unforgiveness against us. I have spent countless hours in the Courts of Heaven for myself and my child and others and their children/families, and the accuser has screamed this at me in the Courts in the spirit. I am grateful I finally know this, and my child is set free. Look at yourself first, and stop blaming others. Instead, destroy the case of the accuser operating and strip him of his legal right!

Remember that most likely the issue that you are dealing with that you need a breakthrough in is usually connected to a sin in that area. For example, if you need a breakthrough with finances, there is usually sin in your life or your bloodline with money or not being good stewards to the Lord with your money. This is how I have learned and been set free of these accusations and see breakthroughs within weeks of repenting in the Courts.

HOW TO APPEAR IN THE COURT OF HEAVEN – GUIDE BY FAITH AND VICTORY COACH ANNAMARIE

Prepare And Pray

Ask the Holy Spirit what is holding back your breakthrough or causing a negative issue in your life or family. Tell Him of your specific issue or need and ask if the enemy — the accuser — is using a legal right to hold you captive to this, and what is the accuser accusing you of? Then ask the Holy Spirit for a court appearance in the Courts of Heaven. Take notes.

THE COURT OF JUDGMENT/ACCUSATION

Just Before Your Appearance - (Pray Out Loud)

- ☐ *"Holy Spirit, I am asking, in Jesus' name, that You will reveal all to me clearly during my court appearance so that I can repent clearly for my wrongdoings and follow through after the verdict is rendered. I am also asking for my angels to accompany me. Thank You for your help, Holy Spirit. Amen."*

- Picture yourself standing in a courtroom with your angels and the Holy Spirit beside you assisting you - (I physically stand while doing this)
- Picture yourself facing the Father God on His throne
- Picture Jesus to the right of the Father
- Picture the Mercy Seat just to the front of the Father near Jesus and in front of you (Ark of the Covenant)
- Picture Jesus' blood on the Mercy Seat
- Picture the accuser's place on the other side of Jesus - (Jesus stands for you in between the accuser and Almighty God, our Righteous Judge)
- Picture the recording angels with desks and scrolls and pens recording what is being said in the courtroom
- Picture the cloud of witnesses witnessing in your case and agreeing with Jesus and the verdict

Ask Jesus To Be Your Intercessor In This Case And For The Court To Convene

- Thank and praise the Father for allowing you to come to Court and for hearing your case
- Thank and praise Jesus for being your intercessor and attorney with your case
- Thank the Holy Spirit for His help in showing you and telling you what is being said
- Ask the Father, in Jesus' name, to demand that the accuser be summoned to appear
- Ask what the accusation against you is (things you have said or done against God or His commandments or someone in your bloodline has done)
- In the spirit, you may hear, remember, or even see a visual of that accusation
- Agree with the accusation
- Confess to the accusation and the sin associated with it — express fully that you are very sorry
- Repent to the Father for this sin against Him and His word
- Renounce all your actions or words connected to this sin
- Ask the Father for His grace, mercy, and forgiveness
- State that the blood of Jesus is your ONLY defense
- State that the blood of Jesus on the Mercy Seat speaks for you now
- Ask Jesus to cover your sins with His blood
- Wait while Jesus does this and thank and praise Him
- Thank the Father for His grace, mercy, and forgiveness
- Ask the Father for His judgment in your case
- Ask to be found "not guilty" because of the blood of Jesus
- You will receive a "not guilty" verdict — agree with this (because of Jesus we are all found not guilty)
- Thank the Father and Jesus that because of His blood, you are not guilty
- Ask the Father, in Jesus' name, to tell the accuser of His judgment and "not guilty" verdict in your case
- Ask the Father to now move you from the Court of Judgment/Accusation to beside His Throne of Grace and Mercy with Jesus
- Ask the Father, in Jesus' name, to strip the enemy of his accusation and any legal rights he has to you because the blood of Jesus is now covering these sins
- Ask the Father, in Jesus' name, to tell the recording angels to wipe your record books/scroll clean of these accusations because they are now under the blood of Jesus
- Ask, in Jesus' name, for all curses connected to this accusation to be removed and rendered null and void on earth and in Heaven, and ask the Father to release you and your family bloodline from all consequences of these sins
- Ask, in Jesus' name, for this new "not guilty" verdict regarding your case to be written in your record book/scroll
- Ask for a new document to be rendered for you from the Court with the new verdict for you to take with you
- Reach out and receive your document with your new "not guilty" verdict
- Ask the Father, in Jesus' name, if you can tell the accuser to leave and never accuse you or any of your descendants ever again of this same thing because the blood of Jesus has spoken on your and their behalf

- Turn to the accuser and tell him his assignment is over. He no longer has a case. By the blood of Jesus and this "not guilty" verdict rendered by the Court of Heaven and God Almighty in your hand, he must leave! Every curse and demonic assignment has been canceled according to the word of God. A curse causeless cannot light! Then in the name of Jesus, forbid him from accusing you or any of your descendants ever again — no recourse! Tell him this case is OVER and He has NOTHING on you because of the BLOOD and the righteous judgment of God!! Tell him he is FIRED and to take his curses with him, in Jesus' name! (You may see him stomp out of the Court!)
- Ask, in Jesus' name, for the Father to command His angels to decree your new "not guilty" verdict out loud in the Heavens
- Ask for any restitution that is available to you and your family (from the curses being removed, there may be blessings, healings, etc. that have been held back)
- Ask if there will be a need for specific angels to be assigned to you to carry out restitution

Upon Preparing To Leave The Court

- Thank the Father and praise Him for His grace and mercy, and thank Him for allowing you to come before Him with your case
- Thank Jesus for interceding for you, and thank Him for the power of His blood which is your only defense
- Thank the Angels who are recording, thank your angels for accompanying you, and thank the Holy Spirit for His help
- Ask the Father, in Jesus' name, for the verdict to immediately be fully carried out and enforced on earth and in your life and family line by the authority of Jesus Christ, the angels on assignment from God, and the by the anointing of the Holy Spirit
- Hold up your verdict and decree: "By the blood of Jesus and the grace and mercy of Almighty God, I am no longer guilty of this sin. I am free of all accusation and curses, in Jesus' name!

COURTS OF HEAVEN RESOURCES

Jeanette Strauss
Prayers/Petitions Written for You – By Jeanette Strauss From the Courtroom of Heaven & Prayers and Petitions www.gloriouscreations.net

Praying Medic
Books By Praying Medic: Defeating Your Adversary in the Court of Heaven by Praying Medic

Robert Henderson
Prayers & Declarations That Open the Courts of Heaven

Gatekeepers Prayer Guide And Decrees

A new wave of God's presence is coming to America! Wave your American flags and welcome the Lord! Decree your faith in His power and might! God's people are rising UP! We stand at the foot of the Cross and on the word of God! We are calling in the angel armies, taking the gates of America for the purposes of God, and claiming the land for the Lord Jesus Christ!

Psalm 24:7-10 (KJV): "Lift up your heads, O ye gates; and be ye lift up, ye everlasting doors; and the King of glory shall come in. Who is this King of glory? The Lord strong and mighty, the Lord mighty in battle. Lift up your heads, O ye gates; even lift them up, ye everlasting doors; and the King of glory shall come in. Who is this King of glory? The Lord of hosts, He is the King of glory. Selah."

Across the United States of America, there are strategic cities considered "gateways" that the enemy wants to take control of and has taken control of. Gates are very important to God and are mentioned many times in the Bible. Whoever controls the gate controls the city, region, or territory. The enemy wants to take over these "gates" and territories to cause problems for the people in these areas and to usher in sin and ungodliness. When this goes unchecked by the faithful people of God in that area, it will try and take over. Jesus told us to advance the kingdom of God and to OCCUPY until He comes.

You have downloaded this prayer guide because you feel called to do this for the kingdom and are asking the Father to guide you as you take your authority in Jesus Christ as a prayer leader and intercessor for the land and nation. I am so glad you are here! Get ready to take the gates for Christ and His kingdom!

Many "main" gates and territories have been infiltrated and taken over by demonic strongholds in America. This affects everything within your area — government, schools, businesses, homes and properties, public events, and churches. Many of our cities and regions across our great land have been overcome by crime, and our schools have been subject to violence and moral breakdown. Many times this will also reflect in land and property values, farming harvests, violent weather, and can also open the door for terrorism.

When there is a demonic stronghold in your city, county, or state, you will see local government leaders and protesters push for everything to be taken down that has to do with God, faith, prayer, and history. You will see that sin and un-repentance have caused God to lift His hand from the region. You will see discord, crime, more occultic practices, and shops and businesses closing in your area.

As a gatekeeper of my region, I want to do exactly that — let the good in and keep the bad out! I am sure you do too.

Our country was founded on biblical values. We are one Nation under God, indivisible, with liberty and justice for all, but this has been under attack.

There is a heated battle right now going on in the spiritual realm over the USA. Do you sense it? Satan wants America because America has been chosen by God to spread the Gospel of Jesus Christ across the world and to stand side by side and support Israel, who are still God's beloved chosen people.

The Holy Spirit began to show and teach me about "gates" and territorial strongholds back in the summer of 2016 right before the presidential election.

First, I was shown my "spiritual weapons." I had been using these in my personal life over my home, business, and family. Soon God began expanding me outward to use these weapons of warfare and started to teach me about taking my authority as a believer in Jesus Christ.

Next, the Lord showed me that we are His army. Jesus said, "Occupy until I come," NOT lay down and get run over till I come! OCCUPY. As believers, we must be strong, VIGILANT, and unified for the purposes of Almighty God and His kingdom, on earth as it is in Heaven. (1 Peter 5:8-9)

We Are Boots On The Ground For God!

Friends, we cannot fight evil with "tolerance and understanding." We are not fighting against flesh and blood but against demonic powers and principalities. The enemy wants our country and our kids. We have to stand up, speak up, and use our spiritual authority through Jesus Christ our King! We are seated in Him! We have the power to stop the devil in his tracks. God still loves America! He still has great plans for us and His people!

The enemy is also looking for his "legal right" to come into your areas. This comes from sin and curses upon the land that give the devil a foothold there.

I started using prayer strategies, declarations of the Word, and a deep desire and love for Jesus to be at the center of my life, in my family, and in my community. I started to see shifts happening in my region for the better!

I asked the Holy Spirit to show me the areas to pray and how to pray and to give me discernment on what was happening in the spirit realm. Maybe you have already been praying and asking God to intervene for America and our president. Maybe you have been praying for the Church to wake up and stand up. Maybe you are like me and you are sick and tired of the enemy having a foothold of your region and you are ready to stand up, take action in faith, and claim your region for the purposes of God!

You are reading this right now because you care about the safety and well-being of your country, your community, your family, and your children. Most of all, you are passionate about God's will and Christian values being revived and honored across this land.

**"Seek peace and well-being for the city where I have sent you into exile, and pray to the Lord on its behalf; for in its peace (well-being) you will have peace."
Jeremiah 29:7**

I was thinking about the harvest of souls for Jesus that America is aligned to do for the kingdom of God across the world. I feel strongly that is why the Lord put President Donald Trump in office — so the church will be awakened to stop hiding and waiting for the rapture and start fighting for Jesus. America will be the leader for the kingdom to rise up for Jesus and His reward.

In the book of Joel, it is written and prophesied in Chapter 2 about a time very much like today, and an army of God's people rose up — a remnant — and God blessed them greatly. My fellow gatekeepers, we are the remnant — a body of faithful believers in Jesus Christ who want to see the will of God done in this world, and those who are also patriotic Americans who believe that we are still one nation under God.

We must take up our divine weapons of warfare and take authority in Christ over our land. God has a divine destiny for America. We are still able to fight for this destiny! We are here to be an ally to Israel and spread the Gospel of Jesus Christ for the end-time harvest. This is why the enemy is coming at us so hard.

While at Jamestown, Virginia, last summer, the Holy Spirit told me to go into the old chapel there and kneel at the altar and just say "YES." This started with an assignment from the Lord back in November of 2016 to go to a main American gateway to pray — the First Landing Cross at Cape Henry, Virginia. I led our church congregation in repentance, warfare, prayer, and decrees over our nation and our people to claim the land once again for the Lord Jesus Christ. Then in July, the Lord led me to go and stand on the soil in Appomattox, Virginia, and decree unity in Christ and bind the spirit of division. I surrendered the land to God as a nation once again — standing in the gap for all Americans. Since then, the Holy Spirit has urged me relentlessly to take this further and create American Gatekeepers. He has shown me that there are powerful prayer leaders all across this nation who want to rise up and take the land again for the kingdom of God and His purposes! Are you with me?

We have got to claim our cities and regions for the purposes of Jesus Christ so the angel armies can be released. God bless you on this assignment. Let's take the gates and cities back for the Lord!

Decree Out Loud

☐ *"Father, in the name of Your Son, Jesus Christ, I say YES to this assignment of becoming a gatekeeper and prayer leader for my city of _____ in the region or county of _____ in the state of _____ and on behalf of the United States of America. Father, fill me with Your Holy Spirit. Pour Your wisdom into me and align my purposes with Yours. Cover me and my family with Your supernatural protection as I embark on this divine assignment for your kingdom and glory. I thank You, Father, for my Seat of Authority in Christ Jesus at Your right hand. I am ready to use this authority, and I truly want Your will to be done on earth as it is in Heaven. I agree with Your plans and purposes for all of America and our people, Father! I decree this now in the name above all names, Jesus Christ of Nazareth, Yeshua HaMashiach, King Of kings, and Lord of lords. Amen!"*

YES!! NOW YOU ARE READY!

1. Consult The Holy Spirit - Do Your Research

First, ask the Holy Spirit to come upon you and guide you and reveal to you if your city or territory is a "gateway." These cities in America have been revealed to me as "main gates": Virginia Beach, Virginia (Cape Henry); Jamestown, Virginia; Boston, Massachusetts; New York, New York; Chicago, Illinois; New Orleans, Louisiana; St. Louis, Missouri; San Francisco, California; and Seattle, Washington. You will see a lot of spiritual warfare happening in these areas.

If your city or territory is not a main gate, it still has a "gate" to the city or region in the spiritual realm. We must release the hosts of Heaven to take these gates, but first we need to bind the demonic spirits behind this.

Ask the Holy Spirit to reveal historical things or any things hidden that have happened in your city or territory that may have opened the door to the enemy. You can also research your city to see if it was the "first" of anything in history (good or bad). Look for laws that were started or passed there that are unbiblical or against God. Search for anything that has to do with witchcraft/occult and New Age practices as well, and find out if they are still active in your area. Believe it or not, Yoga is an occultic practice and can open up a door to the demonic. Look for areas where businesses keep closing or the housing market is failing. Is there an issue with strife in the churches or pastors coming and going a lot? Are there abandoned neighborhood areas, factories, farms, or stores? Are there drugs or gangs? Have there been murders, suicides, or even epidemic illnesses or violence? Are there bad things happening to families who were once successful? Are there unforeseen tragic circumstances coming to families who are losing their land and property? Weather in your area can also be affected by these strongholds. Have there been many floods, droughts, or tornadoes?

Check with the history of government or activist groups in your area — is there a history of corruption? Have any groups been against the Jewish people (God's people) in your area? These things can bring darkness, despair, and depression into your region. When we take authority over them, in Jesus' name — who came to bring life, light, and abundance — these dark things must leave.

Our Lord Jesus explains this in John 10: "Truly, truly, I tell you, I am the gate for the sheep. All who came before Me were thieves and robbers, but the sheep did not listen to them. I am the gate. If anyone enters through Me, he will be saved. He will come in and go out and find pasture. The thief comes only to steal and kill and destroy. I have come that they may have life, and have it in all its fullness."

There is the "gate" reference again in the bible. Gates are in the authority of Jesus Christ. This is why we must take the gates in HIS name for a divine shift to come to your areas and regions.

It's amazing what you will find out when you start to research the history of your city and region — even more amazing what the Holy Spirit will reveal when you ask Him. Get clear on these strongholds and make a list for your intercession.

I ask like this: "Holy Spirit, it is written in 1 Corinthians 2:10 that 'God has revealed them to us through His Spirit. For the Spirit searches all things, yes, the deep things of God.' So, Holy Spirit, I ask You to search all things in my city and region that are hidden in the darkness bringing evil, sin, curses, strife, dangerous plans, ungodly laws, or anything that is not of God into our area that is causing the enemy to have a foothold and stronghold over our gates and our region. Yes, Holy Spirit, lead and guide me, show me exactly what we must pray to be revealed and dealt with by our prayers, declarations, and intercessions, in Jesus' Name. Amen!"

For America itself, we have opened a door to the enemy through our national laws of abortion and gay marriage, as well as taking God out of our schools and town halls. Ask the Holy Spirit to search out and reveal what we need to pray and ask Jesus for in America. We can also ask the Holy Spirit and the angel armies to seek out what is hidden and bring it to light, to thwart the plans of the enemy, and convict the hearts of the people who are plotting these plans or promoting sinful practices across the land through our intercessions.

REPENTANCE FIRST AND FOREMOST!

Once you know what these sins and curses/strongholds are in your city/region, or county, make a list so you can do laser targeted repentance and pulling down of these particular strongholds in your area. The more you laser in on these things the more authority you can administer to bind these strongholds and get specific with your requests for the Holy Spirit and angel armies. You ask for this help by your authority in Jesus Christ.

"So Jesus called them together and began to speak to them in parables: 'How can Satan drive out Satan? If a kingdom is divided against itself, it cannot stand. If a house is divided against itself, it cannot stand. And if Satan is divided and rises against himself, he cannot stand; his end has come. Indeed, no one can enter a strong man's house to steal his possessions unless he first ties up the strong man. Then he can plunder his house.'" - Mark 3:23-27

Get ready to bind the strongman and plunder the strongman's house in your region!

2. Gather Your Prayer Group

There is power in numbers because Jesus said when two or more are gathered in My Name I am in their midst (Matt 18:20). Also the power of agreement: "Again I say to you, if two of you agree on earth about anything they ask, it will be done for them by my Father in heaven." (Matt 18:19)

I have prayed these prayers and spoken these decrees on my own as well. But a group of dedicated prayer leaders is best because God wants His people to lead and grow in influence across the land for His purposes. He has called us to be bold and courageous as a people! (Joshua 1:9)

If you don't have a group at home, our prayer group on Facebook will come into agreement with you with your prayers and declarations over your region.

Gather your prayer leaders who are in agreement with this important assignment, and plan your meetings to decree these prayers as well as your own over your regions. You can meet in homes, churches, or strategic places in your region to "stand upon the soil and decree."

We want to create a prayer shield over this nation with a coast to coast network!

Jesus said we are to pray "on earth as it is in Heaven." We are encouraged by Jesus to ask God to bring heaven to earth and decree it as so.

3. Prepare For Your Intercession

Claim Your Authority In Christ And Set Yourself And Your Home Under God's Protection

- Put on the full armor of God - decree out loud Ephesians 6:10-20
- Take your Seat of Authority in Christ - decree out loud Ephesians 1:17-23 and Ephesians Chapter 2
- Apply the blood of Jesus over yourself, your family members, and everything in your household.
- Repent for your own sins and the sins of your ancestors
- Make sure you renounce any unholy covenants with freemasonry
- Ask God to expand your territory outside of your own property, and decree 1 Chronicles 4:10: "Now Jabez called on the God of Israel, saying, 'Oh that You would bless me

indeed and enlarge my border, and that Your hand might be with me, and that You would keep me from harm that it may not pain me,' and God granted him what he requested."

Decree

- ☐ *"Father, I cover myself and everyone and everything in my household with the blood of Jesus Christ today and every day. I cover all of the members of my family (call them by name) with the blood of Jesus Christ. I cover my home, my land, my car, my finances, my marriage, my children, my pets, my livestock, my properties, my inheritances, my work, and my ministry with the powerful blood of Jesus. In the name of Jesus Christ of Nazareth, by the power of His blood, I break off every power of the kingdom of darkness and cancel every argument in heaven that has established itself against the plans of God in my life, and I spoil every attack of the enemy right now. I call forth, in the name of Jesus, all of God's plans and purposes for my life and my family. As for me and my house, we serve the one true God of Israel — the God of Abraham, Isaac, and Jacob — and His only Son, the Lord Jesus Christ of Nazareth! The only spirit operating in my house and in me and my family is the Holy Spirit! Holy Spirit, in the name of Jesus, I invite You now to take over my home and family and come inside of us. Thank You, Holy Spirit!*

- ☐ *"Now, I take my authority in Christ Jesus over all the power of the enemy! Listen to me, kingdom of darkness, the blood of Jesus is against you, and you have no authority over my life. I take authority over you. I forbid you to touch me or my family on this day or ever again! I am seated in Christ Jesus at the right hand of God the Father, and I put you, Satan, and all your demons and demonic assignments under the feet of Jesus Christ! I command you to stay there and do what Jesus tells you to do, go where Jesus tells you to go, and never return near me or my family or household! It is written: NO WEAPON FORMED AGAINST ME (OR MY FAMILY) SHALL PROSPER, IN JESUS' NAME! AMEN."*

You Can Also Prepare By

- Playing a recording of the shofar out loud in your home and into the atmosphere of your prayer areas. Here is a recording you can find and loop on YouTube: "The Powerful Sound of the Shofar 'Heavenly call'"
- Applying anointing oil over you and your home/property. This is the oil I use: The Light of Jerusalem anointing oil from the Judaica Webstore.

- Putting up a Mezuzah on your front door for protection of your "gate" to your house and to dedicate your home to God
- Fasting before your intercession over your region (optional); doing a vegetarian fast can help you hear the Holy Spirit with more clarity
- Repenting for your sins and the sins of your family bloodline - ask the Father for grace, mercy, and forgiveness by applying the blood of Jesus to all these sins
- Cleansing your own land and property - stand on your property with your family and repent for any sins against God that ever happened on that land and property since it's creation.
- Taking Communion and giving the land Communion by pouring the blood of Christ — Communion grape juice — into the soil of the land. Here is a good resource for cleansing the land - Books By Jeanette Strauss Cleansing the Land Kit www.gloriouscreations.net/
- Making sure you do a "spiritual house cleaning" of your home - get rid of anything from the occult, anything that has the demonic attached to it such as video games, horror movies etc. You don't want anything in common with the enemy because it gives him a foothold against you and can hinder your prayers. I ask the Holy Spirit to show me things that must go.
- Making a verbal covenant with God and renouncing any ungodly covenants. Do every task and assignment in your community in the name of the Lord. Fill yourself with the word and invite the Holy Spirit inside you. Be bold and courageous for He is with you. Remember David only thought about Almighty God who was with him when he approached Goliath! You are not facing giants alone. God does not look for the biggest, strongest person. He looks at your heart and your willingness to do His will. He will have your back all the way! GOD'S GOT YOU, AND YOU WILL BE VICTORIOUS!!
- Praising and worshiping the Lord. That is your biggest weapon against the enemy. Jehoshaphat said to the people of Judah who were up against a great army: "Listen, my friends, if we trust the Lord God and believe what these prophets have told us, the Lord will help us, and we will be successful." Then he explained his plan and appointed men to march in front of the army and praise the Lord for his holy power by singing: "Praise the Lord! His love never ends." As soon as they began singing, the Lord confused the enemy camp so that the Ammonite and Moabite troops attacked and completely destroyed those from Edom. Then they turned against each other and fought until the entire camp was wiped out! - 2 Chronicles 20-23

Now That You Have Done Your Preparations, You Are Ready To Do Your Intercession For Your Region And Take Territory For The Purposes Of God!

First, you want to go to the location of the area you are praying with your group so your feet are on the land/soil, or go outdoors at your home and stand on the soil that is within the borders of the region you are interceding for. If you have a group going to a location, bring your anointing oil, a shofar to blow, or a shofar recording. Take Communion with you (bread pieces and grape juice/cups) and your bibles and copies of your decrees that are here for you below.

Your Plan

1. Pinpoint and gather at your "gateway" spot. Your gateway spot is an area where the town was founded or an entry point to the city, a city monument, sign, or building where the city, town, or county was dedicated. If you are doing this yourself, make sure you are standing on soil that is within the borders of the region for which you are praying.
2. Be clear on your reason for being there and what the strongholds are to declare out loud to the heavens and to release the angel armies to pull them down specifically.
3. Targeted Repentance - It is important that you ***do not judge the sins*** of your region or area, only **repent** for them. Understand and be clear on what the specific sins are in your region to ask for forgiveness from God. Keep these sins to yourself and your prayer group. These are secrets that the Holy Spirit has shared with you. You are called to pray, repent, and ask for healing in all these situations in order for a move of God to happen.

"If my people, which are called by my name, shall humble themselves (repent), and pray, and seek my face, and turn from their wicked ways; then will I hear from heaven, and will forgive their sin, and will heal their land." 2 Chronicles 7:14 (KJV)

Understand that your authority comes from Jesus Christ. It is through HIM that you have all power, dominion, and authority OVER all the power, dominion, and authority of the enemy. Thank you, Jesus!

Here Is Your Plan Outline

- Repent for the sins of the government - for laws and actions that were against the will, word, and commandments of God (past and present)
- Repent for leaders not relying on God
- Repent for broken covenants or treaties with native leaders and lands
- Repent for any idolatry, witchcraft, murders, anti-semitism, and all sin that happened in the area
- Repent for all the sins of all the inhabitants, past and present - "stand in the gap"
- Ask the Father for mercy and forgiveness
- Renounce and nullify all negative words spoken over the area
- Take Communion - focus on Jesus and the power of the Cross
- Pour one cup of Communion into the soil - cleanse the land
- Cover the land, government, and all the people (inhabitants) in the blood of Jesus
- Ask for an open Heaven - King of glory, Jesus, to come In
- Command and send angel armies (shofar)
- Command the angel armies (hosts) to pull down/cast out the demonic- all strongholds/assignments and put them under the feet of Jesus Christ
- Break any curses off of the land and the area and cancel all demonic assignments
- Bind and renounce all spirits of death, suicide, pornography, etc, and command them to leave the region and go to the uninhabited dry place and stay there! Ask Father God to send His Arresting Angels to chain and shackle these demons so they never come back!

- Claim the land — region, borders, and gates — for Jesus Christ!
- Ask for the heavenly anointing to take the "gates"
- Apply the oil to the "gates" (or pour oil on the ground)
- Submit to the purposes of God for the region
- Bless the land and the people - decree life, peace, and prosperity
- Dedicate and consecrate the city/region to God
- Ask God for a covenant of great favor and blessing for the region
- Invite the Holy Spirit — the presence of God — to inhabit the entire region
- Give an offering to a church or ministry in the area in the name of "blessing for the region"
- Thank God for the good things He is doing
- Give thanks and praise To God

Prayers And Declarations To Be Spoken

- ☐ *"Father God, O Righteous Judge, we come to You today in the name of Your Son, Jesus Christ. We humbly ask You, Father, to bring Your presence and Your glory to this place of prayer. Holy Spirit, You are welcome here. Come fill this place and fill us today. We praise You, Father, for Your goodness and thank You for hearing the prayers of Your people. We ask You, Lord Jesus, as our intercessor, to be with us today, for You have told us, Lord, that where two or more are gathered in My name, I am in their midst. (If you are alone you ask your helper, the Holy Spirit, to be with you. He is a person, a helper, and a witness.)*

- ☐ *"Today, we stand as we ask Jesus in prayer for our region/city of _____. Your word, Father, tells us to let our light shine before men in such a way that they may see our good works and to glorify our Father who is in heaven! We have come to be that light and put our prayers and petitions before You, Father, and stand in the gap on behalf of all the people of this region/city of _____. Father, we give You thanks for our city/region of _____. We lift up our city/region of _____ to You, Father God. Father, we repent for any covenants, agreements, judgments, laws, or treaties that were made by our government all the way back to it's beginnings, in Jesus' name. Father, we repent for the sins of the inhabitants upon this land all the way back to it's creation.*

- ☐ *"We ask for Your grace and mercy upon this land and upon the people, Father God, O Righteous Judge, Lord God Almighty! Lord Jesus, we ask that You intercede for our region and our people and that Your blood speaks for us on the Mercy Seat before the*

Courts of Heaven. We cover the land, the people, and all that we speak of here in the blood of Jesus. Cleanse it all with Your precious and powerful blood, Lord Jesus!"

Take Communion

Decree Out Loud

- ☐ *"We decree that our region of _____ is covered and cleansed by the blood of the Lamb of God — Jesus Christ — redeemed from the hand of the devil and set apart for the purposes of Almighty God, in Jesus' name! Lord Jesus, change the hearts and heal the soul wounds of the land and the family blood lines of this region all the way back to their beginnings with Your resurrection power of the Holy Spirit.*

- ☐ *"We decree awakening, revival, and restoration in our region for the purposes of God! Bring forth Your plans, purposes, and agenda for this region and it's people, Lord! Your word says in Jeremiah 29:7 'Also, seek the peace and prosperity of the city to which I have carried you into exile. Pray to the LORD for it, because if it prospers, you too will prosper.' We speak divine prosperity, life, peace, and blessings over our city/region and all the inhabitants now and all future inhabitants! Raise up a hedge of supernatural protection, Lord, over our region! No weapons formed against us will prosper!*

- ☐ *"We decree Psalm 91 over our region and all the people of our region of _____. We that dwelleth in the secret place of the most High shall abide under the shadow of the Almighty. We will say of the Lord, He is my refuge and my fortress: my God; in him will we trust. Surely he shall deliver us from the snare of the fowler, and from the noisome pestilence. He shall cover us with his feathers, and under his wings shalt we trust: his truth shall be our shield and buckler. We the people of _____ shalt not be afraid for the terror by night; nor for the arrow that flieth by day; nor for the pestilence that walketh in darkness; nor for the destruction that wasteth at noonday. A thousand shall fall at our side, and ten thousand at thy right hand; but it shall not come nigh our region of _____. Only with our eyes shalt thou behold and see the reward of the wicked. Because we, the people of _____, hast made the Lord, which is our refuge, even the most High, our habitation; There shall no evil befall us, neither shall any plague come nigh our region of _____. For he shall give his angels charge over our region of _____, to keep us in all our ways. They shall bear us up in their hands, lest thou dash thy foot against a stone. We shalt tread upon the lion and adder: the young lion and the dragon shalt thou trample under our feet. Because we hath set our love upon me, says the Lord, therefore will I deliver them: I will set them on high, because they hath known my name. They of the region of _____ shall call upon me, and I will answer them says the Lord, I will be with them in trouble; I will deliver them of the region of _____, and honour them. With long life will I satisfy them, and shew him my salvation, says the Lord of Hosts!*

- ☐ *"Father God, we decree that Your chosen generation rises up from this region to do mighty works for the kingdom of God! Father, according to Peter 2:9, we are a chosen generation, a royal priesthood, a holy nation, a unique people; that we should show forth the praises of Jesus Christ who has called us out of darkness into his marvelous light!*

- ☐ *"Right now, in the name of Jesus Christ, we ask that every citizen of our region who is stuck in the darkness has the marvelous light of Jesus Christ revealed to them. Let them have a Damascus-Road experience Lord! Take the scales from their eyes and put them in divine appointments of opportunity for followers of Jesus to minister to them and show them the love of Christ Jesus! Yes, Lord, let our community and region be known as a region filled with the Holy Spirit! Come, Holy Spirit, we invite You now to fill our city and region! Holy Spirit, be the ONLY spirit operating in _____, in Jesus' name!*

Updated: How To Do A Land Assignment For Blessing And Cleansing Your Land

If you are here because you want to be a faithful and willing intercessor to pray over your cities, regions, states, and nation, this is the time the Lord is calling up His people to STAND IN THE GAP and pray, ask for forgiveness, and to redeem the land, according to 2 Chronicles 7:14, "If my people, who are called by my name, will humble themselves and pray and seek my face and turn from their wicked ways, then I will hear from heaven, and I will forgive their sin and will heal their land."

I have had many "land assignments" around the country, including my own land and home. Many of you have asked me to teach you how to do this. I have put together some video teachings and resources for you right here so you can begin with your own home and land, and then be prepared to pray over other locations the Lord sends you to. Taking Communion and getting the Communion that represents the blood of Jesus Christ into the soil was something the Holy Spirit made VERY CLEAR to me that He wanted to be done at each land assignment. It's the blood of Christ that speaks and makes intercession for the land and for us as a people of God!

The kingdom of darkness is helpless against the blood of Jesus Christ, and by applying it, we have by faith activated the finished work of the Cross against the enemy. It's a LEGAL transaction against the enemy, and they can no longer hold dominion in the land because the blood of Jesus takes over all authority, breaks all curses, cleanses sin, and destroys all demonic assignments that were once operating there.

Most of my land assignments from the Lord have been at key gateway locations — entrances to cities, an old ferryboat landing in my region that once was a main gate, bridges, post offices, schools, courthouses, on the beach in Sandbridge, Virginia (coastal borders assignment), and all the way to the west coast too in Atascadero, California, and San Francisco.

I found out that Daniel Boone had intended to build a road from the east coast of Virginia Beach, Virginia, all the way to a point between those two cities on the west coast! There are still some old markers across the US where he intended to build. These early places in our history have to be re-dedicated to God, especially if they were corrupted or used for sinful things.

Daniel Boone was a righteous man; however, not every settler or leader was across these states. These sins against the land must be repented for as well. Sinful transactions could have even happened on your own land that need to be repented of. These sins can give a legal right of the demonic to hold a curse against the land and the region! These curses cannot be removed until they are covered in the blood of Jesus.

One thing I have learned is that each assignment can be different depending on the history of the place, so get yourself educated with these teachings. I know that the Lord wants me to give these to you so that more intercessors will be powerfully equipped to do this. Start with your own homes and properties, and then, if you are led, you can go and do bigger land assignments over a special location. I am so excited that you are here to learn this. I told God that it was the goal of my heart back in 2016 to have "boots on the ground" intercessors all over America and the nations doing land assignments and getting the land redeemed and healed by taking Communion and blessing the land! How glorious is this now that we are all doing this?! God is so faithful!

I had a prophetic word from the Lord that in this year — 2020, Hebrew year 5780 — it was very important that we as believers in Yeshua, Jesus Christ, take Communion on our land and also apply the Communion to our door posts as an act of faith and reconciliation before Passover coming up on April 8, 2020.

We do this to repent of the sins of our land, cleanse our land, and dedicate it to God. We also apply the blood of the Lamb — our Lamb, Jesus Christ — our Communion — over the door like the Israelites did at Passover as a prophetic act of faith to declare that our homes belong to God and are in covenant with God through the blood of Christ. Therefore, our homes are marked and covered in the blood of Jesus.

The activated words I give you today as you do this will send the message to all of Heaven and earth that you and your household belong to God and are blessed and that no curses or pestilence or disease can touch your home. They must "pass over," in Jesus' name! This is a powerful time of DELIVERANCE for all of God's people. If we do these prophetic acts of faith, we will see God move in our lives and households and in our land!

PREPARATION FOR YOUR LAND PRAYER ASSIGNMENT

1. First discern the land God wants you to pray and the location. Agree out loud to God for the assignment. Set a time and date to go pray and decree, ideally, Sunday night during the fourth watch (3:00 am - 6:00 am). The fourth watch is the time of deliverance. God will deliver the land and His people at this time out of the hands of the enemy and it's also a time for miracles and resurrection. This is the time of the night that Jacob wrestled with the angel and became Israel, the time of the night that the people of Israel crossed the Red Sea, the time of night that Jesus walked on the water, and the time that the stone was rolled from the tomb and Jesus rose from the dead.

2. Get supplies ready: bottle of Communion — grape juice, bread or crackers — unbreakable cup, recording of shofar (or actual shofar), plain paper and red sharpie pen, fruit seeds, anointing oil, garden trowel, and copy of your prayers and decrees. (The paper can have the new name of the divine purpose of the region that you are proclaiming, such as, revival for Jesus Christ, Hub for the Outpouring of The Holy Spirit, etc. God may give you the

name/purpose he has for it.) If you don't have this, it's okay. The main thing is to get the Communion on the land and repent for it.

3. Go to Google Earth and print out a picture of the area you are called to pray and decree over. Mark the areas where you will stand. Lift up the image to the Lord, thank Him out loud for this assignment, and ask for His Holy Spirit to come and help you and for His angelic hosts to be assigned to you for protection and to carry out the decrees.

4. Ask God out loud to send His hornets ahead to the area. According to Exodus 23:28 and Joshua 24:12, God sent His hornets ahead of His people to drive out the enemies of God and prepare the way of His people before they got there.

5. Ask God to release His "sound" into the region. Call forth the Victory Trumpets of the Lord to be sounded over the region. Ask the Lion of Judah to come and roar over the region.

6. Come into the Courts of Heaven before the Father and repent for your own sins. Get yourself clean and ready. Make sure you are suiting up each day. Get covered in the blood of Jesus, take your Seat of Authority in Christ Jesus, and put on the full armor of God.

7. Ask the Courts of Heaven to be opened for this specific land assignment and the books for this land and region to be opened. Ask for Jesus to intercede on behalf of the region and for you. Ask the blood of Jesus to speak in the courts on your behalf and on behalf of the land. Ask for the cloud of witnesses to be present. Ask angels assigned to this land's divine purpose to be activated to accompany you. Ask for Sentry Angels to surround and protect you.

8. Get ready to head out to your location. Anoint yourself (forehead and feet/shoes) and your vehicle (front and back, sides, and all four tires) asking for God's blessing and that you go forth in the Name of the Lord Jesus Christ.

9. When you get to the land where you will pray, first thank God for this assignment. Then, ask again for the Courts of Heaven to be opened and the books to be opened regarding this land/property/region etc.

10. Repent for the sins of the land. Ask Father God to open His heavenly courts and repent for all the sins, known and unknown, since the birth of that land going back to Adam. Repent for all of the sins of the people who lived or governed or passed through the land — anything they did that was a sin against God and His word. Repent for any specific sins you found in your research. Repent for adultery, blood curses, broken treaties, injustices, murders, unholy and ungodly covenants, Freemasonry, dishonest dealings, etc. Anyone who farms or has farmland needs to repent for reading or putting their faith in the Farmers' Almanac instead of in God — for themselves, past generations, or anyone on that land before them going all the way back to the origination of that land. The Farmers' Almanac uses horoscopes and other things that really are considered sorcery and witchcraft!

11. Take Communion — drink part of the juice and pour the rest in the land. Decree that the land is now being cleansed by the blood of Jesus, and ask Jesus for His blood to speak for the land for grace, mercy, and forgiveness. Decree that the land is cleansed and redeemed by the blood of Jesus! Ask for Jesus' blood to be spread all the way to the borders of that region/city.

12. Claim that the land and the region is now in one covenant with Almighty God through the blood of Jesus and that any other unholy or ungodly covenants are now canceled and made null and void and under the blood of Jesus, including all verbal or written farming contracts, agreements, or leases. Declare that the land is 100 percent free and clear. Claim the land/region for the plans and purposes of God, and call forth the divine destiny and purpose for that land to be activated as written in the books in heaven, in Jesus' name.

13. Ask Father God to send the Hosts of heaven to come and go on a search and destroy mission to clean out and unroot and remove anything that is still in the area from the kingdom of darkness. Then post Sentry Angels of God to come and stand guard at the gates and borders of the region. Play a recording of the shofar loud into the atmosphere, and proclaim that Jesus Christ is Lord and King of this land.

14. Praise and worship God, decree Psalm 24 over the land, and if you have oil, pour it on the land and invite the Holy Spirit to come and do creative miracles and stand hold in the land/region from this day forward.

RESOURCES FOR PRAYER INTERCESSORS AND LAND OWNERS

Suggested Books and Land Kit
From God's Hands To Your Land, Blessings By Jeanette Strauss
www.gloriouscreations.net

Additional Prayer Strategy
Prayer To Remove Ungodly Relationships And Influences (Axe Of God's judgment)

Prayer For Schools And Us Dept Of Education – Courts Of Heaven Repentance And Land Assignment

United States (Us) School System And Dept Of Education
(Us School System And Dept Of Education Prayer Assignment)

Taking The Case To The Courts Of Heaven

Spoken Prayers And Holy Spirit Strategies For Deliverance
Communion – Anointing The Land

If following along on the video broadcast, just come into agreement with these prayers as Annamarie reads them, or you may speak out loud later with your printable copy. Please have Communion elements ready.

Enter Courts Of Heaven - (Pray Out Loud)

- ☐ *"Almighty God, O Righteous Judge, Heavenly Father, we come to You today in the name of Jesus Christ asking to enter Your Heavenly Court and appear before You, O Righteous Judge, with our petition regarding the US SCHOOL SYSTEM AND DEPT OF EDUCATION. We ask You, Lord Jesus, to represent and intercede for us as our high priest with Father God and for Your blood to speak for us and the US SCHOOL SYSTEM AND DEPT OF EDUCATION, including universities, colleges, educational institutions, learning centers, medical schools, public and private schools, Christian schools, Bible schools and seminaries, military schools, trade schools, daycare facilities, residential and specialized schools for the disabled, school boards and all leadership, teachers, administrators, teacher unions, students and employees, contractors at every level, and libraries — both public and on these campuses — on the Mercy Seat.*

- ☐ *"We invite the Holy Spirit to assist and guide us in our heavenly court appearance, repentance, and prayer. We ask for Your angels to surround us, protect us, and assist us to fully complete this from start to finish with the guidance of the Holy Spirit according to Your will, Father God. We ask, in Jesus' name, as we enter Your courts, Father God, for our books to be opened for ourselves, our cities and states, and for our nation, the United States of America, and The US SCHOOL SYSTEM AND DEPT OF EDUCATION, including all universities, all public and private schools, homeschools, preschools, religious schools, Bible schools and seminaries, military schools, trade schools, daycare facilities, residential and specialized schools for the disabled, school board members, teachers, administrations, coaches, parent teacher organizations, and all leadership at every level, including libraries and all extracurricular student activities including clubs, sports, dance, music, arts and all after school programs, summer programs and children's camps — both public and private and on and off these campuses — on the Mercy Seat.*

- ☐ *"We ask, in Jesus' name, for the cloud of witnesses and also the faithful men and women who were righteous believers in Christ Jesus to be present witnessing to this case in the Courts of Heaven, to witness to our intercession and the intercession of Jesus Christ for the United States of America school systems and United States Dept of Education, founded in 1979 by President Jimmy Carter and the First Secretary, Shirley M. Hustedler, and all therein, since its original inception in 1867 by President Andrew Jackson and even before this time, with all teaching and schools, including one-room school houses and universities and colleges that were established and operating in America, even Colonial America before 1867 to this day.*

- ☐ *"We also come into agreement with the intercession of Jesus' prayers. We would be honored to have Your intent revealed, Lord Jesus, for the US SCHOOL SYSTEM AND DEPT OF EDUCATION in the Courts today. Father God, through this time in the Courts, we pray that all people can now come into alignment with Your will and plan. We also ask for Your recording angels to be present. We ask for any and all records of repentance for the sins of our nation regarding the schools and education systems and learning institutions and organizations that have already been repented for to also be taken into consideration today.*

- ☐ *"We ask, Father God, that You demand that the accuser in this case regarding the sins of the US SCHOOL SYSTEM AND DEPT OF EDUCATION and everything associated with it be present in the Court. May this establish precedence in this Court today. We ask in the name of Jesus for the Courts of Heaven to be in session for our case and petition today and the Court to be seated.*

- ☐ *"Because of the blood of Jesus and the finished work of the Cross, we are able to enter Your holy Courts as it is written in Your word, in Hebrews 10:19, "And so, dear brothers and sisters, we can boldly enter Heaven's most holy place because of the blood of Jesus." We now ask to present our case before Your Court. Thank You, Father God. Thank You, Lord Jesus. Thank You, Holy Spirit. Amen!"*

Personal Prayer Of Cleansing

- ☐ *"Almighty God, O Righteous Judge, Heavenly Father, I humbly come before You in Your heavenly Courts and repent for all of my sins and the sins of my ancestors and family bloodline. I specifically repent for my sins and the sins of my ancestors and family bloodline that are sins that were committed through the United States SCHOOL SYSTEM AND DEPT OF EDUCATION, including all types of schools and education systems, learning institutions and organizations. If there are any sins in my life and the life of my ancestors and family bloodline that were done against You, Father God, or against Your word through the US SCHOOL SYSTEM AND DEPT OF EDUCATION, I repent for these sins right now. I am sorry for sinning against You, Father God. I am sorry for any sins I committed or my ancestors or anyone in my family bloodline committed with or through the US SCHOOL SYSTEM AND DEPT OF EDUCATION.*

- ☐ *"Father God, I ask today for grace, mercy, and forgiveness for myself and my ancestors and family bloodline. Lord Jesus, I ask for You to put Your blood on all these sins for me and my ancestors and family bloodline and wash us clean. I ask that these sins be remembered no more for Your sake, Father God, and be wiped clean from the record books of Heaven and earth by the blood of Jesus. I ask now that these sins and any repercussions from these sins be made null and void.*

- ☐ *"Now that the blood of Jesus has covered these sins, I ask that they can no longer be held against me, my family bloodline, or my ancestors ever again, on earth or in Heaven. I ask for the accuser to be stripped of any legal rights and that any curses and demonic assignments be removed and canceled, in Jesus' name. I ask today, Father God, in Jesus' name, that my ancestors, my family line, and I be found "not guilty" by the blood of Jesus — our only defense. I also ask for this new "not guilty" verdict to be written in our books and proclaimed in your Courts today. Father God, it is written in Your word in Proverbs 26:2 that 'a curse causeless cannot stand.' Therefore, the blood of Jesus is now covering all these sins. The blood of Jesus removes all sin, curses, and demonic assignments. Therefore, there is no longer any cause for any curses or repercussions against me or my family bloodline. I ask, in Jesus' name, for my family bloodline, all my ancestors, and I to now be released from any curses, entanglements, repercussions, or consequences from these sins.*

- ☐ *"My request here in Your Heavenly Court, Almighty God, O Righteous Judge, is that the sins that I have repented for today would now be covered in the blood of Jesus, and that my family bloodline, my ancestors, and I be moved from the Court of Judgment to the Throne of Grace and Mercy because our spiritual debt has been paid in full by the precious blood of Jesus, and now there can be no recourse from the accuser.*

- ☐ *"Almighty God, O Righteous Judge, I ask You to silence the voice of the accuser forever, regarding these sins. I ask for Your Holy Spirit to now fill all the places where these sins and curses once were and to stay in that place and fill it forever with Your presence and protection. In Jesus' name, I ask that my books and the books of my ancestors and family bloodline be fully reconciled back to the will of God here in the Courts and my record of repentance be recorded for my future court appearances here in Your spiritual Court of law and my high priest, the Lord Jesus Christ, will confirm for me and my cloud of witnesses in Heaven as a witness to all that was done here today. Thank You, Father God, for Your grace, mercy, and forgiveness. Thank You, Lord Jesus, for Your precious blood that has set me free. Thank You, Holy Spirit, for Your guidance in the Courts. Amen!"*

You are now cleansed, forgiven, redeemed, and you are ready to intercede and to present the main case for the US SCHOOL SYSTEM AND DEPT OF EDUCATION to the Courts of Heaven.

Ambassador Of Reconciliation

- ☐ *"Almighty God, O Righteous Judge, In the name of and with the intercession of Jesus Christ my Lord and high priest, I come before Your Court today (as well as my group of intercessors) asking to be recognized as an "ambassador(s) of reconciliation" to stand in the gap to present a petition of repentance and reconciliation on behalf of the US SCHOOL SYSTEM AND DEPT OF EDUCATION, including universities, medical schools, public and private schools, Christian schools, Bible schools and seminaries, military schools, trade schools, daycare facilities, residential and specialized schools for the disabled, school boards and all leadership at every level, and libraries — both public and on these campuses.*

- ☐ *"Father God, Your word states in Ephesians 6:18-20: 'Praying always with all prayer and supplication in the Spirit, and watching thereunto with all perseverance and supplication for all saints; and for me, that utterance may be given unto me, that I may open my mouth boldly, to make known the mystery of the Gospel, for which I am an ambassador in bonds: that therein I may speak boldly, as I ought to speak.' Also in Your word, Father God, You tell us in Hebrews 4:15-16: 'For we do not have a high priest who is unable to sympathize with our weaknesses, but we have one who was tempted in every way that we are, yet was without sin. Let us then approach the throne of grace with confidence, so that we may receive mercy and find grace to help us in our time of need.' Also, it is written in Hebrews 10:18-20: And where these have been forgiven, an offering for sin is no longer needed. Therefore, brothers, since we have confidence to enter the most holy place by the blood of Jesus, by the new and living way opened for us through the curtain of His body ....'*

- ☐ *"Therefore, according to Your word, Almighty Father God, O Righteous Judge, our group of intercessors and I come before You today as redeemed souls of Jesus Christ, citizens of Heaven and earth, citizens of the United States of America, and patrons of the US SCHOOL SYSTEM AND DEPT OF EDUCATION. Father God, I (we) are here today to present my (our) petition before Your Court as my (our) obligation by faith according to Your word and to receive grace, mercy, and forgiveness on behalf of the US SCHOOL SYSTEM AND DEPT OF EDUCATION.*

- ☐ *"I (we) ask the Lord Jesus Christ and His blood to speak for me (us) and The US SCHOOL SYSTEM AND DEPT OF EDUCATION today before Your Court, in Jesus' name, as I (we) present this case. I (we) ask for all the books to be opened, regarding this case and for the witnesses, the recording angels, and the accuser to be present in the Court, in Jesus' name. I (we) ask You, Lord Jesus, to stand and intercede for me (us) before Father God. Thank You, Father God, O Righteous Judge, for recognizing me (and our group of intercessors) in Your Heavenly Court as an Ambassador(s) of Reconciliation for the US SCHOOL SYSTEM AND DEPT OF EDUCATION, including universities, medical schools, public and private schools, Christian schools, Bible schools and seminaries, military schools, trade schools, daycare facilities, residential and specialized schools for the disabled, school boards and all leadership at every level, and libraries — both public and on these campuses. Thank You, Father God. Thank You, Lord Jesus, and thank You, Holy Spirit. Amen."*

Repentance For Us School System And Dept Of Education

- ☐ *"Almighty God, O Righteous Judge, Heavenly Father, in the name of Jesus Christ, we come to You in Your Heavenly Courts today in repentance for the sins of the US SCHOOL SYSTEM AND DEPT OF EDUCATION, including universities, medical schools, public and private schools, Christian schools, Bible schools and seminaries, military schools, trade schools, daycare facilities, residential and specialized schools for the disabled, school boards and all leadership at every level, and libraries — both public and on these campuses.*

- ☐ *"We ask, in Jesus' name, for the Court to be seated and the books to be opened. As we repent for these sins today, we ask, Father God, O Righteous Judge for the blood of Jesus Christ to speak for us and the US SCHOOL SYSTEM AND DEPT OF EDUCATION on the Mercy Seat. We ask, in Jesus' name, Father God, that You would send Your Holy Spirit upon each person affiliated or connected in any way with the US SCHOOL SYSTEM AND DEPT OF EDUCATION, including universities, medical schools, public and private schools, Christian schools, Bible schools and seminaries, military schools, trade schools, daycare facilities, residential and specialized schools for the disabled, school boards and all leadership at every level, and libraries — both public and on these campuses.*

- ☐ *"Holy Spirit, remove any veils of deception that may be on their eyes because of their sins. Please remove all veils from their eyes of understanding so they can see the truth, know the truth, embrace the truth, stand up for the truth, and boldly speak the truth. Holy Spirit, we ask that You will bring all these people to repentance and give them an encounter with the Lord Jesus Christ that they will leave all sinful ways, seek deliverance, and come to the salvation of the Lord Jesus Christ to walk fully in the righteousness of God's will for their lives, in Jesus' name. Amen.*

- ☐ *"Almighty God, O Righteous Judge, Heavenly Father, in the name of Jesus Christ, we come to You in Your Courts today in repentance for the sins of the US SCHOOL SYSTEM AND DEPT OF EDUCATION. We confess, repent, and ask for grace, mercy, and forgiveness of these sins on their behalf today by the cleansing power of the blood of Jesus Christ to cover these sins we have listed:*

LIST OF REPENTANCE FOR THE US SCHOOL SYSTEM AND DEPT OF EDUCATION

1. Removing God, the Bible, Ten Commandments, and prayer out of the classroom
2. Teachers and administrators knowingly and intentionally teaching lies, political correctness, propaganda, and false religions
3. Causing division between races and sexes
4. Teaching feminism and emasculating-ideologies against God's word for men and women
5. Teaching darwinism-evolution instead of biblical creationism
6. Allowing boys into girls' restrooms and locker rooms
7. Allowing transgenderism and the LGBTQ, etc. agenda to be embraced and promoted by schools and pushed on children and faculty through ungodly teachings, programs, and entitlements, as well as taking the rainbow, which is a symbol of God's covenant, and making an abomination of it
8. Allowing pornographic material in textbooks and reading materials
9. Bringing in New Age practices, occultic and witchcraft practices, and Buddhist meditation
10. Political bribery and manipulation with teacher groups and teacher unions
11. Taking away of parental rights and telling children not to tell parents what is being taught
12. Violating constitutional rights of children and parents and not teaching them their constitutional rights
13. Punishing or firing teachers and coaches for praying and sharing their faith in God and the Bible
14. School shootings and murders
15. Sexual abuse acts on kids from teachers, leaders, religious mentors, and professors
16. Yoga and Buddhist practices in schools
17. Teaching perversion and promoting perversion to young children
18. Having secret societies and Freemasonry practices embedded in school administration and doctrine (especially universities), including staff, CPS, and bus companies.
19. Idols and idolatry practices in schools, universities, and libraries
20. Parents and leaders being lukewarm, complacent, and not speaking up for righteousness in schools
21. Teaching socialism, communism, and ungodly/unbiblical ideologies to children and forcing teachers and administrators to implement it
22. Manipulating textbooks and history books for political and ideological reasons for control of thought
23. Pushing and promoting books and activities in schools and libraries that exalt witchcraft and sorcery (Harry Potter, etc)
24. Pushing secular and antichrist agenda in all schools, including public and private, as well as religious schools and universities
25. Worshipping the mind and created things above the creator
26. Forcing vaccinations and masks on students and not allowing unvaccinated children to enroll in schools
27. Leading children astray and away from the God of the Bible
28. Christians and the Church's complicity in allowing these and other things to be tolerated and brought in, specifically administrators and people in positions of authority, not willing to speak up in truth even many years ago

29. For teaching children to go against God and their parents' rules and ideas and punishing them if they discuss what goes on in the classroom at home
30. Intentionally dumbing down children by lowering standards in reading, writing, and math to make more room for their ungodly programs
31. Indoctrinating and creating spiritual confusion and lukewarmness (compromising — so many young people who believe in Christ but are still following New Age rituals and are caught up in all the racial divides)
32. Lowering the grades of kids who would not wear the mask "properly"
33. Allowing kids to receive birth control, get HIV tests, pregnancy tests, and STD tests, all without a parent's knowledge
34. Undermining parental authority by actively teaching children that their parents can't be trusted and asking children to report their parents
35. Deceiving students about our founding fathers and American history and indoctrinating young minds by elevating anti-God, anti-family, and anti-American nations over our own
36. Manipulating teachers and children by using mind control and doling out unjust punishments
37. Teaching humanistic, worldly curriculums
38. Receiving outside funds from outside governments and organizations to force their agendas
39. Allowing verbal abuse and bullying of children
40. American university labs and professors being involved, in any way, with the beginnings of COVID 19, other bio weapons, and vaccines
41. Students taking oaths with secret societies and entering into unholy, ungodly covenants with fraternities and sororities
42. Adults, leaders, and teachers holding back or shutting down children when they have a desire to pray and learn about Jesus, the Bible, and the the Holy Spirit
43. Keeping children from participating in spiritual gifts of the holy spirit, Communion, and Bible learning
44. Mistreatment or abuse of children according to Matt 18:6
45. Christian schools, universities, and ministries that are educating children under 501c3 tax-exempt status, making the government their leader instead of God
46. Christian schools and universities and their leadership getting into unholy, ungodly covenants with the government through the 501c3 tax-exempt status
47. Christian schools and universities that have been allowing unholy, ungodly, and unbiblical activities, practices, and curricula on their campuses that have caused the staff and students to become lukewarm and to go into sin
48. Medical schools prohibiting biblical and godly healing practices and natural remedies from being taught to medical students and unleashing the spirit of pharmakeia by using sorcery as medicine and manipulating man's minds and bodies with man-made drugs produced by deep-state-controlled big pharma
49. Native American Indian reservation schools where students were often severely abused, abducted from parents, trafficked, and murdered
50. Indoctrinating, coercing, and forcing students to commit blasphemy and sin to graduate or pass

Declare: "WE REPENT FOR THE SINS OF THE CHURCH AND THOSE OF US IN CHRIST FOR BEING SILENT ON ALL THESE MATTERS!"

Asking For The Blood Of Jesus

- ☐ *"Lord Jesus, we ask that You cover all these sins repented of today regarding the US SCHOOL SYSTEM AND DEPT OF EDUCATION with Your blood. Wash these sins clean and wipe them from the record books of Heaven with Your blood, Lord. Father God, we ask that You remember these sins no more for Your sake, in Jesus' name. We ask that the blood of Jesus speak on the Mercy Seat for the US SCHOOL SYSTEM AND DEPT OF EDUCATION. We ask, in Jesus' name, for grace, mercy, and forgiveness of all sins today that have been repented and also any sins that may have unknowingly been omitted.*

- ☐ *"We ask You, Lord Jesus, to intercede for us and cover these sins also with Your blood that all sins, spoken and unspoken, are fully covered by the blood of Jesus on behalf of the US SCHOOL SYSTEM AND DEPT OF EDUCATION. Thank You, Jesus, for Your precious blood! Thank You, Father God, O Righteous Judge, for Your grace, mercy, and forgiveness of the sins of the US SCHOOL SYSTEM AND DEPT OF EDUCATION in this case we have brought forth. We are grateful, and as we stand in the gap for the US SCHOOL SYSTEM AND DEPT OF EDUCATION, we give You, Father God and Lord Jesus Christ, all the praise and glory for this divine opportunity in Your Courts!"*

Receiving The Verdict

- ☐ *"Almighty God, O Righteous Judge, we ask now by the blood of Jesus Christ — our only defense — that You would render a verdict of "not guilty" for the US SCHOOL SYSTEM AND DEPT OF EDUCATION. We also ask that The US SCHOOL SYSTEM AND DEPT OF EDUCATION and everything affiliated with it in this case be moved now from the Court of Judgment to the Throne of Grace and Mercy, in Jesus' name."*

Stripping/Silencing The Accuser

- ☐ *"Almighty God, O Righteous Judge, we ask, in Jesus' name, that You would silence the voice of the accuser and strip him of any legal rights coming against the US SCHOOL SYSTEM AND DEPT OF EDUCATION because their sins are now covered by the blood* of Jesus Christ. It is written in Your word, Father God, that a curse causeless cannot stand, therefore the blood of Jesus Christ has covered the sin and there is no cause for a curse. We ask now, in Jesus' name, for every curse and demonic assignment against the US SCHOOL SYSTEM AND DEPT OF EDUCATION and everything affiliated with it be canceled and made null and void in both the spiritual realm and natural realm.

- ☐ "Father God, In the name of Jesus, we ask for You to dispatch Your mighty angel armies to go forth and remove all demons, demonic principalities, and demonic platforms surrounding the US SCHOOL SYSTEM AND DEPT OF EDUCATION, including anything of the kingdom of darkness operating through universities, medical schools, public and private schools, Christian schools, Bible schools and seminaries, military schools, trade schools, daycare facilities, residential and specialized schools for the disabled, school boards and all leadership at every level, and libraries — both public and on these campuses. We ask that these demonic entities, assignments, strongholds, and their demonic altars and platforms be dismantled, rooted out, bound, and cast out forever to the uninhabited dry place by Your heavenly hosts and warrior angels, in Jesus' name! We ask that these evil demonic forces be blocked now from any and all access to the US SCHOOL SYSTEM AND DEPT OF EDUCATION by Your heavenly hosts and warrior angels from this day forward!

- ☐ "Father God, I ask, in Jesus' name, for Your heavenly hosts and warrior angels to take all US SCHOOL SYSTEM AND DEPT OF EDUCATION, including universities, private schools, religious schools, trade schools, daycare facilities, residential and specialized schools for the disabled, school boards and all leadership at every level, and libraries — both public and on these campuses off the frequency of the demonic so the kingdom of darkness cannot see, hear, or perceive anything having to do with the US SCHOOL SYSTEM AND DEPT OF EDUCATION ever again!

- ☐ "We ask, Father God, for Your angelic armies to stand and hold now over every place they removed these demonic entities and for Your mighty angels to occupy and protect from all evil regarding all areas and to NOT allow any more sinful practices to happen through the US SCHOOL SYSTEM AND DEPT OF EDUCATION ever again, all for Your kingdom and glory, in Jesus' name!"

Renouncing Unholy Covenants

- ☐ *"Almighty God, O Righteous Judge, Heavenly Father, we come before You and, in Jesus' name, on behalf of the US SCHOOL SYSTEM AND DEPT OF EDUCATION, we renounce, rebuke, revoke, divorce, cancel, and come out of agreement with any and all unholy covenants that the US SCHOOL SYSTEM AND DEPT OF EDUCATION, including all types of schools and education systems and learning institutions and organizations, has entered into at any time in history up to this current time. We specifically renounce any agreements or covenants that any representatives or leaders of the US SCHOOL SYSTEM AND DEPT OF EDUCATION made with any secret societies, and particularly renounce, cancel, and divorce all covenants and agreements they made with the Masons/Masonic Lodge.*

- ☐ *"Father God, we ask that all records of unholy covenants be wiped off the record books and the record books of all past leadership and history of the US SCHOOL SYSTEM AND DEPT OF EDUCATION on all levels, including rural, local, regional, national, and international, in the Courts of Heaven by the blood of Jesus and remembered no more for Your sake!*

- ☐ *"Father God, we also ask that the US SCHOOL SYSTEM AND DEPT OF EDUCATION would now be fully released and set free from all entanglements, repercussions, and consequences of these sins and unholy covenants, in Jesus' name! We ask that one NEW HOLY COVENANT with You, Father God, through Jesus Christ be written and decreed for The US SCHOOL SYSTEM AND DEPT OF EDUCATION in the record books in Heaven, and for this to be recorded and proclaimed today to commence on earth as it is in Heaven, Father God, from this day forward, in Jesus' name. Amen!"*

Justice/Enforcement

- ☐ *"Almighty Father God, O Righteous Judge, Heavenly Father, In the name of Jesus Christ and by His authority and by the anointing of Your Holy Spirit and Your angels on assignment, we ask that today this "not guilty" verdict rendered in Your Court be fully enforced in the spiritual and the natural realm and in the heavens and the earth. We also ask that justice be carried out fully in the spiritual and the natural regarding any injustices, sins and crimes regarding the US SCHOOL SYSTEM AND DEPT OF*

EDUCATION. We ask, in Jesus' name, Father God, that You would assign and dispatch your angels of justice to go forth and bring exposure and justice according to Your laws and the laws of the United States of America to those who have done injustices against your people and this nation of the United States of America using the US SCHOOL SYSTEM AND DEPT OF EDUCATION. We ask for this to be fulfilled swiftly, in Jesus' name. Amen."

Restitution

- ☐ "Almighty Father God, O Righteous Judge, we now ask in the name of Jesus Christ for Your angels of restitution to be assigned to this case. Our request is that full restitution of everything that was stolen or lost or even destroyed by or through The US SCHOOL SYSTEM AND DEPT OF EDUCATION, including universities, medical schools, public and private schools, Christian schools, Bible schools and seminaries, military schools, trade schools, daycare facilities, residential and specialized schools for the disabled, school boards and all leadership at every level, and libraries — both public and on these campuses, or any loss including time, be given to the proper recipient, even those who are the descendants of those who are due restitution from any loss, past or present, and that it shall be redeemed to them swiftly, in Jesus' name."

Blessing

- ☐ "Father God, we ask now if You would pour out a blessing and restore your original intention and plans for the US SCHOOL SYSTEM AND DEPT OF EDUCATION. We cancel and renounce any negative words or curses that have been spoken or written about the US SCHOOL SYSTEM AND DEPT OF EDUCATION, in Jesus' name. We specifically cancel the words ever spoken or written. We ask You, Lord Jesus, to cover any negative words or curses that have ever been spoken or written against the US SCHOOL SYSTEM AND DEPT OF EDUCATION with Your blood, Lord, and that these words are now null and void, in Jesus' name. We speak blessing and prosperity to the US SCHOOL SYSTEM AND DEPT OF EDUCATION and all those affiliated with these universities, medical schools, public and private schools, Christian schools, Bible schools and seminaries, military schools, trade schools, daycare facilities, residential and specialized schools for the disabled, school boards and all leadership at every level, and libraries — both public and on these campuses.

- ☐ *"Father God, we ask for You to surround the US SCHOOL SYSTEM AND DEPT OF EDUCATION with Your favor and that Your Holy Spirit come upon it and everyone shall see and know that the righteousness and blessings and gifts of God are covering and working in and through everything having to do with the US SCHOOL SYSTEM AND DEPT OF EDUCATION, all for Your glory and honor, God, in Jesus' name! People will once again have good things to say and write and enjoy and trust in the US SCHOOL SYSTEM AND DEPT OF EDUCATION!"*

Protection Of The Gates Of The Us School System And Dept Of Education

- ☐ *"Father God, in the name of Jesus Christ, we ask for You to post Your sentry angels to the natural, spiritual, and digital gates in all locations and property of the US SCHOOL SYSTEM AND DEPT OF EDUCATION or any place/location where they are operating both publicly and privately to keep watch and guard around the clock and protect these gates from all evil!*

- ☐ *I ask that the sentry angels of Almighty God would stop and destroy any evil or demonic assignments that would attempt to go in or out though any and all gateways of the US SCHOOL SYSTEM AND DEPT OF EDUCATION with their supernatural, fiery swords and shields from this day forward, in Jesus' name! Thank You, Father God, for sending your angels to keep us in all our ways!"*

Dominion/Dedication

- ☐ *"In the name of Jesus Christ, King of kings, Lord of lords, the name above all names, by His authority we claim, consecrate and dedicate THE US SCHOOL SYSTEM AND DEPT OF EDUCATION in its entirety to Almighty God. We place it all in the blood of Jesus Christ. This includes all universities, medical schools, public and private schools, Christian schools, Bible schools and seminaries, military schools, trade schools, daycare facilities, residential and specialized schools for the disabled, school boards and all leadership at every level, and libraries — both public and on these campuses of the US SCHOOL SYSTEM AND DEPT OF EDUCATION into the dominion and kingdom of Almighty God to now only be used for the plans and purposes of God and the kingdom and glory of God from this day forward, in Jesus' name!"*

The Scepter Of Righteousness

- *"In the name of Jesus Christ, King of kings, Lord of lords the name above all names, by His authority, we claim that the US SCHOOL SYSTEM AND DEPT OF EDUCATION including universities, medical schools, public and private schools, Christian schools, Bible schools and seminaries, military schools, trade schools, daycare facilities, residential and specialized schools for the disabled, school boards and all leadership at every level, and libraries — both public and on these campuses — and services belong to Almighty God and are now allotted to the righteous! Therefore, it is written in Psalm 125:3 that 'the scepter of wickedness will not remain over the land allotted to the righteous.' So we declare, in Jesus' name, that the SCEPTER OF RIGHTEOUSNESS RULES over all land, buildings, services, and properties of the US SCHOOL SYSTEM AND DEPT OF EDUCATION, and we renounce and beat down the scepter of wickedness and command it to leave for it no longer has power or authority to remain, in Jesus' name!"*

Ax Of God's Judgment

- *"Father God, Your word says in Matthew 3:10, 'And now also the axe is laid unto the root of the trees: therefore every tree which bringeth not forth good fruit is hewn down, and cast into the fire.' Father God, I believe Your word, and I want to activate it right now in the spiritual and in the natural! Father, in Jesus' name, I ask You to take Your ax of judgment, according to Matthew 3:10, and chop and pull up at the root any and all unholy ungodly influences that are in and around the US SCHOOL SYSTEM AND DEPT OF EDUCATION that are not there to produce good fruit! Remove those unholy, ungodly influences at the root, pull the stumps up out of the ground, shake the stumps with no roots remaining in the ground and any of its branches, vines, or, seeds, and cast it all into the fire to burn to ashes, in Jesus' name! We do not have to accept anything that is not the will of God for our nation, our school system, our community, or our people, in Jesus' name! Father God, I ask You to replace all those areas of influence in and around the US SCHOOL SYSTEM AND DEPT OF EDUCATION with Holy Spirit-filled, righteous influences that will bear and multiply good Holy Spirit-fruit for Your kingdom and glory, in Jesus' name!"*

Take Group Communion — Prepare Your Communion Bread And Juice And Pray

☐ *"Heavenly Father, in the name of Jesus, we take Communion together as a prophetic act of faith to seal and confirm our prayers and this time in the Courts of Heaven. Father God, we lift up this bread to You and we give You thanks and praise. We dedicate and consecrate this bread to You, Father God, and we ask You to bless this bread as it represents the body of Your Son — the bread of life — Jesus Christ. Lord Jesus, You told us to remember You this way and remember what You did on the Cross for us. Lord, we invite You to our table because you invited us to Yours. We understand that Your sacrifice on the Cross, Lord, was for our sins and the sins of the world and we are grateful. Thank You, Lord Jesus, and we ask You, Lord, to cleanse this bread with Your blood, and sanctify it. We proclaim this bread is holy and sanctified by the blood of Jesus. Thank You, Lord. Thank You, Father God. We bless this bread, in Jesus' name."* (Eat bread)

☐ *"Heavenly Father, in the name of Jesus, we take Communion together as a prophetic act of faith to seal our prayers and this time in the Courts of Heaven. Father God, we lift up this cup and grape juice to You, and we give You thanks and praise. We dedicate and consecrate this cup and grape juice to You, Father God, and we ask You to bless this as it represents the blood of Your Son, Jesus Christ. Lord Jesus, You told us to remember You this way and remember that You shed Your blood for us and our sins. Your blood, Lord, cleanses us of all sin and iniquities, heals us, protects us, and redeems us out of the hand of the devil and back to God to be set aside for the plans and purposes of Father God, all because of Your blood, Lord!*

☐ *"Thank You, Lord Jesus, and we ask You, Lord, to cleanse this cup and grape juice with Your blood and sanctify it. We proclaim by faith that this grape juice is holy and sanctified by the blood of Jesus and that everywhere it touches, the power of the blood of Jesus is released! Thank You, Lord. Thank You, Father God. We bless this cup and juice and partake, in Jesus' name."* (Drink juice)

Taking Authority As A King And Priest For Land Assignment
Make sure before you go to land prayer location you put on your full armor of God and do my Suit Up Prayer here in the book.

☐ *"Almighty Father God, O Righteous Judge, in the name of Jesus Christ, Your word says in Revelation 1:6, 'And hath made us kings and priests unto God and his Father; to him be glory and dominion for ever and ever. Amen.' Therefore, we do now take our kingly and priestly place and authority right here and now in Christ Jesus and through Christ Jesus as we stand at this educational institution location for zip code _____ in _____ (City/State) and claim this land and this educational institution for Your plans and purposes, Almighty God, for Your kingdom and Your glory from this day forward, in Jesus' name!"*

Local United States Department of Education, Schools and School systems, and Educational Organizations Repentance

If you cannot go to the location, you can do this in your own yard or in the spirit if you live within the zip code area.

- ☐ *"Father God, we also come to You, in the name of Jesus Christ, repenting for the sins of this particular educational institution location for zip code _____ in _____ (City/State) since its founding. We have repented of all sinful acts against You, Father God, and all sinful acts against Your word that have transgressed through the US SCHOOL SYSTEM AND DEPT OF EDUCATION in its entirety and now also repent for the sinful acts that have transgressed through this educational institution location for zip code _____ in _____ (City/State). We come into agreement with all of the repentance that was done in the Courts of Heaven today (on March 9, 2021) with our group of intercessors across the nation and ask that our petition for repentance and forgiveness locally here also be honored in Your Courts, Father God.*

- ☐ *"We ask now for grace, mercy, and forgiveness for these sins. We ask now, Lord Jesus, for You to put Your blood on all these sins and wash them clean. Father God, now that the blood of Jesus is on these sins, we ask that this educational institution location for zip code _____ in _____ (City/State) be released of all consequences of these sins and all accusations, curses, and demonic assignments be canceled off of this educational institution location for zip code _____ in _____ (City/State) by the redeeming power of the blood of Jesus. We ask now, Father God, for your plans and purposes and blessings to go forth through this educational institution location for zip code _____ in _____ (City/State) from this day forward. So be it, in Jesus' name. Amen."*

Pour Communion In The Land

At your educational institutional location, you will pray the prayer below over the Communion cup filled with grape juice. Then you partake first and pour the rest on the ground.

- ☐ *"Father God, we lift up this cup and grape juice to You, and we give You thanks and praise. We dedicate and consecrate this cup and grape juice to You, Father God, and we ask You to bless this as it represents the blood of Your Son, Jesus Christ. Lord Jesus, You told us to remember You this way and remember that You shed Your blood for us and our sins. Your blood, Lord, cleanses us of all sin and iniquities, heals us, protects us, and redeems us out of the hand of the devil and back to God to be set aside for the plans and purposes of Father God, all because of Your blood, Lord! Lord Jesus, Your blood poured into the ground at Your crucifixion when You proclaimed, "It Is finished." We understand that Your precious blood not only redeemed us that day but that when it touched the earth, the land was also redeemed back to God. We ask today for Your blood to cleanse, sanctify, and redeem this land upon which we stand today. Thank You, Lord Jesus, and we ask You, Lord, to cleanse this cup and grape juice with Your blood and to sanctify it. We proclaim by faith that this grape juice is holy and sanctified by the blood of Jesus, and that everywhere it touches, the redeeming and cleansing power of the blood of Jesus is released! Thank You, Lord. Thank You, Father God. We bless this cup and juice and partake, in Jesus' name."* (Drink juice and leave some to pour on the ground after the next declaration below.)

Declare As You Pour The Communion

- ☐ *"Father God, Your word says in Hebrews 12:24, "To Jesus the mediator of a new covenant, and to the sprinkled blood that speaks a better word than the blood of Abel." Let this land receive the blood of Jesus Christ. Let the blood of Jesus Christ speak for this land, this property, and everything on this property to be cleansed of all sins and iniquities! By the blood of Jesus, this land and property and everything on the land, above the land, and below the land is now redeemed out of the hand of the devil back to God and set aside for the plans and purposes of God by the power of the blood of Jesus all for the glory of God! So be it. Amen!"* (Pour Communion in the land. You do not need much — just enough to soak into the soil.)

Pour/Apply Anointing Oil To The Land

Bless and dedicate the oil FIRST. See my "How To Pray Over And Apply Anointing Oil Prayer" here in the book.

Next, apply the oil to yourself and dedicate yourself to God and His plans and purposes in Jesus' name. Apply to your forehead, palms of your hands, and tops of your feet. Also, put some on the tops and bottoms of your shoes so you release the anointing wherever you walk and whatever you touch.

Declare As You Pour The Oil On The Ground - (You Just Need A Few Drops)

- ☐ *"In the name of Jesus Christ, we pour the anointing oil into this land and educational institutional property of zip code _____ in _____ (City/State). We declare as it is written that the anointing breaks the yoke, and we proclaim that every yoke of bondage, slavery, and sin is now shattered off this land, the property upon it, and this educational institution, in Jesus' name. We declare this land, educational institution, and everything on it, along with all services being provided here, is now only yoked to Jesus Christ and the kingdom of Almighty God. We dedicate and consecrate this land, property, educational institution, all buildings and everything on this property, the services being provided here, and every gateway — natural, digital, and spiritual — to Almighty God. Let every gateway on this land and property receive the anointing of the Holy Spirit! We invite the Holy Spirit to come upon this land and property and do creative healing and deliverance miracles. Let the power of the Holy Spirit be released upon everyone and everything on this property, this educational institution, and this land!*

- ☐ *From this day forward, let the power of the Holy Spirit be released upon everything coming in and going out from this place, in Jesus' name! We declare that this educational institution property of zip code _____ in _____ (City/State) is now anointed, blessed, and set aside to be used for the plans and purposes of Almighty God, all for the kingdom and glory of God from this day forward, in Jesus' name!"*

Asking For Angel Armies Of The Lord For Your Local Educational Institution

- ☐ *"Father God, In the name of Jesus, we ask for You to dispatch Your heavenly hosts and warrior angels to come now and remove all demons, demonic principalities, and demonic platforms surrounding this educational institution location in the region of the zip code of _____ in _____ (City/State), including anything of the kingdom of darkness operating through its services, leaders, employees, trainees, contractors, curricula, equipment, patrons, customers, clients, land, and properties here. We ask that these demonic entities, assignments, strongholds, and their demonic altars and platforms be dismantled, rooted out, bound, and cast out forever to the uninhabited dry place by the heavenly hosts and warrior angels of Almighty God, in Jesus' name! Let the heavenly hosts and warrior angels of Almighty God take this educational institution location in zip code _____ in _____ (City/State) off the frequency of the demonic forever! We ask, Father God, for Your angelic armies to stand and hold now over every place they removed these demonic entities from and for Your mighty angels to now occupy and protect this educational institution and zip code region from all evil regarding all areas of this educational institution and its services, leaders, employees, trainees, contractors, curriculum, equipment, land, and property here in zip code _____ in _____ (City/State) for Your kingdom and glory, in Jesus' name!"*

Blessing Your Local US Department of Education, Schools and School Systems, and Educational Organizations

- ☐ *"Father God, we ask now if You would pour out a blessing and restore Your original intention and plans for this educational institution here in zip code _____ in _____ (City/State). We cancel and renounce any negative words or curses that have been spoken or written about this educational institution here in zip code _____ in _____ (City/State), in Jesus' name. We ask You, Lord Jesus, to cover any negative words or curses that have ever been spoken here or over this place with Your blood, Lord, and that these words would now be null and void, in Jesus' name. We speak blessing and prosperity to this educational institution located here in zip code _____ in _____ (City/State) and to all of the employees and patrons!*

- ☐ *"Father God, we ask for You to surround this educational location here in zip code _____ in _____ (City/State) with Your favor and that Your Holy Spirit would come upon it, and everyone shall see and know that the righteousness and blessing and gifts of God are covering and working in and through everything having to do with this educational location here in zip code _____ in _____ (City/State) all for Your glory and honor, God, in Jesus' name! People will once again have good to say and write and enjoy and trust about this educational location and its leaders and employees here in zip code _____ in _____ (City/State), in Jesus' name!"*

Dedicate Your Local US Dept of Education, Schools and School Systems, and Educational Organizations

Apply the prayed-over oil with your fingertips/hands on a structure on the property as you pray.

- ☐ *"Father God, I thank You for this _____ with the address of _____. In the name of Jesus Christ, I dedicate and consecrate this _____ at this address _____ to You, Father God, and declare that it is designated and set aside for Your plans and purposes. I place this _____ at this address _____ in the blood of Jesus Christ. Lord Jesus, release the power of Your blood over this _____ at this address _____. Your blood, Lord Jesus, destroys all darkness, cleanses all sins, and breaks all curses and demonic assignments. I declare by the blood of Jesus, this _____ at this address _____ is now sanctified. I anoint this _____ in the name of Jesus, and I invite You, Holy Spirit, to come upon this _____ with your power, protection, and presence. I declare this _____ at this address _____ is now anointed. Let the power of the Holy Spirit come upon this _____ at this address of _____. Father God, bless this _____, and let it be used only for Your glory. I bless this _____. Let the blood of Jesus and the power of the Holy Spirit be released upon everything coming in and going out from this _____ at this address _____ from this day forward, in Jesus' name. Amen."*

Mail Anointed Prayer Letter

This is a powerful prophetic act of faith to release the power and the authority of the Lord Jesus Christ and of the Holy Spirit throughout the inner workings of the US SCHOOL SYSTEM AND DEPT OF EDUCATION. Every place and every person that comes in contact with your anointed letter there will encounter the presence of the Holy Spirit as in Acts 19:12 when Apostle Paul anointed the aprons: "They were brought to the sick, and diseases departed from them, and evil spirits went out of them."

You will also release an authority and blessing of the Lord by speaking over the letter. Isaiah 55:11 says: "His word will not return void but will accomplish that which he pleases and shall prosper in the thing whereto he SENT it."

Together as the Body of Christ, we are going to compose a letter with an anointing that carries God's word and His Holy Spirit throughout the US SCHOOL SYSTEM AND DEPT OF EDUCATION with a blessing and declaration. See below for the letter and the anointing prayer and decree.

If You Feel Led, You Can Also Dab Some Communion On The Letter And Pray This Prayer

Take Communion yourself and speak prophetically with a drop on the letter as an act of faith.

- ☐ *I apply the blood of Jesus to my life and to this letter and all that is written in it and to every place this letter travels. It will release the cleansing and redeeming power of the blood of Jesus. I decree that we are redeemed by the blood of Jesus out of the hand of the devil back into the hands of Almighty God and now set aside for the plans and purposes of God, all by the blood of Jesus, from this day forward, in Jesus' name!*

- ☐ *I decree that the power of the blood of Jesus will be carried and released into and through this letter everywhere it goes! Lord Jesus, by faith and as an act of my will, I pour a drop of this Communion juice on this letter. Let the power of Your blood, Lord, be upon this letter. Lord Jesus, release the power of Your blood to cleanse the sin, break all curses and demonic assignments, and destroy all demonic strongholds everywhere this letter travels! Let the power of Your blood, Lord Jesus, sanctify and reconcile everything this letter touches and every place this letter passes through all back to God for HIS plans and purposes!*

- ☐ *I proclaim by the authority of Jesus Christ and by the power of His blood, DOMINION OF Almighty God over the US SCHOOL SYSTEM AND DEPT OF EDUCATION and everywhere this letter travels. I pray that every person who touches this letter comes to the salvation of the Lord Jesus Christ, in Jesus' name. Amen.*

Your Handwritten Or Typed Letter May Be Something Like This

Dear friend in Christ,

I am writing and mailing you this letter as an act of faith to release the anointing of the Holy Spirit along with a blessing and word of the Lord upon the US SCHOOL SYSTEM AND DEPT OF EDUCATION. By faith and by the authority of Jesus Christ, I ask you to please join me in claiming the US SCHOOL SYSTEM AND DEPT OF EDUCATION, including all of its leaders, teachers, administrators, employees, students, and anything affiliated with it at every location in the nation for the kingdom of Almighty God.

This is a prophetic act of faith. We have come together and repented for the sins against God regarding the US SCHOOL SYSTEM AND DEPT OF EDUCATION and asked God, by the blood of Jesus, to cleanse the US SCHOOL SYSTEM AND DEPT OF EDUCATION of all evil and sinfulness and bring everything having to do with the US SCHOOL SYSTEM AND DEPT OF EDUCATION back into the will of God to be used only for righteous purposes.

Our prayer group felt led by the Lord to send out these anointed letters to travel through the US SCHOOL SYSTEM AND DEPT OF EDUCATION SYSTEM. We ask the angels of the Lord to protect this letter as it travels. We declare Psalm 91 protection over this letter and over the US SCHOOL SYSTEM AND DEPT OF EDUCATION, including its leadership, employees, and all its works.

We proclaim Psalm 91:4, "He shall cover thee with his feathers, and under his wings shalt thou trust: his truth shall be thy shield and buckler." We proclaim Exodus 23:20, "Behold, I send an angel before thee, to keep thee in the way, and to bring thee into the place which I have prepared." We proclaim Isaiah 55:1, "His word will not return void and will accomplish that which he pleases and shall prosper in the thing whereto he SENT it."

We proclaim and dedicate the US SCHOOL SYSTEM AND DEPT OF EDUCATION, including its leaders, employees and all its works for the plans and purposes of Almighty God, all for the glory of God.

This letter has been anointed with anointing oil that has been dedicated to God. It is written in Isaiah 10:27 that the anointing breaks all yokes of slavery and bondage, and anything anointed shall be set aside for God's purposes. Would you faithfully come into agreement in prayer for the US SCHOOL SYSTEM AND DEPT OF EDUCATION when you receive this letter?

We bless you and your household, and we bless the US SCHOOL SYSTEM AND DEPT OF EDUCATION, including its leadership, its employees, and all its works and affiliations from this day forward. So be it, in Jesus' mighty name! Amen.

Yours In Christ Jesus,

Signed: _____

Feel free to add any personal prayer or scripture to your letter. It is important that you hand sign your name. This is a symbol of covenant with God. Then you will put a small dab of prayed-over anointing oil on your letter and envelope and seal it. You don't have to soak it in oil; it carries the power of the Holy Spirit and just a small amount will do nicely. I just put some on my hands and touch the edges.

If you don't have anointing oil you can use plain prayed-over olive oil. Pray my anointing oil prayer in this book to dedicate your oil to God. This is an important step, so please follow these instructions. The purpose of this letter is that the anointing goes through the system to release the healing and restoring power of the Holy Spirit as we have released our faith and authority in Christ.

Jesus did not have to personally touch each person to heal them. He sent the Holy Spirit to be our helper in all of these things. The oil represents the presence of the Holy Spirit. Our faith and authority in Jesus Christ is what activates it.

You want your oil to carry the power of the anointing, so pray over it and bless it in faith. Make sure your oil is prayed over using my anointing oil prayer, then apply some oil to your hands and fingertips.

Put Your Anointed Hands On The Letter And Addressed/Stamped Envelope And Declare

- ☐ *"Father God, I thank You for this letter addressed to _____. In the name of Jesus Christ, I dedicate and consecrate this letter and envelope to You, Father God, and declare that it is designated and set aside for Your plans and purposes for the US SCHOOL SYSTEM AND DEPT OF EDUCATION. Through the sending and delivery of this letter, we ask for the power of Your Holy Spirit to be upon it. I place this letter and everything on it in the blood of Jesus Christ. Lord Jesus, release the power of Your blood over this letter. Your blood, Lord Jesus, destroys all darkness and breaks all curses and demonic assignments. By the blood of Jesus, this letter is now sanctified.*

- ☐ *"I anoint this letter and envelope in the name of Jesus, and I invite You, Holy Spirit, to come upon it with your power, protection, and presence. Holy Spirit, release your dunamis power and presence everywhere this letter goes — upon every person and place it touches and passes! As this letter is mailed and travels through the US SCHOOL SYSTEM AND DEPT OF EDUCATION, let the power of Your Holy Spirit flow and be released and activated at each place and upon each person in the travels of this letter, in Jesus' name!*

- ☐ *"Holy Spirit, bring deliverance, healing, restoration, and encounters with the Lord Jesus Christ in each place along the way to the destination of this letter! Holy Spirit, bring Your light, Your living waters, Your healing oil, Your breath of life, and Your holy refining fire into all the dark, damaged, and lost places and hearts this letter encounters!*

- ☐ *"Holy Spirit, bring complete divine alignment, restoration, restitution, righteousness, and renewal to the US SCHOOL SYSTEM AND DEPT OF EDUCATION and everything connected to it according to the will and word of God! Let the original intent and plan of God come forth for the US SCHOOL SYSTEM AND DEPT OF EDUCATION! Holy Spirit, give every person involved with the US SCHOOL SYSTEM AND DEPT OF EDUCATION a heart to know and receive the presence of the living God and the salvation of the Lord Jesus Christ!*

- ☐ *"In Jesus' name, Holy Spirit, I ask You to restore everything to God's divine order along the way through the educational locations and curriculum with Your resurrection power that this letter now carries! Father God, dispatch Your angels to protect and accompany this letter to make sure it gets to its destination of _____. Father God, bless this letter, and let Your hand be upon it and let it be used only for Your plans, purposes and glory, Almighty God, from this day forward, in Jesus' name. Amen."*

Please mail your anointed, hand-signed, stamped, and prayed-over letter through your local post office to another brother or sister in Christ, and then ask them to receive the letter and come into agreement with the prayer.

Optional Offering

After you finish this US SCHOOL SYSTEM AND DEPT OF EDUCATION assignment, give an offering to God into a ministry or church that is fertile soil for the kingdom thanking Him for opening His Courts to you and for His grace, mercy, and forgiveness, or sow a seed into God's kingdom and name the seed, "Righteousness of Almighty God takes over the US SCHOOL SYSTEM AND DEPT OF EDUCATION and multiplies throughout the world in all educational systems for a great harvest for Jesus Christ and for the kingdom and glory of Almighty God."

If you desire, you can sow into Life In The Faith Lane Ministry

By US Mail:
Annamarie Strawhand
P.O Box 7068
Virginia Beach, VA 23457

US Judicial System Prayer Assignment – Repentance In The Courts Of Heaven

The Judicial And Court System Of The United States Of America
(Us Judicial System Prayer Assignment)

Taking The Case To The Courts Of Heaven

Spoken Prayers And Holy Spirit Strategies For Deliverance

Blessing The Land – Courthouse Locations

Let's help you all have some clarity between prayer and entering the Courts of Heaven with a petition and prayer. The Courts of Heaven are when we ask the Father God to approach His throne as Judge in a case that the accuser the (devil) is using to keep a stronghold on something because of sin.

We ask through Jesus Christ to enter the Courts to repent for these sins before God, our Righteous Judge, and ask Jesus to wash the sins with His blood and for His blood to speak in our defense and in defense of the sins in which we are interceding for in our nation because the blood of Jesus is the ONLY defense that can redeem us from sin, even of the land and a nation. We are deemed innocent when the blood of Jesus is applied and we ask for the judgment verdict to be not guilty because the blood of Jesus has spoken, and then and only then can the accuser be stripped of his curses and the person/land can be set free and delivered out of any demonic strongholds.

Note: On February 1,1790, the first session of the US Supreme Court was held in New York City's Royal Exchange Building. The Judiciary Act of 1789 established the federal court system separate from individual state courts. It was one of the first acts of the First Congress. President George Washington signed it into law on September 24, 1789.

Opening Prayer

- ☐ *Matthew 6:9-13 (KJV): "After this manner therefore pray ye: Our Father which art in heaven, Hallowed be thy name. Thy kingdom come, Thy will be done in earth, as it is in heaven. Give us this day our daily bread. And forgive us our debts, as we forgive our debtors. And lead us not into temptation, but deliver us from evil: For thine is the kingdom, and the power, and the glory, for ever. Amen."*

Enter Courts Of Heaven - (Speak Out Loud)

- ☐ *"Almighty God, O Righteous Judge, Heavenly Father, we come to You today, in the name of Jesus Christ, asking to enter Your Heavenly Court and to appear before You, O Righteous Judge, with our petition regarding the JUDICIAL AND COURTS SYSTEMS OF THE JUDICIARY BRANCH OF UNITED STATES OF AMERICA. This includes everything pertaining to the US JUDICIAL SYSTEM – UNITED STATES SUPREME COURT- ALL COURT LEVEL SYSTEMS AND LEVELS OF THE JUDICIAL BRANCHES and MILITARY COURTS, FISA COURT on all levels of federal, state, county, city and internationally where the United States of America is involved judicially and has jurisdiction to give rulings and judgments from the court and laws and constitutional government of this land. This shall be referred to as the United States Judicial System as a whole as we present this case in Your holy Courts today, Father God.*

- ☐ *"We are including all US courts, judges, clerks, officials, rulings, documents, laws, and jurisdictions since the official founding of the Federal Judicial System in 1789 and all other Judicial levels before and after in the United States Of America. This includes early Colonial law and judiciary and law under English rule in the original 13 colonies and any reception of law and judiciary practices of the Crown of England that may be still in use today in the United States.*

- ☐ *"We ask You, Lord Jesus, to represent and intercede for us as our high priest with Father God and for Your blood to speak for us and the US Judicial System on the Mercy Seat. We invite the Holy Spirit to assist and guide us in our Heavenly Court appearance, repentance, and prayer. We ask for Your angels to surround us to protect us and assist us to fully complete this from start to finish with the guidance of the Holy Spirit according to Your will, Father God. We ask, in Jesus' name, as we enter Your Courts, Father God, for our books to be opened for ourselves, our cities and states, our nation — the United States of America — and the US Judicial System including all of the courthouses, buildings, offices, documents, rulings, correspondence, laws, land, judges, clerks, officials, and people associated with it.*

- ☐ *"We realize there has already been much repentance for the sins of the United States Supreme Court, and we ask for all of those records of repentance to be considered today. We ask, in Jesus' name, for the Cloud of Witnesses and also the faithful men and women who were righteous believers in Christ Jesus, to be present witnessing to this case and that those who were righteous judges in America to witness to the intercession of Jesus Christ for the US Judicial System for which we come into agreement with the intercession of Jesus' prayers.*

- ☐ *"We would be honored to have Your intent revealed for the US Judicial System in the Courts today, Father God, and through this time in the Courts, we pray that all can now come into alignment with Your will and plan. We also ask for Your recording angels to be present. We ask for any repentance for the sins of our nation — the United States of America — and courts, courthouses, judges, clerks, officers, employees, buildings, offices, judgments, documents, laws, correspondence, land, leaders, citizens of any jurisdiction, and ANY people publicly known and secretly associated past and present with it that have already been repented for or unrepented, to be taken into consideration today as we desire to have full and complete repentance for every sin, known and unknown to us, as we come before you again today, O Righteous Judge.*

- ☐ *"We ask, Father God, in Jesus' name, that You demand the accuser in this case regarding the sins of the United States Judicial System and everything associated with it to be present in the Court. We ask, in the name of Jesus, for the Courts of Heaven to be in session for our case and petition today and the Court to be seated. Because of the blood of Jesus and the finished work of the Cross, we are able to enter Your holy Courts as it is written in Your word in Hebrews 10:19: "And so, dear brothers and sisters, we can boldly enter heaven's Most Holy Place because of the blood of Jesus." We now ask to present our case before Your Court. Thank You, Father God. Thank You, Lord Jesus. Thank You, Holy Spirit. Amen!"*

Personal Prayer Of Cleansing

- ☐ *"Almighty God, O Righteous Judge, Heavenly Father, I humbly come before You in Your Heavenly Courts and repent for all my sins and the sins of my ancestors and family bloodline. I specifically repent for my sins and the sins of my ancestors and family bloodline that are sins that were committed through the United States Judicial System or any sins of agreement with the sins of the United States Judicial System. If there are any sins in my life or the lives of my ancestors and family bloodline that were done against You, Father God, or against Your word regarding the United States Judicial System, I repent for these sins right now. I am sorry for sinning against You, Father God. I am sorry for any sins that my ancestors — anyone in my family bloodline — or I committed with or through the United States Judicial System and any sins of agreement with any evil that the US Judicial System or its judges have been doing or have done.*

- [ ] *"Father God, I ask today for grace, mercy, and forgiveness for my ancestors, my family bloodline, and myself. Lord Jesus, I ask for You to put Your blood on all of these sins for my ancestors, my family bloodline, and myself and wash us clean. I ask that these sins be remembered no more for Your sake, Father God, and that they be wiped clean from the record books of Heaven and earth by the blood of Jesus. Now that the blood of Jesus has covered these sins, I ask that they will no longer be held against my family bloodline, my ancestors, or me ever again on earth or in Heaven. These sins are now null and void.*

- [ ] *"In Jesus' name, I ask for the accuser to be stripped of any legal rights and that any curses and demonic assignments be removed and canceled, in Jesus' name. I ask today, Father God, in Jesus' name, that my ancestors, my family line, and I be found "not guilty" by the blood of Jesus — our only defense. I also ask for this new "not guilty" verdict to be written in our books and proclaimed in your Courts today. Father God, it is written in Your word in Proverbs 26:2 that a curse causeless cannot stand. Therefore, the blood of Jesus is now covering all these sins. The blood of Jesus removes all sin, curses, and demonic assignments. Therefore, there is no longer any cause for any curses or repercussions against me or my family bloodline. I ask in Jesus' name for myself, my family bloodline, and all my ancestors to now be released from any curses, entanglements, repercussions, or consequences from these sins.*

- [ ] *"My request here in Your Heavenly Court, Almighty God, O Righteous Judge, because these sins I have repented for today are now covered in the blood Of Jesus, is that my family bloodline, my ancestors, and I be moved from the Court of Judgment to the Throne of Grace and Mercy because our spiritual debt has been paid in full by the precious blood of Jesus, and now there can be no recourse from the accuser. Father God, O Righteous Judge, I ask for You to silence the voice of the accuser forever regarding these sins.*

- ☐ *"I ask for Your Holy Spirit to fill all the places now where these sins and curses once were and stand hold there with Your presence and protection. In Jesus' name, I ask that my books and the books of my ancestors and family bloodline be fully reconciled back to the will of God here in the Courts and my record of repentance be recorded for my future court appearances here in Your Spiritual Court of Law, and my high priest, the Lord Jesus Christ, will confirm for me and my cloud of witnesses in Heaven as a witness to all that was done here today.*

- ☐ *"Thank You, Father God, for Your grace, mercy, and forgiveness. Thank You, Lord Jesus, for Your precious blood that has set me free. Thank You, Holy Spirit, for Your guidance in the Courts. Amen!"*

You are now cleansed, forgiven, redeemed, and ready to intercede and present the main case for the US JUDICIAL SYSTEM into the Courts of Heaven.

Ambassador Of Reconciliation

- ☐ *"Almighty God, O Righteous Judge, in the name of and with the intercession of Jesus Christ, my Lord and high priest, I come before Your Court today (as well as my group of intercessors) asking to be recognized as an Ambassador(s) of Reconciliation to stand in the gap to present a petition of repentance and reconciliation on behalf of the United States Judicial System, its justices and judges, its history, its employees, clerks and officers, its locations — jurisdictions, courthouses, offices, correspondence, rulings, laws, documents, and properties — and all of its works and affiliations today on all levels — city, state, county, federal, military, FISA courts, and international courts — since its founding in 1789, even before that of any courts operating in the 13 colonies, now in all 50 states and the United States of America and our interests abroad.*

- ☐ *"Father God, Your word states in Ephesians 6:18-20: 'Praying always with all prayer and supplication in the Spirit, and watching thereunto with all perseverance and supplication for all saints; And for me, that utterance may be given unto me, that I may open my mouth boldly, to make known the mystery of the gospel, For which I am an ambassador in bonds: that therein I may speak boldly, as I ought to speak.' Also, in Your word, Father God, You tell us in Hebrews 4:15-16: 'For we do not have a high priest who is unable to sympathize with our weaknesses, but we have one who was tempted in every way that we are, yet was without sin. Let us then approach the throne of grace with confidence, so that we may receive mercy and find grace to help us in our time of need. And it is written in Hebrews 10:18-20: 'And where these have been forgiven, an offering for sin is no longer needed. Therefore, brothers, since we have confidence to enter the Most Holy Place by the blood of Jesus, by the new and living way opened for us through the curtain of His body ...'*

- ☐ *"Therefore, according to Your word, Almighty Father God, O Righteous Judge, I (and our group of intercessors) come before You today as a redeemed soul(s) of Jesus Christ, and as citizens of Heaven and Your kingdom and citizens of the United States of America — a nation that has been dedicated to You, Father God, through our founders and again in this generation. I (we) am (are) here today to present my (our) petition before Your court as my (our) obligation by faith according to Your word and to receive grace, mercy, and forgiveness on behalf of the US Judicial System — a main branch of the government of The United States of America.*

- ☐ *"I (we) ask the Lord Jesus Christ and His blood to speak for me (us), and the US Judicial System today before Your Court, in Jesus' name, as I (we) present this case. I (we) ask for all the books to be opened regarding this case and for the witnesses, the recording angels, and the accuser to be present in the Court, in Jesus' name. I (we) ask You, Lord Jesus, to stand and intercede for us before Father God.*

- ☐ *"Thank You, Father God, O Righteous Judge, for recognizing me (and our group of intercessors) in Your Heavenly Court as an Ambassador(s) of Reconciliation for the US Judicial System and its leaders, its justices and judges, its attorneys, its officials, its employees, its juries, its plaintiffs, its defendants, its witnesses, its representatives, its locations — courts, courthouses, and jurisdictions — and everything regarding it since its founding in 1789 and anything before or after that. Thank You, Father God. Thank You, Lord Jesus, and thank You, Holy Spirit. Amen."*

Repentance For US Judicial System

- ☐ *"Almighty God, O Righteous Judge, Heavenly Father, in the name of Jesus Christ, we come to You in Your Heavenly Courts today in repentance for the sins of the US Judicial*

System, of its attorney generals and district attorneys, its justices and judges, the attorneys, court clerks, paralegals, court reporters, liaison officers, mediators, juries, justices of the peace, deputies, witnesses, plaintiffs and defendants, employees, interns, officers, law enforcement, the sins of its locations — courthouses, office buildings and properties — and the sins of all involved in this system and the judicial branch of our government of the United States of America, including all city, county, state, federal, military, international, and FISA levels that the US JUDICIAL SYSTEM provides publicly and anything that they have been doing in secret. We are repenting for these sins since its founding in 1789 up to this very moment.

☐ *"We ask, in Jesus' name, for Your Heavenly Court to be seated and the books to be opened. As we repent for these sins today, we ask Father God, O Righteous Judge, for the blood of Jesus Christ to speak for us and the US Judicial System on the Mercy Seat. We ask, in Jesus' name, Father God that You would send Your Holy Spirit upon each person affiliated or connected in any way with the US Judicial System, including current and former leadership, justices and judges, attorneys, court clerks, paralegals, officers of the court, justices of the peace, court reporters, mediators, juries, witnesses, plaintiffs, defendants, interns, bailiffs, law enforcement, political leaders, law professionals, and all individuals involved past and present who are still alive on the earth for the Holy Spirit to encounter them and remove any veils of deception that may be on their eyes because of their sins.*

☐ *"Please remove all veils off their eyes of understanding so they can see the truth, know the truth, embrace the truth, stand up for the truth, and boldly speak the truth. Holy Spirit, we ask that You bring all of these individuals to repentance and give them an encounter with the Lord Jesus Christ and that they will leave all sinful ways, seek deliverance, and come to the salvation of the Lord Jesus Christ to walk fully in the righteousness of God's will in every aspect of their lives, in Jesus' name. Amen."*

☐ *"Almighty God, O Righteous Judge, Heavenly Father, in the name of Jesus Christ, we come to You in Your Courts today in repentance for the sins of the US Judicial System. We confess, repent, and ask for grace, mercy, and forgiveness of these sins on their behalf today by the cleansing power of the blood of Jesus Christ to cover these sins we have listed:*

US JUDICIAL SYSTEM ALL COURT LEVEL SYSTEMS AND LEVELS OF THE JUDICIAL BRANCHES

The Federal Court System
- District courts
- Circuit courts
- Supreme Court of the United States

Local Court System
- City courts
- County courts
- State courts
- State supreme courts

Judges – elected and appointed
Attorney generals
District attorneys
Court clerks
Officers of the courts
Paralegals
Interns
Court reporters
Juries
Mediators
Justices of the peace
Law enforcement

All jurisdictions
All courthouses in America and abroad – US law

United States military courts
Foreign Intelligence Surveillance Court (FISA)
International courts – embassies

LIST OF REPENTANCE FOR THE JUDICIAL SYSTEM OF THE UNITED STATES OF AMERICA

1. Corrupt judges, fraudulent activity
2. Bribery, greed, pride, manipulation, blackmail
3. Putting politics before truth and honor, treating ethical lawyers with disdain
4. Family court injustice and taking children to traffick them, corrupt judges working with corrupted DHS, children being removed from good parents, children being adopted out unlawfully, endangering children
5. Ungodly and unbiblical policies and rulings

6. Secretive system in place to conceal the misconduct of judges
7. Abortion, Roe v. Wade, all rulings in favor of abortion, all rulings supporting or in favor of anything to do with planned parenthood
8. Unjust rulings against churches
9. Lying under oath after swearing-in on a Bible, treason, making false statements
10. Innocent people being executed, convicted, or imprisoned wrongfully
11. Any unjust ruling associated with or concerning any government agency including the military
12. Anyone being elected through fraud, any type of involvement in election fraud, refusing to see evidence of election fraud, unethical election laws
13. Sexual misconduct
14. Being silent when they know the truth — those who remain silent in crucial criminal cases are accomplices
15. Racial injustices and immigration injustices
16. FISA Court's illegal surveillance of President Trump and US citizens
17. Eldercare fraud, taking estates in unjust rulings
18. Anything in favor of the Equality Act or LGBTQ rulings
19. Unfair judgment associated with Foreign Corrupt Practices Act (FCPA)
20. Unjust rulings over zoning, real estate, city council, ordinances, budgets
21. Any association with secret societies/Masons
22. Attempting to remove GOD from everything
23. Unjust rulings in school cases — public, private, and universities.
24. Unjust rulings over parents and legal guardians concerning medical conditions, living wills, advance directives
25. Judges being in violation of their covenant oath of office on a Bible to protect the Constitution
26. Perversion of what our founding fathers established to be the promise of equal justice under the law
27. Any association with the Monarchy that is corrupt
28. Rulings in favor of sexual sin, pornography, and strip clubs,
29. Rulings in favor of bars, nightclubs, casinos, marijuana, drugs, liquor licenses, entertainment industry
30. Sinful and unjust rulings concerning other US Government agencies
31. Anything unjustly ruled against Israel
32. Anything in favor of satanic rituals and worship
33. Attempting to change or rewrite the Constitution, unjust rulings of our constitutional rights and human rights
34. Unjust sentences to mental facilities and nursing homes
35. Passing laws to aid in human trafficking, unprotected borders
36. Illegal land grabs and ill-gotten gains
37. Involvement in assassinations or attempted assassinations of judges, lawmakers, presidents, politicians, and unjust rulings in such cases
38. Unjust rulings in Market Integrity and Major Frauds Unit (MIMF) cases — specializes in fraud related to Department of Defense and other contracting agencies, as well as

corporate accounting fraud among defense contractors; also securities fraud and insider trading and market manipulation and other schemes deceiving investors in connection with the covid 19 crisis
39. Any corrupt or unfair military rulings
40. Unjust rulings in the Court of Appeals
41. Unjust rulings in favor of Big Tech and Big Pharma
42. Paying off juries and letting dangerous criminals go free
43. Unjust rulings to remove indigenous tribes from their land
44. Unjust rulings of conservatorship to control a person's life and finances
45. Laws that infringe on our personal privacy
46. Fear of man instead of fear of God, mocking the Holy Bible, blasphemy
47. People being forced to testify against their will for fear of harm or even death
48. Rulings that allow ungodly or unholy monuments to be constructed
49. Rulings that align with a one-world government and a cashless society
50. Any unjust rulings against any other nation
51. Rulings that allow for toxins to be placed in food, air, land, and water
52. Rulings that align with depopulation or sterilization
53. Any rulings that align with chemical or biological warfare
54. Unjust rulings concerning domestic terrorism and Homeland Security
55. Unjust rulings concerning health care and the CARES Act
56. Unfair or unjust rulings in alimony, palimony, divorce cases, or inheritance cases.
57. Unjust IRS rulings, tax evasion, etc.
58. Unjust rulings concerning trade
59. Unjust rulings concerning police brutality cases
60. Unjust insurance settlements — individual, class action, and corporate
61. Unlawful mask mandates
62. Unjust rulings concerning unions, labor, and pensions
63. Unjust rulings concerning financial institutions, corporations, and businesses
64. Unjust rulings concerning utilities, telecommunications, internet, servers, and the dark web
65. Unjust rulings concerning ports, airports, trucking, trains, freight, and commerce
66. Using the Corporate Administrative Procedure Act to corrupt justice and sidestep all legalities, corporate administrative courts
67. All sins and iniquities of the judicial branch of the Government of the United States of America
68. Anything that is a sin or an injustice against You, Your people, and Your word that is missing on this list, Lord, we ask for grace, and we ask for You to cover those sins in the blood of Jesus and that they be remembered no more for Your name's sake.

Asking For The Blood Of Jesus

☐ *"Lord Jesus, we ask that You cover all these sins repented for today regarding the US Judicial System with Your blood. Wash these sins clean and wipe them from the record books of Heaven with Your blood, Lord. Father God, we ask that You remember these sins no more for Your sake, in Jesus' name. We ask for the blood of Jesus to speak on the Mercy Seat for the US Judicial System. We ask, in Jesus' name, for grace, mercy, and forgiveness of all sins today that have been repented for and also any sins that may have unknowingly been omitted. We ask You, Lord Jesus, to intercede for us and cover these sins also with Your blood and that all sins, spoken and unspoken, be fully covered by the blood of Jesus on behalf of the US Judicial System since our 13 Colonies to the founding in 1789 up to this very moment — everything connected to it all today.*

- ☐ *"Thank You, Jesus, for Your precious blood! Thank You, Father God, O Righteous Judge, for Your grace, mercy, and forgiveness of the sins of the US Judicial System in this case that we have brought forth. We are grateful; and as we stand in the gap for the US Judicial System, we give You, Father God and Lord Jesus Christ, all the praise and glory for this divine opportunity in Your Courts!"*

Receiving The Verdict

- ☐ *"Almighty God, O Righteous Judge, we ask now by the blood of Jesus Christ, our only defense, that You would render a verdict of "not guilty" for the US Judicial System. We also ask that the US Judicial System and everything affiliated with it that pertains to this case be moved now from the Court of Judgment to the Throne of Grace and Mercy, in Jesus' name."*

Stripping/Silencing The Accuser

- ☐ *"Almighty God, O Righteous Judge, we ask, in Jesus' name, that You would silence the voice of the accuser and strip him of any legal rights coming against the US Judicial System because now their sins are covered by the blood of Jesus Christ. It is written in Your word, Father God, that a curse causeless cannot stand; therefore, the blood of Jesus Christ has covered the sin and there is no cause for a curse. We ask now, in Jesus' name, for every curse and demonic assignment against the US Judicial System and everything affiliated with it to be canceled and made null and void in both the spiritual realm and natural realm.*

- ☐ *"Father God, in the name of Jesus we ask for You to dispatch Your mighty angel armies to go forth and remove all demons, demonic principalities, and demonic platforms surrounding the US Judicial System, including anything of the kingdom of darkness operating through the US Judicial System and all the courthouses, buildings, offices, documents, rulings, correspondence, laws, land, judges, clerks, officials and people associated with its services, leaders, employees, lawyers and clients, law enforcement, and properties on all levels. We ask that these demonic entities, assignments, strongholds, and their demonic altars and platforms be dismantled, rooted out, bound, and cast out forever to the uninhabited dry place by Your heavenly hosts and warrior angels, in Jesus' name! We ask for these evil demonic forces to now be blocked from any and all access to the US Judicial System by Your heavenly hosts and warrior angels from this day forward!*

- ☐ *"Father God, I ask, in Jesus' name, that Your heavenly hosts and warrior angels take all US Judicial System judges and justices, attorneys, officials, officers, paralegals, mediators, juries, interns, plaintiffs, defendants, witnesses, representatives, law enforcement, courthouses, office buildings and properties of the US Judicial System and everything and everyone connected to it off the frequency of the demonic so the kingdom of darkness cannot see, hear or perceive anything having to do with the US Judicial System ever again! We ask, Father God, for Your angelic armies to stand hold now over every place they removed these demonic entities and for Your mighty angels to occupy and protect from all evil regarding all areas and to NOT allow any more sinful practices to happen through the US Judicial System ever again, all for Your kingdom and glory, in Jesus' name!"*

Renouncing Unholy Covenants

- ☐ *"Almighty God, O Righteous Judge, Heavenly Father, we come before You and, in Jesus' name, on behalf of the US Judicial System, we renounce, rebuke, revoke, divorce, cancel, and come out of agreement with any and all unholy covenants that the US Judicial System and any of their leaders ever made or agreed to before or since their founding by President George Washington. We specifically renounce any agreements or covenants any justices or judges, representatives, or leaders of the US Judicial System made with any secret societies. We particularly renounce, cancel, and divorce all covenants and agreements they made with Baal, Satan, Masons/Masonic, the Crown of England, or any foreign entities.*

- ☐ *"Father God, we ask that all records of unholy or secret covenants be wiped off the record books of all current and past leadership and history of the US Judicial System on all levels — city, state, federal, and international — in the Courts of Heaven by the blood of Jesus and remembered no more for Your sake! Father God, I also ask for the US Judicial System to now be fully released and set free from all entanglements, repercussions, and consequences of these sins and unholy covenants, in Jesus' name! I ask that one NEW HOLY COVENANT with You, Father God, through Jesus Christ, be written and decreed for The US Judicial System in the record books in Heaven and be recorded and proclaimed today to commence on earth as it is in Heaven, Father God, from this day forward, in Jesus' name. Amen!"*

Justice/Enforcement

- ☐ *"Almighty Father God, O Righteous Judge, Heavenly Father, in the name of Jesus Christ and by His authority and by the anointing of Your Holy Spirit and Your angels on assignment, we ask that today this "not guilty" verdict rendered in Your Court be fully enforced in the spiritual and the natural realm and in the heavens and the earth. We ask also that justice be carried out fully in the spiritual and the natural regarding any injustices, sins, and crimes regarding the US Judicial System. We ask, in Jesus' name, Father God, that You would assign and dispatch your angels of truth and justice to go forth and bring exposure and justice according to Your laws and the laws of the United States of America to those who have done injustices against your people and this nation of the United States of America using the US Judicial System. We ask for this to be fulfilled swiftly, in Jesus' name. Amen."*

Angels Of Restitution

- ☐ *"Almighty Father God, O Righteous Judge, we now ask, in the name of Jesus Christ, for Your angels of restitution to be assigned to this case. Our request is that everything that was stolen, lost, or even destroyed by or through The United States Judicial System because of its sins and injustices be fully restored to all who were victims of these sins and injustices such as families, children, businesses, churches, those who suffered the loss of property — buildings, homes, land, or livestock — those who suffered the loss of income or support, loss of life, health, or physical injuries, loss of inheritances, loss of silver and gold and/or mineral rights, wrongful arrest or wrongful imprisonment, loss of child or loss of child custody, or any loss including time and finances. We ask for full restitution to be given to the proper recipient, even those who are the descendants of those who are due restitution from any loss, past or present, and that it would be redeemed to them swiftly and fully, in Jesus' name."*

Blessing

- *"Father God, we ask now if You would pour out a blessing and restore Your original intention and plans for the US Judicial System. You are the SUPREME JUDGE OVER EVERYTHING, Almighty God, so let Your judgments RULE over all the land and all the Courts in America. What is ruled in Your Heavenly Courts shall be ruled in the earth, in Jesus' name. As Your word says in "The Lord's Prayer" — "on earth as it is in Heaven." Let it be in the United States Judicial System as it is in Heaven!*

- *"On behalf of our nation, we cancel and renounce any negative words or curses that have been spoken or written about the US Judicial System, in Jesus' name. We specifically cancel the words ever spoken or written against righteous judges and righteous rulings, that they will no longer have negative meanings or be used as curses. We ask You, Lord Jesus, to cover any negative words or curses that have ever been spoken or written against any righteous judges or rulings in the US Judicial System with Your blood, Lord, and that these words would now be null and void, in Jesus' name. We speak blessings, wisdom, righteousness, justice, and alignment with the word and will of God to the US Judicial System and all who work there.*

- *"Father God, we ask for You to surround the US Judicial System with Your favor and protection and that Your Holy Spirit will come upon it and everyone shall see and know that the righteousness, blessing, protection, wisdom, justice, and will of God are covering and working in and through everything having to do with the US Judicial System all for Your glory and honor, God, in Jesus' name! People will once again have godly things to say and write – trusting in truth and justice in the US Judicial System!"*

Protection Of The Gates Of The Us Judicial System

- ☐ *"Father God, in the name of Jesus Christ, we ask for You to post Your sentry angels to the gates in both the natural and the spiritual, and the digital gateway areas of every US Judicial System courthouse location and every judge's home, judge's office, and employee's' office of the US Judicial System or any place/location where they are operating both publicly and privately to keep watch and guard around the clock and protect these gates from all evil! Protect these judges and courtrooms from any threats so they can peacefully and righteously do what they have been called to do for this nation and Your kingdom, O God.*

- ☐ *"We ask for the sentry angels of Almighty God to stop and destroy any evil or demonic assignments that would attempt to go in or out though any and all gateways of the US JUDICIAL SYSTEM with their supernatural fiery swords and shields from this day forward, in Jesus' name! Father God, in the name of Jesus, we ask You to send Your heavenly hosts and warrior angels to go and take every US Judicial System Court location and every judge and judge's office of the US Judicial System or any place/location where they are operating both publicly and privately, including their homes and families, off of the radar of the demonic! O God, arise and scatter Your enemies far, far away from every US Judicial System Court location and every judge and judge's office of the US Judicial System or any place/location where they are operating both publicly and privately, including their homes and families, and keep them under the protection of Your angel armies and on the frequency of the Holy Spirit! Thank You, Father God, for sending Your angels to keep us in all of our ways!"*

Dominion/Dedication

- ☐ *"In the name of Jesus Christ, King of kings, Lord of lords, the Name above all names, by His authority, we claim, consecrate and dedicate The US Judicial System, IN ITS ENTIRETY, TO ALMIGHTY GOD. We place it all in the blood of Jesus Christ, including all courthouses, judges, officials, clerks, cases, services, property, land, buildings, offices, documents, records — even those records and documents that have been thrown away or attempted to be destroyed or hidden, both past and present — along with all assets and communications — public and hidden — both in the physical or digital, that are of the US Judicial System, and into the dominion and kingdom of*

Almighty God to now only be used for the plans and purposes of God and the kingdom and glory of God from this day forward, in Jesus' name!"

The Scepter Of Righteousness

☐ *"In the name of Jesus Christ, King of kings, Lord of lords, the name above all names, by His authority, we claim that the US Judicial System and all its couthouses, properties, land, buildings and anything that proceeds on these jurisdictions belong to Almighty God and are now allotted to the righteous! Therefore, it is written in Psalm 125:3 that the scepter of wickedness will not remain over the land allotted to the righteous. So we declare, in Jesus' name, that the SCEPTER OF RIGHTEOUSNESS RULES over all jurisdictions, courthouses, land, office buildings, judges, employees, officers and all rulings, cases, records and documents, and anything to do with the US Judicial System on all levels — city, county, state, federal, military, FISA, and International US Jurisdictions — and we renounce and beat down the scepter of wickedness and command it to leave for it no longer has power or authority to remain, in Jesus' name!"*

Ax Of God's Judgment

☐ *"Father God, Your word says in Matthew 3:10, "And now also the axe is laid unto the root of the trees: therefore every tree which bringeth not forth good fruit is hewn down, and cast into the fire." Father God, I believe Your word, and I want to activate it right now in the spiritual and in the natural! Father, in Jesus' name, I ask You to take Your ax of judgment, according to Matthew 3:10, and chop and pull up at the root any and all unholy, ungodly influences that are in and around the US Judicial System that are not there to produce good fruit! Remove those unholy, ungodly influences at the root, pull the stumps up out of the ground, shake the stumps with no roots remaining in the ground and its branches, vines, or seeds, and cast it all into the fire to burn to ashes, in Jesus' name!"*

We do not have to accept anything that is not the will of God for our nation, our judicial system, our community and our people, in Jesus' name! Father God, I ask You to replace all those areas of influence in and around the US Judicial System with Holy Spirit-filled, righteous influences that will bear and multiply good Holy Spirit-fruit for Your kingdom and glory, in Jesus' name!

Declare

- ☐ *"Holy Spirit, take over and flow into all the halls of justice in this nation, in Jesus' name!"*

Take Group Communion - Prepare Your Communion Bread And Juice And Pray

- ☐ *"Heavenly Father, in the name of Jesus, we take Communion together as a prophetic act of faith to seal and confirm our prayers and this time in the Courts of Heaven. Father God, we lift up this bread to You and give You thanks and praise. We dedicate and consecrate this bread to You, Father God, and we ask You to bless this bread as it represents the body of Your Son — the bread of life — Jesus Christ. Lord Jesus, You told us to remember You this way and remember what You did on the Cross for us. Lord, we invite You to our table because You invited us to Yours. We understand that Your sacrifice on the Cross, Lord, was for our sins and the sins of the world and we are grateful. Thank You, Lord Jesus, and we ask You, Lord, to cleanse this bread with Your blood, and sanctify it. We proclaim this bread is holy and sanctified by the blood of Jesus. Thank You, Lord. Thank You, Father God. We bless this bread, in Jesus' name."* (Eat bread)

- ☐ *"Heavenly Father, in the name of Jesus, we take Communion together as a prophetic act of faith to seal our prayers and this time in the Courts of Heaven. Father God, we lift up this cup and grape juice to You, and we give You thanks and praise. We dedicate and consecrate this cup and grape juice to You, Father God, and we ask You to bless this as it represents the blood of Your Son, Jesus Christ. Lord Jesus, You told us to remember You this way and remember that You shed Your blood for us and our sins. Your blood, Lord, cleanses us of all sin and iniquities, heals us, protects us, and redeems us out of the hand of the devil and back to God to be set aside for the plans and purposes of Father God, all because of Your blood, Lord!*

- ☐ *"Thank You, Lord Jesus, and we ask You, Lord, to cleanse this cup and grape juice with Your blood and sanctify it. We proclaim by faith that this grape juice is holy and sanctified by the blood of Jesus and that everywhere it touches, the power of the blood of Jesus is released! Thank You, Lord. Thank You, Father God. We bless this cup and juice and partake, in Jesus' name."* (Drink juice)

Taking Authority As A King And Priest For Land Assignment

Make sure that before you go to the land prayer location you put on your full armor of God and do my "Daily Suit Up Prayer" here in the book.

- ☐ *"Almighty Father God, O Righteous Judge, in the name of Jesus Christ, Your word says in Revelation 1:6, 'And hath made us kings and priests unto God and his Father; to him be glory and dominion for ever and ever. Amen.' Therefore, we do now take our kingly and priestly place and authority right here and now in Christ Jesus and through Christ Jesus. As we stand at this United States Judicial System courthouse location in the jurisdiction of _____ (City/State/County), we claim this land and this United States Judicial System courthouse location for Your plans and purposes, Almighty God, for Your kingdom and Your glory from this day forward, in Jesus' name!"*

Local US Judicial System Repentance

If you cannot go to the location, you can do this in your own yard in the spirit if you live within the jurisdiction area.

- ☐ *"Father God, we also come to You in the name of Jesus Christ repenting for the sins of this particular judicial and courthouse location, in the jurisdiction of _____ (City/State/County) since its founding. We have repented of all sinful acts against You, Father God, and all sinful acts against Your word that have transgressed through the US Judicial System in its entirety and now also repent for the sinful acts that have transgressed through this judicial and courthouse location in the jurisdiction of _____ (City/State/County). We come into agreement of all the repentance that was done in the Courts of Heaven today (March, 15, 2021) with our group of intercessors across the nation and ask that our petition for repentance and forgiveness locally here also be honored in Your Courts, Father God. We ask now for grace, mercy, and forgiveness for these sins. We ask now, Lord Jesus, for You to put Your blood on all of these sins and wash them clean.*

- ☐ *"Father God, now that the blood of Jesus is on these sins, we ask that this judicial and courthouse location, in the jurisdiction of _____ (City/State/County), be released of all consequences of these sins and all accusations, curses, and demonic assignments be canceled off of this United States judicial and courthouse location, in the jurisdiction of _____ (City/State/County), by the redeeming power of the blood of Jesus. We ask now, Father God, for Your plans and purposes and blessings to go forth through this judicial and courthouse location, in the juristiction of _____ (City/State/County), from this day forward. So be it, in Jesus' name. Amen."*

Pour Communion In The Land

At your local judicial and courthouse location, you will pray the prayer below over the Communion cup filled with grape juice. You will partake first, and then pour the rest on the ground.

- ☐ *"Father God, we lift up this cup and grape juice to You, and we give You thanks and praise. We dedicate and consecrate this cup and grape juice to You, Father God, and we ask You to bless this as it represents the blood of Your Son, Jesus Christ. Lord Jesus, You told us to remember You this way and remember that You shed Your blood for us and our sins. Your blood, Lord, cleanses us of all sins and iniquities, heals us, protects us, and redeems us out of the hand of the devil and back to God to be set aside for the plans and purposes of Father God all because of Your blood, Lord!*

- ☐ *"Lord Jesus, Your blood poured into the ground at Your crucifixion when You proclaimed, "It Is finished." We understand that Your precious blood not only redeemed us that day, but also when it touched the earth, the land was also redeemed back to God. We ask today for Your blood to cleanse, sanctify, and redeem this land upon which we stand today. Thank You, Lord Jesus, and we ask You, Lord, to cleanse this cup and grape juice with Your blood and sanctify it. We proclaim by faith that this grape juice is holy and sanctified by the blood of Jesus, and that everywhere it touches, the redeeming and cleansing power of the blood of Jesus is released! Thank You, Lord. Thank You, Father God. We bless this cup and juice and partake, in Jesus' name."* (Drink juice and leave some to pour on the ground after the next declaration below.)

Declare As You Pour The Communion

- ☐ *"Father God, Your word says in Hebrews 12:24, 'And to Jesus the mediator of a new covenant, and to the sprinkled blood that speaks a better word than the blood of Abel.' Let this land receive the blood of Jesus Christ. Let the blood of Jesus Christ speak for this land, this jurisdiction and courthouse property, and everything on this property that it be cleansed of all sins and iniquities! By the blood of Jesus, this land and property and everything on the land, above the land, and below the land is now redeemed out of the hand of the devil, back to God, and set aside for the plans and purposes of God by the power of the blood of Jesus all for the glory of God! So be it. Amen!"* (Pour Communion in the land. You do not need much, just enough to soak into the soil.)

Pour/Apply Anointing Oil To The Land

Bless and dedicate the oil FIRST. See my "How To Pray Over And Apply Anointing Oil Prayer" here in the book.

Then apply the oil to yourself and dedicate yourself to God and His plans and purposes in Jesus' name. Apply to your forehead, palms of your hands, and tops of your feet. Also, put some on the tops and bottoms of your shoes so you release the anointing wherever you walk and whatever you touch.

Declare As You Pour The Oil On The Ground - (You Just Need A Few Drops)

- ☐ *"In the name of Jesus Christ, we pour the anointing oil into this land of the judicial and courthouse location, in the jurisdiction here in _____ (City/State/County). We declare as it is written that the anointing breaks the yoke and we proclaim that every yoke of bondage, slavery, and sin is now shattered off of this land, the property upon it, and this judicial and courthouse location, in Jesus' name. We declare that this land here at this judicial and courthouse location and everything on it, along with all being provided here, is now only yoked to Jesus Christ and the kingdom of Almighty God. We dedicate and consecrate this land, property, courthouse, all buildings, offices, and everything on this property, the services being provided here, and every gateway — natural, digital and spiritual — to Almighty God. Let every gateway on this land and property receive the anointing of the Holy Spirit! We invite the Holy Spirit to come upon this land and property and do creative healing and deliverance miracles and let the power of the Holy Spirit be released upon everyone and everything on this property, this US Judicial System, and land! From this day forward, let the power of the Holy Spirit be released upon everything coming in and going out from this place, in Jesus' name! We declare this judicial and courthouse location, in the jurisdiction of _____ (City/State/County), is now anointed, blessed, and set aside to be used for the plans and purposes of Almighty God all for the kingdom and glory of God from this day forward, in Jesus' name!"*

Asking For Angel Armies Of The Lord For Your Local Us Judicial System

- ☐ *"Father God, In the name of Jesus, we ask for You to dispatch Your heavenly hosts and warrior angels to come now and remove all demons, demonic principalities, and demonic platforms surrounding this judicial and courthouse location in the jurisdiction of _____ (City/State/County), including anything of the kingdom of darkness operating through the land, buildings, people, and properties here, so that these demonic entities, assignments, strongholds, and their demonic altars and platforms will be dismantled, rooted out, bound, and cast out forever to the uninhabited dry place by the heavenly hosts and warrior angels of Almighty God, in Jesus' name!*

- ☐ *"Let the heavenly hosts and warrior angels of Almighty God take this judicial and courthouse location, in the jurisdiction of _____ (City/State/County), off the frequency of the demonic forever! We ask, Father God, for Your angelic armies to stand hold now over every place where they removed these demonic entities and for Your mighty angels to now occupy and protect this judicial and courthouse location and region from all evil regarding all areas — the land, buildings, people, and properties operating at this courthouse location in the jurisdiction of _____ (City/State/County) — for Your kingdom and glory, in Jesus' name!"*

Blessing Your Local US Judicial System – Courthouse

- ☐ *"Father God, we ask now if You would pour out a blessing and restore Your original intention and plans for this US Judicial System and courthouse location in the jurisdiction of _____ (City/State/County). We cancel and renounce any negative words or curses that have been spoken or written about this US Judicial System and courthouse here in _____ (City/State/County), in Jesus' name. We ask You, Lord Jesus, to cover any negative words or curses that have ever been spoken here or over this place with Your blood, Lord, and that these words would now be null and void, in Jesus' name. We speak blessing and prosperity to this judicial and courthouse location, in the jurisdiction of _____ (City/State/County), and to all who are employed here and all citizens who come through here!*

- ☐ *"Father God, we ask for You to surround this US Judicial System and courthouse location here in _____ (City/State/County), with Your favor and that Your Holy Spirit will come upon it and everyone shall see and know that the righteousness and blessings and gifts of God are covering and working in and through everything having to do with this US Judicial System and courthouse location in the jurisdiction of _____ (City/State/County), all for Your glory and honor, God, in Jesus' name! People will once again have good to say and write and enjoy and trust in this US Judicial System and courthouse location — this jurisdiction, this courthouse, land, buildings, properties, offices, and its leaders, judges, clerks, officers, employees, and all proceedings here in _____ (City/State/County), in Jesus' name!"*

Dedicate Your Personal Legal Documents

If you have any legal documents issued to you by your local or state courts or even the federal judicial system in your possession that are signed by a judge or clerk of the courts, you can dedicate those documents to God. (Apply the prayed-over oil with your fingertips/hands on the item as you pray.)

Pray Out Loud

- ☐ *"Father God, I thank You for this _____ with the address of _____. In the name of Jesus Christ, I dedicate and consecrate this _____ at this address _____ to You, Father God, and declare that it is designated and set aside for Your plans and purposes. I place this _____ at this address _____ in the blood of Jesus Christ. Lord Jesus, release the power of Your blood over this _____ at this address _____. Your blood, Lord Jesus, destroys all darkness, cleanses all sins, and breaks all curses and demonic assignments. I declare by the blood of Jesus that this _____ at this address _____ is now sanctified. I anoint this _____ in the name of Jesus, and I invite You, Holy Spirit, to come upon this _____ with Your power, protection, and presence. I declare that this _____ at this address _____ is now anointed. Let the power of the Holy Spirit come upon this _____ and this address of _____. Father God, bless this _____, and let it be used only for Your glory. I bless this _____. Let the blood of Jesus and the power of the Holy Spirit be released upon everything coming in and going out from this _____ at this address from this day forward, in Jesus' name. Amen."*

Mail Anointed Prayer Letter To The United States Supreme Court or Local State Courts

This is a powerful prophetic act of faith to release the power and the authority of the Lord Jesus Christ and of the Holy Spirit throughout the inner workings of the UNITED STATES OF AMERICA JUDICIAL COURTS SYSTEM. Every place and every person that comes in contact with your prayed-over, anointed letter will experience the presence of the Holy Spirit as in Acts

19:12 when Apostle Paul anointed the aprons: "They were brought to the sick and diseases departed from them, and evil spirits went out of them."

You will also release an authority and blessing of the Lord by speaking over the letter. Isaiah 55:11 says, "His word will not return void but will accomplish that which he pleases and shall prosper in the thing whereto he SENT it."

Together, as the Body of Christ, we can compose a letter with an anointing that carries God's word and His Holy Spirit throughout the US Judicial System with a blessing, prayer and declaration.

Take Communion And Speak Over The Letter And Pray This Prayer, If You Feel Led

First, take Communion yourself, and then speak prophetically holding up the letter as an act of faith.

Decree Out Loud

- ☐ *"I apply the blood of Jesus to my life and to this letter and all that is written in it and to every place this letter travels, and declare that it will release the cleansing and redeeming power of the blood of Jesus. I decree that we are redeemed by the blood of Jesus out of the hand of the devil, back into the hands of Almighty God, and are now set aside for the plans and purposes of God all by the blood of Jesus from this day forward, in Jesus' name! I decree that the power of the blood of Jesus will be carried and released into and through this letter everywhere it goes!*

- ☐ *"Lord Jesus, by faith and as I apply the blood of Jesus, let the power of Your blood, Lord, be upon this letter. Lord Jesus, release the power of Your blood to cleanse the sin, break all curses and demonic assignments, and destroy all demonic strongholds everywhere this letter travels and upon its destination! Let the power of Your blood, Lord Jesus, sanctify and reconcile everything this letter touches and every place this letter passes through all back to God for HIS plans and purposes!*

- ☐ *"I proclaim, by the Authority of Jesus Christ and by the power of His blood, DOMINION of Almighty God over the US Judicial System and The United States Supreme Court and everywhere this letter travels. I pray that every person who touches this letter comes to the salvation of the Lord Jesus Christ, in Jesus' name. Amen."*

Feel free to add any personal prayer or scripture to your letter. It is important that you hand sign your name. This is a symbol of covenant with God. Then put a small dab of prayed-over anointing oil on the edges of your letter and envelope and seal it. You don't have to soak it in oil; it carries the power of the Holy Spirit and just a small amount will do nicely. I just put some on my hands and touch the edges. If you don't have anointing oil you can use plain prayed-over olive oil.

See my "How To Pray Over And Apply Anointing Oil Prayer" here in the book.

This is an important step, so please follow these instructions. The purpose of this letter is that the anointing goes through the system to release the healing and restoring power of the Holy Spirit, as we have released our faith and authority in Christ. Jesus did not have to personally touch each person to heal them. He sent the Holy Spirit to be our helper in all of these things. The oil represents the presence of the Holy Spirit. Our faith and authority in Jesus Christ is what activates it.

You want your oil to carry the power of the anointing so pray over it and bless it in faith. Make sure your oil is prayed over using my anointing oil prayer; then apply some oil to your hands and fingertips.

Put Your Anointed Hands On The Letter And Addressed/Stamped Envelope And Declare

- ☐ *"Father God, I thank You for this letter addressed to _____. In the name of Jesus Christ, I dedicate and consecrate this letter and envelope to You, Father God, and declare that it is designated and set aside for Your plans and purposes for the US Judicial System, The United States Supreme Court, and the local courts. Through the sending and delivery of this letter, we ask for the power of Your Holy Spirit to be upon it. I place this letter and everything on it in the blood of Jesus Christ. Lord Jesus, release the power of Your blood over this letter. Your blood, Lord Jesus, destroys all darkness and breaks all curses and demonic assignments. By the blood of Jesus, this letter is now sanctified.*

- ☐ *"I anoint this letter and envelope in the name of Jesus, and I invite You, Holy Spirit, to come upon it with Your power, protection, and presence. Holy Spirit, release Your dunamis power and presence everywhere this letter goes and upon every person and place it touches and passes! As this letter is mailed and travels through the US Judicial System, let the power of Your Holy Spirit flow and be released and activated at each place and upon each person in the travels of this letter, in Jesus' name! Holy Spirit, bring deliverance, healing, restoration, and encounters with the Lord Jesus Christ in each place along the way to the destination of this letter! Holy Spirit, bring Your light, Your living waters, Your healing oil, Your breath of life, and Your presence into all the dark, damaged, and lost places and hearts this letter encounters!*

- ☐ *"Holy Spirit, bring complete divine alignment, restoration, restitution, righteousness, and renewal to the US Judicial System and everything connected to it according to the will and word of God! Let the original intent and plan of God come forth for the UNITED STATES OF AMERICA JUDICIAL SYSTEM! Holy Spirit, give every person involved with the UNITED STATES OF AMERICA JUDICIAL SYSTEM a heart to know and receive the presence of the living God and the salvation of the Lord Jesus Christ!*

- ☐ *"In Jesus' name, Holy Spirit, I ask You to restore everything to God's divine order along the way through the US Judicial System locations and carriers with Your resurrection power, Holy Spirit, that this letter now carries! Father God, dispatch Your angels to protect and accompany this letter to make sure it gets to its destination of _____. Father God, bless this letter; let Your hand be upon it, and let it be used only for Your plans, purposes and glory, Almighty God, from this day forward, in Jesus' name. Amen."*

Please mail your anointed, hand signed, stamped, and prayed-over letter to your local county, state, or federal US Judicial Court System. I encourage you to put your words of faith and let them know you have been praying for them. I would also add in the letter whatever you want to share as a Christian and as an American citizen. Our voices must go forth in the name of Jesus Christ.

Strategies Going Forward

Take the time to continue to enforce the blood of Jesus over the Judicial System of the United States of America. This way, we continue to release our verdict from the Courts of Heaven in a powerful way. We will see the glory of God revealed in many ways through the US Judicial System and the entire Judiciary Court System on all levels! This is how we advance the kingdom of God, the Gospel of the Lord Jesus Christ, and how we shall see righteousness return to our government, our people, and our communities.

Optional Offering

After you finish this United States of America Judicial System Assignment, give an offering to God into a ministry or church that is fertile soil for the kingdom, thanking God for opening His Courts to you and for His grace, mercy, and forgiveness, or sow a seed into God's kingdom and name the seed: "Righteousness of Almighty God takes over the United States of America's

Judicial System and multiplies throughout the nation and the world for the Great Harvest for Jesus Christ and for the kingdom and glory of Almighty God."

You can send your offerings and letters here to my ministry, and I will come into agreement with your prayer.

By US Mail:
Annamarie Strawhand
P.O Box 7068
Virginia Beach, VA 23457

Declare Out Loud

"According to Jeremiah 30:17, ABBA, FATHER, thank You that You restore, refresh, redeem, and renew. We are Your beloved children and You love us. Amen."

USPS Courts Of Heaven Prayer Strategies And Land Assignment

USPS (United States Postal Service Land Prayer Assignment)

Taking The Case To The Courts Of Heaven

Spoken Prayers And Holy Spirit Strategies For Deliverance And Blessing The Land

Let's help you all have some clarity between prayer and entering the Courts of Heaven with a petition and prayer. The Courts of Heaven are when we ask the Father God to approach His throne as Judge in a case that the accuser (the devil) is using to keep a stronghold on something because of sin.

We ask through Jesus Christ to enter the Courts to repent for these sins before God, our Righteous Judge, and ask Jesus to wash the sins with His blood and for His blood to speak in our defense and in defense of the sins in which we are interceding for in our nation because the blood of Jesus is the ONLY defense that can redeem us from sin, even of the land and a nation. We are deemed innocent when the blood of Jesus is applied and we ask for the judgment verdict to be not guilty because the blood of Jesus has spoken, and then and only then can the accuser be stripped of his curses and the person/land can be set free and delivered out of any demonic strongholds.

Enter Courts Of Heaven - (Speak Out Loud)

- ☐ *"Almighty God, O Righteous Judge, Heavenly Father, we come to You today in the name of Jesus Christ asking to enter Your heavenly Court and appear before You, O Righteous Judge, with our petition regarding the United States Postal Service. We ask You, Lord Jesus, to represent and intercede for us as our high priest with Father God and for Your blood to speak for us and the United States Postal Service on the Mercy Seat. We invite the Holy Spirit to assist and guide us in our heavenly court appearance, repentance, and prayer. We ask for Your angels to surround us, to protect us, and assist us to fully complete this from start to finish with the guidance of the Holy Spirit according to Your will, Father God. We ask, in Jesus' name, as we enter Your Courts, Father God, for our books to be opened for ourselves, our cities and states, our nation, the United States of America, and The United States Postal Service, including all the buildings, vehicles, correspondence, land, leaders, and people associated with it. We ask, in Jesus' name, for the Cloud of Witnesses and also the faithful men and women who were righteous believers in Christ Jesus, to be present witnessing to this case, such as*

Benjamin Franklin and Abraham Lincoln, who were righteous postmasters in America, to witness to the intercession of Jesus Christ for the United States Postal Service, and we come into agreement with the intercession of Jesus' prayers.

- ☐ *"We would be honored to have Your intent for the United States Post Office revealed in the Courts today, Father God, and through this time in the Courts, we pray that all can now come into alignment with Your will and plan. We also ask for Your recording angels to be present. We ask for any repentance for the sins of our nation, The United States of America, and the buildings, vehicles, correspondence, land, leaders, patrons, customers, contractors, and ANY people publicly known and secretly associated, past and present, with it to be taken into consideration today. We ask, Father God, that You demand the accuser in this case regarding the sins of the United States Postal Service and everything associated with it to be present in the Court. We ask, in the name of Jesus, for the Courts of Heaven to be in session for our case and petition today and the court to be seated. Because of the blood of Jesus and the finished work of the Cross, we are able to enter Your holy Courts because it is written in Your word in Hebrews 10:19, 'And so, dear brothers and sisters, we can boldly enter heaven's Most Holy Place because of the blood of Jesus.' We now ask to present our case before Your Court. Thank You, Father God. Thank You, Lord Jesus. Thank You, Holy Spirit. Amen!"*

Personal Prayer Of Cleansing

- ☐ *"Almighty God, O Righteous Judge, Heavenly Father, I humbly come before You in Your Heavenly Courts and repent for all of my sins and the sins of my ancestors and family bloodline. I specifically repent for my sins and the sins of my ancestors and family bloodline that are sins that were committed through the United States Postal Service. If there are any sins in my life and the lives of my ancestors and family bloodline that were done against You, Father God, or against Your word through the United States Postal Service, I repent for these sins right now. I am sorry for sinning against You, Father God. I am sorry for any sins I committed or my ancestors or anyone in my family bloodline committed with or through the United States Postal Service. Father God, I ask today for grace, mercy, and forgiveness for me, my ancestors, and family bloodline. Lord Jesus, I ask for You to put Your blood on all of these sins for me, my ancestors, and family bloodline and wash us clean. I ask that these sins be remembered no more for Your sake, Father God, and that they be wiped clean from the record books of Heaven and earth by the blood of Jesus. I ask now that these sins and any repercussions from these sins be made null and void.*

- ☐ *"Now that the blood of Jesus has covered these sins, I ask for them to no longer be held against me, my family bloodline, or my ancestors ever again on earth or in Heaven. In Jesus' name, I ask that the accuser be stripped of any legal rights and that any curses and demonic assignments be removed and canceled, in Jesus' name. I ask today, Father God, in Jesus' name, that my ancestors, my family line, and I be found "not guilty" by the blood of Jesus — our only defense. I also ask for this new "not guilty" verdict to be written in our books and proclaimed in your Courts today.*

- ☐ *"Father God, it is written in Your word in Proverbs 26:2 that '... a curse causeless cannot stand.' Therefore, the blood of Jesus is now covering all these sins. The Blood of Jesus removes all sins, curses, and demonic assignments. Therefore, there is no longer any cause for any curses or repercussions against me or my family bloodline. I ask, in Jesus' name, for my family bloodline, all of my ancestors, and me to now be released from any curses, entanglements, repercussions or consequences from these sins. My request here in Your Heavenly Court, Almighty God, O Righteous Judge, that because these sins that I have repented for today are now covered in the blood of Jesus, that my family bloodline, my ancestors, and I can be moved from the Court of Judgment to the Throne of Grace and Mercy because our spiritual debt has been paid in full by the precious blood of Jesus, and there can now be no recourse from the accuser.*

- ☐ *"Father God, O Righteous Judge, I ask You to silence the voice of the accuser forever regarding these sins. I ask for Your Holy Spirit to fill all the places now where these sins and curses once were and stand hold there with Your presence and protection. In Jesus' name, I ask for my books and the books of my ancestors and family bloodline to be fully reconciled back to the will of God here in the Courts and my record of repentance to be recorded for my future court appearances here in Your Spiritual Court of Law, and that my High Priest, the Lord Jesus Christ, will confirm for me and my cloud of witnesses in Heaven as witness to all that was done here today.*

- ☐ *"Thank You, Father God, for Your grace, mercy, and forgiveness. Thank You, Lord Jesus, for Your precious blood that has set me free. Thank You, Holy Spirit, for Your guidance in the Courts. Amen!"*

You are now cleansed, forgiven, redeemed, and ready to intercede and present the main case for the USPS to the Courts of Heaven.

Ambassador Of Reconciliation

- ☐ *"Almighty God, O Righteous Judge, in the name of and with the intercession of Jesus Christ my Lord and High Priest, I come before Your Court today (as well as my group of intercessors) asking to be recognized as an "Ambassador(s) of Reconciliation" to stand in the gap to present a petition of repentance and reconciliation on behalf of the United States Postal Service, its leaders, its history, its employees, its locations and properties, and all of its works and affiliations today.*

- ☐ *"Father God, Your word states in Ephesians 6:18-20, 'Praying always with all prayer and supplication in the Spirit, and watching thereunto with all perseverance and supplication for all saints; And for me, that utterance may be given unto me, that I may open my mouth boldly, to make known the mystery of the gospel, for which I am an ambassador in bonds: that therein I may speak boldly, as I ought to speak.'*

- ☐ *"Also in Your word, Father God, You tell us in Hebrews 4:15-16, 'For we do not have a high priest who is unable to sympathize with our weaknesses, but we have one who was tempted in every way that we are, yet was without sin. Let us then approach the throne of grace with confidence, so that we may receive mercy and find grace to help us in our time of need.'*

- ☐ *"It is also written in Hebrews 10:18-20, 'And where these have been forgiven, an offering for sin is no longer needed. Therefore, brothers, since we have confidence to enter the Most Holy Place by the blood of Jesus, by the new and living way opened for us through the curtain of His body, ...'*

- ☐ *"Therefore, according to Your word, Almighty Father God, O Righteous Judge, I (and our group of intercessors) come before You today as a redeemed soul(s) of Jesus Christ, a citizen of Heaven and earth, a citizen of the United States of America, and a patron of the United States Postal Service. Father God, I (we) am here today to present my (our) petition before Your Court as my (our) obligation by faith according to Your word, and to receive grace, mercy, and forgiveness on behalf of the United States Postal Service. I (we) ask the Lord Jesus Christ and His blood to speak for me and the United States Postal Service today before Your Court, in Jesus' name, as I (we) present this case. I (we) ask for all the books to be opened regarding this case, and for the witnesses, the recording angels, and the accuser to be present in the Court, in Jesus' name.*

- ☐ *"I (we) ask You, Lord Jesus, to stand and intercede for us before Father God. Thank You, Father God, O Righteous Judge, for recognizing me (and our group of intercessors) in Your Heavenly Court as an Ambassador(s) of Reconciliation for the United States Postal Service, its leaders, its employers, its works, its locations, its contractors, its patrons and customers, users and clients, and everything regarding it since its founding in 1775. Thank You, Father God. Thank You, Lord Jesus, and thank You, Holy Spirit. Amen."*

Repentance For USPS

- ☐ *"Almighty God, O Righteous Judge, Heavenly Father, in the name of Jesus Christ, we come to You in Your Heavenly Courts today in repentance for the sins of the United States Postal Service, the sins of its leaders, the sins of its employees, carriers and contractors, the sins of its locations, buildings, and properties, and the sins of its patrons, customers, users and clients of these services, including all local, rural, regional, national, and international level that the USPS provides publicly and any services that they have been doing in secret. We are repenting for these sins since its founding in 1775 up to this very moment.*

- ☐ *"We ask, in Jesus' name, for the Court to be seated and the books to be opened. As we repent for these sins today, we ask, Father God, O Righteous Judge, for the blood of Jesus Christ to speak for us and the United States Postal Service on the Mercy Seat. We ask, in Jesus' name, Father God, that You would send Your Holy Spirit upon each person affiliated or connected in any way with the United States Postal Service, including current and former leadership, managers, employees, contractors, trainers, carriers, landlords, patrons, customers, clients, and users of their public and and/or secret services to go and remove any veils of deception that may be on their eyes because of their sins. Please remove all veils off their eyes of understanding so they can see the truth, know the truth, embrace the truth, stand up for the truth, and boldly speak the truth.*

☐ *"Holy Spirit, we ask that You will bring all these people to repentance and give them an encounter with the Lord Jesus Christ so that they will leave all sinful ways, seek deliverance, and come to the salvation of the Lord Jesus Christ to walk fully in the righteousness of God's will for their lives, in Jesus' name. Amen."*

☐ *"Almighty God, O Righteous Judge, Heavenly Father, in the name of Jesus Christ, we come to You in Your Courts today in repentance for the sins of the United States Postal Service. We confess, repent and ask for Grace, Mercy and Forgiveness of these sins on their behalf today by the cleansing power of the Blood of Jesus Christ to cover these sins we have listed:*

LIST OF REPENTANCE FOR THE UNITED STATES POSTAL SERVICE

1. Drug trafficking - pharmakeia
2. Pornography and child pornography
3. Child/human trafficking
4. Voter fraud
5. Taking bribes and payoffs
6. DNC and RNC bribery or control
7. Getting paid for illegal activities
8. Purposeful destruction of mail
9. Stealing mail and packages
10. Sins on the land and properties of post offices
11. Sins of past postmasters and leadership in USPS
12. Bloodshed and murders at post office locations
13. All witchcraft/occult items and activity sent through the mail
14. All types of fraud, including but not limited to insurance, health care, Medicaid, food stamps, prescriptions, credit cards, DMV, birth and death certificates, IRS, banks, social security, VA benefits, and every other type of fraud committed using USPS
15. Identity theft, also fake IDs, green cards, passports
16. Destruction of ballots and destruction of evidence
17. Election fraud in all states, cities, and zip codes
18. Poisons, such as anthrax, being sent through the mail
19. Germ/biological warfare using the mail

20. Ill-gotten gains – raising funds with sinful ways or sales and/or selling services and property that caused harm or loss to innocent people
21. Religious scams
22. Propaganda
23. Assisting the enemies of America, treason
24. Sending hidden chemicals, weapons, ammunition, explosives
25. All corruption of government agencies, both national and international, through the postal service
26. Unholy or ungodly covenants
27. False accusations against President Trump or any innocent person
28. Washington, D.C., corruption
29. Corporate mailrooms and corporate mail carriers
30. Internal mail system corruption
31. Organs sent through mail/planned parenthood
32. US military mail fraud
33. Pony Express and stagecoach fraud/robberies
34. Telegraph and Western Union
35. Ports, train stations, airports, and any vehicles or buildings used to transport and process mail
36. Fiber optics, drones, satellites, and all telecommunications
37. Hidden servers and digital programs with intent of fraudulent activities used by USPS
38. Schools, universities, scams
39. Big pharma bribery and backdoor deals
40. Military industrial complex
41. Casinos, gambling, and organized crime/racketeering
42. Hotels, cruise lines, resorts
43. Hospitals, nursing homes, funeral homes
44. Notary publics, titles, deeds, passports, IDs fraud/fakery
45. Any type of commerce or service that was corrupted
46. Counterfeit money and merchandise
47. Census fraud
48. Pyramid schemes and chain letters
49. Banking/stock scams
50. Prostitution
51. Piracy
52. Employee theft, harassment, violence, murders "going postal"
53. Scams with retailers and online shopping
54. Sweepstake scams
55. Mail order brides
56. Printing/newspaper/magazine false advertising
57. Illegal or endangered species of animals, plants, or insects sent through mail
58. Modified seeds with intent to harm environment or people sent through mail
59. Employee theft/embezzlement
60. Armed robbery

61. Any sins against the word and will of God

Asking For The Blood Of Jesus

☐ *"Lord Jesus, we ask that You cover all of these sins that were repented for today regarding the United States Postal Service with Your blood. Wash these sins clean and wipe them from the record books of Heaven with Your blood, Lord. Father God, we ask that You remember these sins no more for Your sake, in Jesus' name. We ask for the blood of Jesus to speak on the Mercy Seat for the United States Postal Service. We ask, in Jesus' name, for grace, mercy, and forgiveness of all sins today that have been repented for. Any sins that may have unknowingly been omitted, we ask You, Lord Jesus, to intercede for us and cover these sins also with Your blood, and that all sins, spoken and unspoken, be fully covered by the blood of Jesus on behalf of the United States Postal Service since its founding in 1775 and everything connected to it all today. Thank You, Jesus, for Your precious blood! Thank You, Father God, O Righteous Judge, for Your grace, mercy, and forgiveness of the sins of the United States Postal Service in this case we have brought forth. We are grateful, and as we stand in the gap for the United States Postal Service, we give You, Father God and Lord Jesus Christ, all the praise and glory for this divine opportunity in Your Courts!"*

Receiving The Verdict

☐ *"Almighty God, O Righteous Judge, we ask now by the blood of Jesus Christ, our only defense, that You would render a verdict of "not guilty" for the United States Postal Service. We also ask for the United States Postal Service and everything affiliated with it in this case to be moved from the Court of Judgment to the Throne of Grace and Mercy, in Jesus' name."*

Stripping/Silencing The Accuser

☐ *"Almighty God, O Righteous Judge, we ask, in Jesus' name, that You would silence the voice of the accuser and strip him of any legal rights coming against the United States Postal Service because now their sins are covered by the blood of Jesus Christ. It is written in Your word, Father God, that a curse causeless cannot stand; therefore, the blood of Jesus Christ has covered the sin and there is no cause for a curse. We ask now, in Jesus' name, for every curse and demonic assignment against the United States*

Postal Service and everything affiliated with it to be canceled and made null and void in both the spiritual and natural realms. Father God, in the name of Jesus, we ask for You to dispatch Your mighty angel armies to go forth and remove all demons, demonic principalities, and demonic platforms surrounding the United States Postal Service, including anything of the kingdom of darkness operating through its services, leaders, employees, trainees, contractors, carriers, equipment, patrons, customers, clients, land, and properties. Let these demonic entities, assignments, strongholds, and their demonic altars and platforms be dismantled, rooted out, bound, and cast out forever to the uninhabited dry place by Your heavenly hosts and warrior angels, in Jesus' name! Let these evil demonic forces now be blocked from any and all access to the United States Postal Service by Your heavenly hosts and warrior angels from this day forward! Father God, I ask, in Jesus' name, for Your heavenly hosts and warrior angels to take all United States Postal Service services, leaders, employees, trainees, contractors, carriers, equipment, patrons, customers, clients, and land off of the frequency of the demonic so the kingdom of darkness cannot see, hear, or perceive anything having to do with the United States Postal Service ever again! We ask, Father God, for Your angelic armies to stand hold now over every place they removed these demonic entities and for Your mighty angels to occupy and protect from all evil regarding all areas and to NOT allow any more sinful practices to happen through the United States Postal Service ever again, all for Your kingdom and glory, in Jesus' name!"

Renouncing Unholy Covenants

☐ *"Almighty God, O Righteous Judge, Heavenly Father, we come before You, in Jesus' name, on behalf of the United States Postal Service, and we renounce, rebuke, revoke, divorce, cancel, and come out af agreement with any and all unholy covenants that the United States Postal Service and any of their leaders ever made or agreed to since their founding in 1775. We specifically renounce any agreements or covenants any postmasters, representatives, or leaders of the United States Postal Service made with any secret societies. We particularly renounce, cancel, and divorce all covenants and agreements that they made with the Masons/Masonic Lodge.*

☐ *Father God, we ask that all records of unholy covenants be wiped off the record books and the record books of all past leadership and history of the United States Postal*

Service on all levels — rural, local, regional, national, and international — in the Courts of Heaven by the blood of Jesus and be remembered no more for Your sake! Father God, I also ask that the United States Postal Service now be fully released and set free from all entanglements, repercussions, and consequences of these sins and unholy covenants, in Jesus' Name! I ask that one NEW HOLY COVENANT with You, Father God, through Jesus Christ, be written and decreed for the United States Postal Service in the record books in Heaven and be recorded and proclaimed today to commence on earth as it is in Heaven, Father God, from this day forward, in Jesus' name. Amen!"

Justice/Enforcement

☐ *"Almighty Father God, O Righteous Judge, Heavenly Father, in the name of Jesus Christ and by His authority and by the anointing of Your Holy Spirit and Your angels on assignment, we ask that this "not guilty" verdict rendered in Your Court be fully enforced today in the spiritual and the natural realms and in the heavens and the earth. We ask also that justice be carried out fully in the spiritual and the natural regarding any injustices, sins, and crimes regarding the United States Postal Service. We ask, in Jesus' name, Father God, that You would assign and dispatch your angels of justice to go forth and bring exposure and justice according to Your laws and the laws of the United States of America to those who have done injustices against Your people and this nation of the United States of America using the United States Postal Service. We ask for this to be fulfilled swiftly, in Jesus' name. Amen."*

Restitution

☐ *"Almighty Father God, O Righteous Judge, we now ask in the name of Jesus Christ for Your angels of restitution to be assigned to this case. Our request is that full restitution of everything that was stolen, lost, or even destroyed by or through the United States Postal Service and its leaders, land, locations, employees, carriers, contractors, customers, patrons, or clients, including any stolen or lost mail, letters, cards, gifts, parcels, ballots, checks, inheritances, money, jewelry, packages, or any loss including time, be given to the proper recipients, even those who are the descendants of those who are due restitution from any loss, past or present, and that it shall be redeemed to them swiftly, in Jesus' name."*

Blessing

- *"Father God, we ask now if You would pour out a blessing and restore Your original intention and plans for the United States Postal Service. We cancel and renounce any negative words or curses that have been spoken or written about the United States Postal Service, in Jesus' name. We specifically cancel the words ever spoken or written such as "going postal." That will no longer have a negative meaning or be used as a curse. We ask You, Lord Jesus, to cover any negative words or curses that have ever been spoken or written against the United States Postal Service with Your blood, Lord, and that these words would now be null and void, in Jesus' name.*

- *"We speak blessing and prosperity to the United States Postal Service and all who are employed there and those who are patrons! Father God, we ask for You to surround the United States Postal Service with Your favor and for Your Holy Spirit to come upon it and that everyone will see and know that the righteousness and blessings and gifts of God are covering and working in and through everything having to do the United States Postal Service, all for Your glory and honor God, in Jesus' name! People will once again have good to say and write and enjoy and trust in the United States Postal Service!"*

Protection Of The Gates Of The USPS

- *"Father God, in the name of Jesus Christ, we ask for You to post Your sentry angels to the gates of the natural, spiritual, and digital gateway areas of every post office location and property of the United States Postal Service or any place/location where they are operating, both publicly and privately, to keep watch and guard around the clock and protect these gates from all evil! I ask for the sentry angels of Almighty God to stop and destroy any evil or demonic assignments that would attempt to go in or out through any and all gateways of the USPS with their supernatural fiery swords and shields from this day forward, in Jesus' name! Thank You, Father God, for sending Your angels to keep us in all of our ways!"*

Dominion/Dedication

- *"In the name of Jesus Christ, King of kings, Lord of lords, the Name above all names, by His authority, we claim, consecrate, and dedicate THE UNITED STATES POSTAL SERVICE IN ITS ENTIRETY to Almighty God. We place it all in the blood of Jesus*

Christ, which includes all services, property, land, buildings, offices, retail stores, training centers, warehouses, equipment, resources, files, records, finances, supplies, manpower, machinery, trucks, planes, mail, ballots, packages, and parcels, even those contracted out or those that have been thrown away or attempted to be destroyed or hidden, both past and present, along with all assets and communications, public and hidden, both in the physical or digital, that are of the United States Postal Service. We place it all into the dominion and kingdom of Almighty God to only be used now for the plans and purposes of God and the kingdom and glory of God from this day forward, in Jesus' name!"

The Scepter Of Righteousness

☐ *"In the name of Jesus Christ, King of kings, Lord of lords, the Name above all names, by His authority, we claim that the United States Postal Service and all of its properties, land, buildings, and services belong to Almighty God and are now allotted to the righteous! Therefore, it is written in Psalm 125:3, that the scepter of wickedness will not remain over the land allotted to the righteous. So we declare, in Jesus' name, that the SCEPTER OF RIGHTEOUSNESS RULES over all land, buildings, services, and properties of the United States Postal Service, and we renounce and beat down the scepter of wickedness and command it to leave for it no longer has power or authority to remain, in Jesus' name!"*

Ax Of God's Judgment

☐ *"Father God, Your word says in Matthew 3:10, "And now also the axe is laid unto the root of the trees: therefore every tree which bringeth not forth good fruit is hewn down, and cast into the fire." Father God, I believe Your word, and I want to activate it right now in the spiritual and in the natural! Father, in Jesus' name, I ask You to take Your ax of judgment, according to Matthew 3:10, and chop and pull up at the root any and all unholy, ungodly influences that are in and around the United States Postal Service that are not there to produce good fruit! Remove those unholy, ungodly influences at the root, pull the stumps up out of the ground, shake the stumps with no roots remaining in the ground and any of its branches, vines or seeds, and cast it all into the fire to burn to ashes, in Jesus' name! We do not have to accept anything that is not the will of God for our nation, our mail system, our community, and our people, in Jesus' name! Father*

God, I ask You to replace all of those areas of influence in and around the United States Postal Service with Holy Spirit-filled, righteous influences that will bear and multiply good Holy Spirit fruit for Your kingdom and glory, in Jesus' name!"

Take Group Communion - Prepare Your Communion Bread And Juice And Pray

- ☐ *"Heavenly Father, in the name of Jesus, we take Communion together as a prophetic act of faith to seal and confirm our prayers and this time in the Courts of Heaven. Father God, we lift up this bread to You and we give You thanks and praise. We dedicate and consecrate this bread to You, Father God, and we ask You to bless this bread as it represents the body of Your Son — the bread of life — Jesus Christ. Lord Jesus, You told us to remember You this way and remember what You did on the Cross for us. Lord, we invite You to our table because You invited us to Yours. We understand that Your sacrifice on the Cross, Lord, was for our sins and the sins of the world and we are grateful. Thank You, Lord Jesus, and we ask You, Lord, to cleanse this bread with Your blood, and sanctify it. We proclaim this bread is holy and sanctified by the blood of Jesus. Thank You, Lord. Thank You, Father God. We bless this bread, in Jesus' name."* (Eat bread)

- ☐ *"Heavenly Father, in the name of Jesus, we take Communion together as a prophetic act of faith to seal our prayers and this time in the Courts of Heaven. Father God, we lift up this cup and grape juice to You, and we give You thanks and praise. We dedicate and consecrate this cup and grape juice to You, Father God, and we ask You to bless this as it represents the blood of Your Son, Jesus Christ. Lord Jesus, You told us to remember You this way and remember that You shed Your blood for us and our sins. Your blood, Lord, cleanses us of all sin and iniquities, heals us, protects us, and redeems us out of the hand of the devil and back to God to be set aside for the plans and purposes of Father God, all because of Your blood, Lord!*

- ☐ *"Thank You, Lord Jesus, and we ask You, Lord, to cleanse this cup and grape juice with Your blood and sanctify it. We proclaim by faith that this grape juice is holy and sanctified by the blood of Jesus and that everywhere it touches, the power of the blood of Jesus is released! Thank You, Lord. Thank You, Father God. We bless this cup and juice and partake, in Jesus' name."* (Drink juice)

Taking Authority As A King And Priest For Land Assignment

Make sure that before you go to the land prayer location you put on your full armor of God and do my Suit Up Prayer here in the book.

- ☐ *"Almighty Father God, O Righteous Judge, in the name of Jesus Christ, Your word says in Revelation 1:6, "And hath made us kings and priests unto God and his Father; to him be glory and dominion for ever and ever. Amen." Therefore, we now take our kingly and priestly place and authority right here and now in Christ Jesus and through Christ Jesus as we stand at this post office location for zip code _____ in _____ (City/State) and claim this land and this post office for Your plans and purposes, Almighty God, for Your kingdom and Your glory from this day forward, in Jesus' name!"*

Local Post Office Repentance

If you cannot go to the location, you can do this in your own yard or in the spirit if you live within the zip code area

- ☐ *"Father God, we also come to You, in the name of Jesus Christ, repenting for the sins of this particular post office location for zip code _____ in _____ (City/State) since its founding. We have repented of all sinful acts against You, Father God, and all sinful acts against Your word that have transgressed through the United States Postal Service in its entirety. We now also repent for the sinful acts that have transgressed through this post office location for zip code _____ in _____ (City/State). We come into agreement with all of the repentance that was done in the Courts of Heaven today (March, 8, 2021) with our group of intercessors across the nation and ask that our petition for repentance and forgiveness locally here also be honored in Your Courts, Father God. We ask now for grace, mercy, and forgiveness for these sins. We ask now, Lord Jesus, for You to put Your blood on all of these sins and wash them clean."*

- ☐ *"Father God, now that the blood of Jesus is on these sins, we ask that this post office location for zip code _____ in _____ (City/State) be released of all consequences of these sins and that all accusations, curses, and demonic assignments be canceled off of this post office location for zip code _____ in _____ (City/State) by the redeeming power of the blood of Jesus. We ask now, Father God, for Your plans and purposes and blessings to go forth through this post office location for zip code _____ in _____ (City/State) from this day forward. So be it, in Jesus' name. Amen."*

Pour Communion In The Land

At your post office location, you will pray the prayer below over the Communion cup filled with grape juice. Then you partake first and pour the rest on the ground.

- ☐ *"Father God, we lift up this cup and grape juice to You and we give You thanks and praise. We dedicate and consecrate this cup and grape juice to You, Father God, and we ask You to bless this as it represents the blood of Your Son, Jesus Christ. Lord Jesus, You told us to remember You this way and remember that You shed Your blood for us and our sins. Your blood, Lord, cleanses us of all sin and iniquities, heals us, protects us, and redeems us out of the hand of the devil and back to God, to be set aside for the plans and purposes of Father God, all because of Your Blood, Lord! Lord Jesus, Your blood poured into the ground at Your crucifixion when You proclaimed, "It Is finished." We understand that Your precious blood not only redeemed us that day, but when it touched the earth, the land was also redeemed back to God.*

    "We ask today Lord Jesus for Your blood to cleanse, sanctify, and redeem this land upon which we stand today. Thank You, Lord Jesus, and we ask You, Lord, to cleanse this cup and grape juice with Your blood and sanctify it. We proclaim by faith that this grape juice is holy and sanctified by the blood of Jesus, and that everywhere it touches, the redeeming and cleansing power of the blood of Jesus is released! Thank You, Lord. Thank You, Father God. We bless this cup and juice and partake, in Jesus' name."
    (Drink juice and leave some to pour on the ground after the next declaration below)

Declare As You Pour The Communion

- ☐ *"Father God, Your word says in Hebrews 12:24, "To Jesus the mediator of a new covenant, and to the sprinkled blood that speaks a better word than the blood of Abel." So let this land receive the blood of Jesus Christ. Let the blood of Jesus Christ speak for this land, this property, and everything on this property and be cleansed of all sins and iniquities! By the blood of Jesus, this land and property and everything on the land, above the land, and below the land is now redeemed out of the hand of the devil, back to God, and set aside for the plans and purposes of God by the power of the blood of*

Jesus, all for the glory of God! So be it. Amen!" (Pour Communion in the land – just enough to soak into the soil)

Pour/Apply Anointing Oil To The Land

Bless and dedicate the oil FIRST. See my "How To Pray Over And Apply Anointing Oil Prayer" here in the book.

Then apply the oil to yourself and dedicate yourself to God and His plans and purposes, in Jesus' name. Apply it to your forehead, palms of your hands, and tops of your feet. Also, put some on the tops and bottoms of your shoes so you release the anointing wherever you walk and whatever you touch.

Declare As You Pour The Oil On The Ground - (You Just Need A Few Drops)

- ☐ *"In the name of Jesus Christ, we pour the anointing oil into this land and post office property of zip code _____ in _____ (City/State). We declare as it is written, that the anointing breaks the yoke, and we proclaim that every yoke of bondage, slavery, and sin is now shattered off of this land, property upon it, and this post office, in Jesus' name. We declare that this land, post office, and everything on it, along with all services being provided here, is now only yoked to Jesus Christ and the kingdom of Almighty God."*

- ☐ *"We dedicate and consecrate this land, property, and post office, including all buildings and everything on this property, the services being provided here, and every gateway — the natural, digital, and spiritual — to Almighty God. Let every gateway on this land and property receive the anointing of the Holy Spirit! We invite the Holy Spirit to come upon this land and property and do creative healing and deliverance miracles and let the power of the Holy Spirit be released upon everyone and everything on this property, this post office, and this land! From this day forward, let the power of the Holy Spirit be released upon everything coming in and going out from this place, in Jesus' name! We declare that this post office property of zip code _____ in _____ (City/State) is now anointed, blessed, and set aside to be used for the plans and purposes of Almighty God, all for the kingdom and glory of God, from this day forward, in Jesus' name!"*

Asking For Angel Armies Of The Lord For Your Local Post Office

- ☐ *"Father God, in the name of Jesus, we ask for You to dispatch Your heavenly hosts and warrior angels to come now and remove all demons, demonic principalities, and demonic platforms surrounding this post office location and in the region of the zip code of _____ in _____ (City/State), including anything of the kingdom of darkness operating through its services, leaders, employees, trainees, contractors, carriers, equipment, patrons, customers, clients, land, and properties here. Let these demonic entities, assignments, strongholds, and their demonic altars and platforms be dismantled, rooted out, bound, and cast out forever to the uninhabited dry place by the heavenly hosts and warrior angels of Almighty God, in Jesus' name! Let the heavenly hosts and warrior angels of Almighty God take this post office in zip code _____ in _____ (City/State) off of the frequency of the demonic forever! We ask, Father God, for Your angelic armies to stand hold now over every place they removed these demonic entities and for Your mighty angels to now to occupy and protect this post office and zip code region from all evil regarding all areas of this post office and its services, leaders, employees, trainees, contractors, carriers, equipment, land, and property here in zip code _____ in _____ (City/State) for Your kingdom and glory, in Jesus' name!"*

Blessing Your Local Post Office

- ☐ *"Father God, we ask now if You would pour out a blessing and restore your original intention and plans for this post office here in zip code _____ in _____ (City/State). We cancel and renounce any negative words or curses that have been spoken or written about this post office here in zip code _____ in _____ (City/State), in Jesus' name. We ask You, Lord Jesus, to cover any negative words or curses that have ever been spoken here or over this place with Your blood, Lord, and for these words to now be null and void, in Jesus' name.*

- ☐ *We speak blessing and prosperity to this post office location here in zip code _____ in _____ (City/State) and to all whom are employed here and also to the patrons! Father God, we ask for You to surround this post office location here in zip code _____ in _____ (City/State) with Your favor and for Your Holy Spirit to come upon it, and everyone shall see and know that the righteousness and blessings and gifts of God are covering and working in and through everything having to do with this post office location here in zip code _____ in _____ (City/State), all for Your glory and honor, God, in Jesus' name! People will once again have good to say and write and enjoy and trust in this post office location and its leaders and employees here in zip code _____ in _____ (City/State), in Jesus' name!"*

Dedicate Your Personal And Business P.O. Boxes And Mailboxes

Apply the prayed-over oil with your fingertips/hands on the item as you pray.

- ☐ "Father God, I thank You for this _____ with the address of _____. In the name of Jesus Christ, I dedicate and consecrate this _____ at this address _____ to You, Father God, and declare that it is designated and set aside for Your plans and purposes. I place this _____ at this address _____ in the blood of Jesus Christ. Lord Jesus, release the power of Your blood over this _____ at this address _____. Your blood, Lord Jesus, destroys all darkness, cleanses all sins, and breaks all curses and demonic assignments. I declare by the blood of Jesus, that this _____ at this address _____ is now sanctified. I anoint this _____, in the name of Jesus, and I invite You, Holy Spirit, to come upon this _____ with Your power, protection, and presence. I declare that this _____ at this address _____ is now anointed. Let the power of the Holy Spirit now come upon this _____ and this address of _____. Father God, bless this _____ and let it be used only for Your Glory. I bless this _____ and ask that the blood of Jesus and the power of the Holy Spirit be released upon everything coming in and going out from this _____ at this address from this day forward, in Jesus' name. Amen."

Mail Anointed Prayer Letter

This is a powerful prophetic act of faith to release the power and the authority of the Lord Jesus Christ and of the Holy Spirit throughout the inner workings of the USPS. Every place and every person that comes in contact with your anointed letter will experience the presence of the Holy Spirit as in Acts 19:12 when Apostle Paul anointed the aprons: "They were brought to the sick and diseases departed from them, and evil spirits went out of them."

You will also release an authority and blessing of the Lord by speaking over the letter. Isaiah 55:11 says: "His word will not return void but will accomplish that which he pleases and shall prosper in the thing whereto he SENT it."

Together as the Body of Christ, we are going to compose a letter with an anointing that carries God's word and His Holy Spirit throughout the United States Postal Service with a blessing and declaration. See below for the letter and the anointing prayer and decree.
If you feel led, you can also dab some Communion on the letter and pray the prayer below out loud. First, take Communion yourself and speak prophetically with a drop on the letter as an act of faith.

- ☐ *"I apply the blood of Jesus to my life and to this letter and all that is written in it and to every place this letter travels. It will release the cleansing and redeeming power of the blood of Jesus. I decree that we are redeemed by the blood of Jesus out of the hand of the devil, back into the hands of Almighty God and are now set aside for the plans and purposes of God, all by the blood of Jesus from this day forward, in Jesus' name! I decree that the power of the blood of Jesus will be carried and released into and through this letter everywhere it goes! Lord Jesus, by faith and as an act of my will, I pour a drop of this Communion juice on this letter. Let the power of Your blood, Lord, be upon this letter. Lord Jesus, release the power of Your blood to cleanse the sin, break all curses and demonic assignments, and destroy all demonic strongholds everywhere this letter travels! Let the power of Your blood, Lord Jesus, sanctify and reconcile everything that this letter touches and every place that this letter passes back to God for HIS plans and purposes! I proclaim by the authority of Jesus Christ and by the power of His blood, DOMINION of Almighty God over the United States Postal Service and everywhere this letter travels. I pray that every person who touches this letter comes to the salvation of the Lord Jesus Christ, in Jesus' name. Amen."*

Your Handwritten Or Typed Letter May Be Something Like This

Dear friend in Christ,

I am writing and mailing you this letter as an act of faith to release the anointing of the Holy Spirit along with a blessing and word of the Lord upon the United States Postal Service. By faith and by the authority of Jesus Christ, I ask you to please join me in claiming the United States Postal Service and all its employees, services, and anything affiliated with it, including all post office locations and postal carriers and contractors, for the kingdom of Almighty God.

This is a prophetic act of faith as we have come together and repented for the sins against God regarding the United States Postal Service. We have asked God, by the blood of Jesus, to cleanse the USPS of all evil and sinfulness and to bring everything having to do with the USPS back into the will of God to be used only for righteous purposes.

Our prayer group felt led by the Lord to send out these anointed letters to travel through the USPS system. We ask the angels of the Lord to protect this letter as it travels. We declare Psalm 91 protection over this letter and over the United States Postal Service and its leadership, employees, and all its works. We proclaim Psalm 91:4, "He shall cover thee with his feathers, and under his wings shalt thou trust: his truth shall be thy shield and buckler." We proclaim Exodus 23:20, "Behold, I send an Angel before thee, to keep thee in the way, and to bring thee into the place which I have prepared." We proclaim Isaiah 55:11, "His word will not return void and will accomplish that which he pleases and shall prosper in the thing whereto he SENT it."

We proclaim and dedicate the United States Postal Service, its leaders, employees and all its works for the plans and purposes of Almighty God, all for the glory of God.

This letter has been anointed with anointing oil that has been dedicated to God. It is written in Isaiah 10:27 that the anointing breaks all yokes of slavery and bondage, and anything anointed shall be set aside for God's purposes. Would you faithfully come into agreement in prayer for the United States Postal Service when you receive this letter?

We bless you and your household, and we bless the United States Postal Service, its leadership, its employees, and all its works and affiliations from this day forward. So be it, in Jesus' mighty name! Amen.

Yours In Christ Jesus,

Signed: _____

Feel free to add any personal prayer or scripture to your letter. It is important that you hand sign your name. This is a symbol of covenant with God. Then you will put a small dab of prayed-over anointing oil on your letter and envelope and seal it. You don't have to soak it in oil. It carries the power of the Holy Spirit and just a small amount will do nicely. I just put some on my hands and touch the edges.

If you don't have anointing oil, you can use plain prayed-over olive oil. See my "How To Pray Over And Apply Anointing Oil Prayer" in the book.

This is an important step so please follow these instructions. The purpose of this letter is that the anointing goes through the system to release the healing and restoring power of the Holy Spirit as we have released our faith and authority in Christ. Jesus did not have to personally touch each person to heal them. He sent the Holy Spirit to be our helper in all these things. The oil represents the presence of the Holy Spirit. Our faith and authority in Jesus Christ is what activates it.

You want your oil to carry the power of the anointing, so pray over it and bless it in faith. Make sure your oil is prayed over using my anointing-oil prayer, and then apply some oil to your hands and fingertips.

Put Your Anointed Hands On The Letter And Addressed/Stamped Envelope And Declare
- ☐ *"Father God, I thank You for this letter addressed to _____. In the name of Jesus Christ, I dedicate and consecrate this letter and envelope to You, Father God, and declare that it is designated and set aside for Your plans and purposes for the United*

States Postal Service. Through the sending and delivery of this letter, we ask for the power of Your Holy Spirit to be upon it. I place this letter and everything on it in the blood of Jesus Christ. Lord Jesus, release the power of Your blood over this letter. Your blood, Lord Jesus, destroys all darkness and breaks all curses and demonic assignments. By the blood of Jesus, this letter is now sanctified.

"I anoint this letter and envelope in the name of Jesus, and I invite You, Holy Spirit, to come upon it with Your power, protection, and presence. Holy Spirit, release Your dunamis power and presence everywhere this letter goes and upon every person and place it touches and passes! As this letter is mailed and travels through the United States Postal Service, let the power of Your Holy Spirit flow and be released and activated at each place and upon each person in the travels of this letter, in Jesus' name! Holy Spirit, bring deliverance, healing, restoration, and encounters with the Lord Jesus Christ in each place along the way to the destination of this letter! Holy Spirit, bring Your light, Your living waters, Your healing oil, Your breath of life, Your holy refining fire into all the dark, damaged, and lost places and hearts this letter encounters! Holy Spirit, bring complete divine alignment, restoration, restitution, righteousness and renewal to the United States Postal Service and everything connected to it according to the will and word of God! Let the original intent and plan of God come forth for the USPS! Holy Spirit, give every person involved with the USPS a heart to know and receive the presence of the living God and the salvation of the Lord Jesus Christ! "In Jesus' name, Holy Spirit, I ask You to restore everything to God's divine order along the way through the post office locations and carriers with Your resurrection power that this letter now carries! Father God, dispatch your angels to protect and accompany this letter to make sure it gets to its destination of _____, and, Father God, bless this letter. Let Your hand be upon it, and let it be used only for Your plans, purposes, and glory, Almighty God, from this day forward, in Jesus' name. Amen."

Please mail your anointed, hand signed, stamped, and prayed-over letter through your local post office to another brother or sister in Christ, and then ask them to receive the letter and come into agreement with the prayer. You are welcome to join my free private group on Facebook where we fellowship, and you can share addresses safely.

Strategies Going Forward

Take the time to pray over all your mail going out and even coming in. Dedicate it to God, cover it in the blood of Jesus, and anoint it and ask for the presence of the Holy Spirit to come upon it.

I do this with all my mailings, especially when I mail out my books to a reader. This way, we continue to release our faith in a great way. The USPS and all mailings will continue to be blessed and protected and our country and our people will all benefit greatly!

We will see the glory of God revealed in many ways through the United States Postal Service! This is how we advance the kingdom of God, the Gospel of the Lord Jesus Christ, and how we shall see righteousness return to our government, our people, and our communities.

Optional Offering

After you finish this United States Postal Service Assignment, give an offering to God into a ministry or church that is fertile soil for the kingdom. Thank God for opening His Courts to you and for His grace, mercy, and forgiveness. Or you can sow a seed into God's kingdom and name the seed: "Righteousness of Almighty God takes over the USPS and multiplies throughout the world in all postal systems for a Great Harvest for Jesus Christ and for the kingdom and glory of Almighty God."

You can send your offerings and letters here to my ministry, and I will come into agreement with your prayer.

By US Mail:
Annamarie Strawhand
P.O Box 7068
Virginia Beach, VA 23457

Part 5
Faith Activation

Prayer Activation Strategy: "Marvelous" Faith To Get Prayers Answered!

Stop Waiting And Start Activating

Do you feel like you are waiting and waiting to have your prayer answered? It's time to STOP waiting and START activating. I have learned that God responds to FAITH ACTIVATION. Actually, He MARVELS at it. It's time to show God how faithful you are.

Faith moves God. In the Gospel of Luke, Chapter 7, we read about the Roman centurion who came to Jesus asking Him to heal his servant. Jesus was about to go, and the centurion said to Jesus,"You don't have to go. I know and understand Your authority. Just say the word and I know my servant will be healed right now."

WOW, that's BIG FAITH, and the Bible says Jesus MARVELED at this man's faith. So instead of waiting for a prayer to be answered, activate your faith to marvel the Lord!

Say This Prayer

- ☐ *"Lord Jesus, You know my need for _____ right now. I am believing in faith, without any doubt, that at this very moment my request is being granted because I trust in your complete authority as the Son of Almighty God. Thank You, Jesus! I am excited to see Your power and glory manifested in my life. Amen!"*

Prayer For Discernment

My friends, we are living in times that can be confusing. Propaganda from the media is being thrown at us to play on our emotions, but this is when we go to God and become quiet to hear His voice. What is His truth in all this? Discernment is like gold in these days! I look to the prophet, Jeremiah. He had sharp discernment and asked God for more. God loved that Jeremiah came to Him for all understanding. He even said to Jeremiah, "Ask Me, and I will show you the hidden secrets!" Be like Jeremiah.

Pray Out Loud

- ☐ *"Father God, I come to You today because there are so many confusing things happening in the world. You know the truth, and I want to know the truth too! I'm praying today for discernment — the same discernment of your prophet, Jeremiah. I'm seeking You, God, for the truth. I want to know the truth, see the truth, walk in the truth, understand the truth, and speak the truth!!*

- ☐ *"Father God, You told Your prophet, Jeremiah, in Your word, according to Jeremiah 33:3, to call unto You, Lord God, and ask and You would show him the hidden things, the secret things, the things he did not know. So today, I come to You in faith, Father God, just like Jeremiah did, asking You to show me the hidden things, the secret things, the things I do not know! I'm asking You, Father God, to show me the things that even the devil doesn't want me to know! Show me the hidden secret things that are happening in the world. Show me the hidden and secret things that are happening in my life and in my children! Show me where the enemy is trying to sneak around in my life and in the world!*

- ☐ *"I invite Your Holy Spirit to come and partner with me and guide me in all truth! Father God, In Jesus' name, give me revelation. Give me wisdom. Cover me in Your glory, God, and Your divine protection! I want to see what You see! I am seeking Your heart, Father!! I want divine understanding! I am made in Your image, and I want to represent Your Truth! Father God, thank You for Your truth! I'm going to keep asking. I'm going to keep seeking You, and I'm going keep knocking. I know all these doors will be opened for me because You promised me they would!!*

- ☐ *"Thank You, Father God, that I can come to You today according to Your word and ask for supernatural wisdom and knowledge. I'm excited and in expectation and open to receive the truth!! I will not fear even if the truth is disturbing. I know that You are with me. I know man cannot harm me because You, Almighty God, have Your hand upon me!!*

☐ *"Father God, take the scales off of my eyes, and lift the veils. I ask You to do the same with my loved ones!! Your truth is precious to me, Lord, and I treasure it! I will be a good steward of these secrets and revelations of truth, and I will only use them for Your glory, God!! I ask for all of this today and receive it, in Jesus' name. Amen!!"*

Prayer For Grace
The Meaning Of Seeing The Number 555 Repeatedly

I love the number five because, biblically, number five means grace. Many students ask me about seeing certain numbers over and over, and I love it when they say they are seeing lots of fives — 5, 55, and 555! That is the HOLY SPIRIT reminding you how much grace you have from Father God!

The triumph of faith in Jesus Christ is grace! God pours out His love and grace upon grace to you through His Holy Spirit, and He wants to remind you to come to Him. You can even ask for more when you mess up! God will give you so much grace that He even redeems the time back to you that you lost when you were making those mistakes. WOW.

Pray This Prayer For More Grace

- ☐ *"Father God, thank You for Your grace! Because of Jesus, I have grace. I come to You today, Father, to ask for more grace for these mistakes I have made that cost me some time, pain, and relationships. I ask today, Father, for more grace. I ask for grace upon grace through Your Son, Jesus Christ.*

- ☐ *"I ask, King Jesus, if You would redeem the time and things I have lost because of my sins and mistakes. I do not have to be disappointed or ashamed of my mistakes and shortcomings! I ask for grace to be poured out to me through Your Holy Spirit, according to Your word in Romans 5:5, 'And hope does not make us ashamed, because the love of God has been poured out into our hearts through the Holy Spirit, the One having been given to us.'*

- ☐ *"Thank You, Jesus! Thank You, Holy Spirit!! I have an ABUNDANCE of grace!! I receive the outpouring of Your grace right now, Father God. I love You, Father. Thank You for this precious gift, in Jesus' name. Amen."*

Now you can thank the Holy Spirit for showing you these numbers and for this grace. Remember, He is prompting you and reminding and guiding you of what is promised in the word of God when you see these numbers.

Part 6
Family And Relationships

Five Strategies For Praying Your Prodigals Home
(And Back To God)

I want to share a powerful prayer strategy for those of you praying for your prodigal sons and daughters — or husbands and wives! My experience comes from the revelation and the prayer strategies that I have received from praying for my own daughter who had been struggling with her faith in Jesus.

God is so faithful to give us the steps and strategies from His word and through the Holy Spirit to give us the solutions we need for our families, marriages, and children to be restored. Praise God!

So many of you have been reaching out to me through our prayer requests form asking for us to pray for your prodigal child who is away from God or going into dark and sinful lifestyles. Many of you have asked for the same prayers for a husband or wife. I felt very strongly about asking the Lord for a word to share with you all that would give us a prayer strategy to activate over our prodigals.

Here is the Prodigal Prayer Strategy I received from the revelation of the Holy Spirit giving me direction as I continued to pray for my own daughter. It's something that each of you can combine with your own revelation from the Lord as you spend time in prayer for your prodigal.

1. Send The Holy Spirit

The Holy Spirit is our helper and we have the authority in Christ to send Him to help us in any situation.

Pray Out Loud

> ☐ *"In the name of Jesus, I send the Holy Spirit to hover over my loved one, _____. I ask You, Holy Spirit, to do creative miracles in them today. Remove the scales from their eyes and lift the veils to give them eyes of understanding to see Your truth. Point them to the living God. Reveal the Lord Jesus Christ to them. Holy Spirit, give them a check of conviction in their own spirit when they try to move further away from God's will. Guide them back into God's will for their lives. Holy Spirit, I ask You to completely engulf and surround _____ night and day and pour fresh oil on them to activate their God-given gifts and divine purpose. Remind them why they were created and what they were created to do. Give them dreams and visions for their divine calling and purpose, in Jesus' name!*

- [ ] *Thank You, Holy Spirit, for Your help and faithfulness to my request. Thank You, Jesus, for my authority through You to send the Holy Spirit, my helper, on this assignment for my loved one, in Jesus' name I pray. Amen."*

2. Put Them In The Blood Of Jesus

The enemy is helpless against the blood of Jesus Christ.

Decree Out Loud - (Add The Names Of Your Loved Ones In The Blanks)

- [ ] *I place myself completely in the blood of Jesus.*
- [ ] *I place my motherhood/fatherhood in the blood of Jesus.*
- [ ] *I place my marriage in the blood of Jesus.*
- [ ] *I release the power of the blood of Jesus over me and my family.*
- [ ] *I place my daughter/son/husband/wife, _____, in the blood of Jesus.*
- [ ] *I place my relationship with my _____ in the blood of Jesus.*
- [ ] *I place every influence and friendship in and around _____ in the blood of Jesus.*
- [ ] *I place _____'s divine gifts and anointings in the blood of Jesus.*
- [ ] *I place _____'s life purpose as ordained by God in the blood of Jesus.*
- [ ] *I release the power of the blood of Jesus over and in _____ right now!*
- [ ] *Lord Jesus, let Your blood speak into _____!*
- [ ] *Lord Jesus, Your blood speaks life over _____!*
- [ ] *Lord Jesus, Your blood exposes darkness hiding in and around _____!*
- [ ] *Lord Jesus, Your blood destroys all darkness in and around _____!*
- [ ] *Thank You, Jesus, for the power of Your precious blood!*
- [ ] *Thank You, Jesus, for the authority to release and apply Your blood!*

3. Release Angels On Assignment

Angels are activated by the word of God. The Bible says that the Lord watches over His word to perform it. (Jeremiah 1:12)

Decree the word of God over your prodigal and ask the Lord to release his angels to perform this task by faith.

Builder Angels: Pray This "Hedge Of Thorns" Prayer Out Loud

- ☐ *"Father, in the name of Jesus, I thank You for _____ 's life. I love them very much, Father, but I cannot even fathom how much more You love _____. I know, Father God, that You have a great plan and purpose for their life. Right now, _____ is going away from You, Lord, and their life is not producing the fruit of the Holy Spirit. They have evil influences around them and are chasing evil things. Father, I ask that today You release Your Builder Angels to build a hedge of thorns around them to fence them in to protect them from all evil influences and to keep them from going after things that are not of Your will for their life. Father, Your word in Hosea 2:6-7 states, 'Therefore, I will block her/his path with thornbushes; I will wall her/him in so that she cannot find her way. She/he will chase after her lovers but not catch them; she/he will look for them but not find them. Then she/he will say, 'I will go back to my husband/wife/parents as at first, for then I was better off than now.' I believe Your word, Father, and I ask for that same 'hedge of thorns' fence to be built around my loved one, _____, and for Your Builder Angels to be activated to build this fence of thorns like a barbed wire fence around a fertile field. I decree that my loved one, _____, is like a fertile field that is ripe for harvest for Jesus Christ and that this barbed, thorny fence will protect them from all predators or bad seeds that could defile or ruin the fruit they are meant to produce for the kingdom of God. I ask that this protective barrier be completed around them today, in the name of Jesus. Thank You, Father. Amen."*

Sower Angels: Pray This "Sowing Of Good Seed" Prayer Out Loud

- ☐ *"Father, I thank You for who You are and all that You do for us. Today, I lift up my loved one, _____, to You in prayer. I thank You, Father, for their life and the plans and purposes You have for their life. Father, in the name of Jesus, I decree over _____ that they become the fertile ground that our Lord Jesus speaks about in Matthew 13:8, 'Still other seed fell on good soil, where it produced a crop–a hundred, sixty or thirty times what was sown.' Father, I ask, in the name of Jesus, that You would release Your Sower Angels to sow good seeds into _____. I ask that these seeds would actually be Holy Spirit-filled and godly mentors, friendships, and influences that come into their life. I ask that through the help of Your Holy Spirit working with the Sower Angels, that 'good seeds' would be ushered into _____'s life right now. I ask for the Sower Angels to go and gather these godly people and influences and bring them into the path of _____ as soon as possible. I am also asking, Father, for Your divinely inspired books, videos, music, events, and teachings to come as an opportunity to them in an unexpected way. Usher this in through angelic assistance to plant a good seed in their heart and mind, starting them on their path back to Jesus Christ. I am asking for these new Holy Spirit-filled relationships that You have for their life to take root and grow to help _____ have a closer and deeper relationship with You, Father, and begin to walk in their divine calling and purpose. I pray that all these seeds come to an abundant harvest in their life for Your glory, in Jesus' name. Amen."*

Hunter and Trapper Angels: Pray This "Hunt and Trap The Foxes" Prayer Out Loud

- *"Father, thank You for Your word that teaches and guides us how to pray for our children and marriages. By faith, we know that You want us to bloom and prosper and produce the fruit of the Holy Spirit from walking in our divine purpose and having a close relationship with You, Lord. Father, I am coming to You today decreeing and standing upon Your word in Song of Solomon 2:15, 'Catch for us the foxes — the little foxes that ruin the vineyards — for our vineyards are in bloom.' Father, I can clearly see that there are sneaky little foxes in the spirit realm that are stealing the fruits of the Holy Spirit that my loved one, _____, is meant to produce in their life. My loved one, _____, is gifted and anointed by You, Father, to fulfill their calling in life and to come into a full relationship with Jesus Christ. My loved one, _____, is being hindered by those foxes that are trying to spoil their fruit and the branches that connect them to Christ, who is the vine. According to Your word in John 15:5, Jesus said, 'I am the vine, ye are the branches: He that abideth in me, and I in him, the same bringeth forth much fruit: for without me ye can do nothing.' In the name of Jesus, I ask that Your Hunter and Trapper Angels be released on behalf of my loved one, _____, to hunt and trap those foxes that are coming against Your will and Your plans for their life. I ask that these Hunter and Trapper Angels go now to catch every single sneaky fox that is operating in and around my loved one, _____, and send those foxes far, far away from my loved one,*

_____, forever! I decree that those sneaky foxes will never come near my loved one again and will never be allowed to touch their fruits of the Holy Spirit ever again, in Jesus' mighty name! Amen."_

Harvest Angels: Pray This "Harvest Angels Prayer" Out Loud

- ☐ *"Father, I thank You for the blessings and abundance that You have promised for my life and the life of my loved one, _____. Father, Your word is true and good, and I praise You for Your faithfulness in our lives. Today, Father, I am calling in the Harvest Angels for my loved one, _____, in Jesus' name. In Your word, Jesus teaches us in Matthew 13:24 that the enemy comes in when we are not looking and sows tares and weeds into our harvest fields. I decree that my loved one, _____, is ripe for the harvest for Jesus Christ right now. In the name of Jesus, I ask You, Father, to release Your Harvest Angels into my loved one, _____'s, field. I ask for the Harvest Angels to pull up at the root every weed and tare in their harvest field. Pull up every ungodly relationship and evil influence that is in their life at the roots and bundle them and cast them into Your holy fire to be burned to ashes! I decree that every single relationship and influence in my loved ones life that is not Your will for them, Father God, will be removed at the root and these relationships burned to ashes, in Jesus' name! I decree that those weeds and tares (ungodly relationships) will never come near _____ again, and their weed seeds will never take root in _____'s harvest field again! I decree that _____'s harvest is for the Lord. I also ask, Father, that my loved one, _____, is harvested right now like good wheat by Your Harvest Angels and bundled and put safely into the barn of our Master, Jesus Christ, in Jesus' mighty name! Amen."*

A POWERFUL Act Of Faith

Sow a seed offering to a ministry in the name of your loved one as a seed to come to harvest for the LORD.

4. Prophesy and Decree Over Them

It is extremely powerful when you decree God's word for their life over your loved one, giving Him thanks and praise ahead of time for their breakthrough and deliverance! It is a huge activation of your faith for their life. The word says, in Job 22:28, that if we decree a thing it shall be established. This includes good or bad, so watch what you say even if you are upset with them. Focus on decreeing God's word over them. Then prophesy God's will to be done now to them! I start with decreeing that my loved one is the beautiful feet spoken of in Isaiah 52:7,

"How beautiful upon the mountains are the feet of him that bringeth good tidings, that publisheth peace; that bringeth good tidings of good, that publisheth salvation; that saith unto Zion, Thy God reigneth!" Then I prophesy that my loved one is living in the will of God and producing the fruit of the Holy Spirit in their life right now! I decree that they have realized the pigpen is no good and they have it better at home and better with God! I decree the good things I see in the future for them, such as walking with the Lord, in good health, filled with godly wisdom, and fully using their God-given gifts and anointings. I ask the Holy Spirit to go and hover over them right where they are and for the presence of God to be so strong around them that evil cannot stand to be near them and will flee. I prophesy in faith that the scales have fallen off their eyes right now. The chains are falling off, in Jesus' name, and they see the truth and the truth has set them free!

5. Pray In The Spirit

When you have been baptized in the Holy Spirit, you will receive the gift of praying in a prayer language (tongues). You surrender to the Holy Spirit and ask the Holy Spirit to pray what needs to be prayed for your loved one through you. You can go and lay on their spot on their bed and pray or even sit in their chair or place at the table. If you do not have a prayer language, then come before the Father on your knees or lying on the floor before Him, and praise Him until you feel the presence of the Holy Spirit. Then, surrender yourself and your loved one to God. Repent for any negative words or curses, known or unknown, that you have ever spoken over your loved one. Ask for the blood of Jesus to cover your sins and all those words and wipe them away clean by His blood.

Pray Out Loud

> ☐ *"In the name of Jesus, I repent for every negative word or curse I have ever spoken over _____, and I cancel every negative word or every curse I have ever spoken, over my loved one, in Jesus' name. I mark them null and void and cover them in the blood of Jesus. I loose off my soul all bitterness and unforgiveness I had for my loved one, in Jesus' name and put it on the Cross, and I ask the Holy Spirit to come and hover over me and my loved one and to heal and restore our relationship, in Jesus' name."*

Continue to pray in the Spirit as the Lord guides you. When you have all of your own sin, negative words, and bitterness forgiven and covered in the blood, it will open up the Holy Spirit to flow through you like a vessel to pray strongly in the Spirit for your loved one! Pray until you see breakthrough!

Have Faith And Stay Patient

Keep praying for them and loving them no matter what you see happening in the natural. You have activated the spirit realm and Heaven is fighting for them right now!

Warning

Don't put what God has called you to do in your own life on hold because you are worried about your children or waiting for your spouse to see the light! That would be direct disobedience to God! Your obedience brings breakthrough in ALL areas of your life! Keep moving forward with your own calling in faith and obedience! Matthew 6:33, "Seek first the KINGDOM of God and all these things will be added to you." That means you should always be seeking for yourself as well as for your family members! Also, the will of God for their life might be something you would never expect. If what they are called to do produces fruit for the kingdom of God and the Body Of Christ, then it is of God. Judge only by the fruit like Jesus instructs us.

Prepare The Return Party By Faith

Thank God in advance for bringing your prodigal home and delivering them from darkness and back to Jesus! Thank Him and Praise Him for His faithfulness and goodness in all that He is doing right now! Stay in faith no matter how long it takes. Keep pressing in! God loves them even more than we do and wants them back! Prepare a party by FAITH for your loved one's return! Have it all ready to go. Buy a ring to put on their finger, a new robe or nice outfit for them, and special decorations for their HOMECOMING party. Keep everything in a place where you can see it all the time and decree over it by faith:

- ☐ "Today is the day of celebration! _____ has been delivered by the hand of God! My prodigal is HOME!! Hallelujah!! God DID it!! Romans 8:28, 'And we know that for those who love God all things work together for good, for those who are called according to his purpose.'

- ☐ "My _____ and I are now rich in experiences of joy, peace, faith, love and harmony together! The Lord has redeemed all the time we lost, and we have even more blessings together than ever before! Thank You, Jesus!

Prayer For Unsaved Loved Ones – Decree To See A Loved One Saved Or To Return To Jesus Christ

Decree Out Loud

I put my faith in God and enter His rest!

Pray This Prayer For Your Unsaved Loved Ones

- ☐ "Father, I come to You, in Jesus' name, praying for _____. I ask You, Father, to bring the perfect divine laborer of Your choosing into _____'s path. Let this laborer speak *just the right word to _____ at the right moment, divinely orchestrated by Your Holy Spirit. As I cover _____ with prayer and the blood of Jesus Christ, I thank You, Father, that sin is going to become exceedingly sinful and repungent to them, and _____ will no longer find pleasure in the sinful things that they have enjoyed in the past! _____ will see that they can only enjoy life when they are in a relationship with you, Father God, and in the Lord Jesus Christ!! I thank You, Father God, that Your Holy Spirit is dealing with _____ right now! Your Holy Spirit is dealing with _____ and dealing with _____ and dealing with _____ until _____ gives in and lets You, Father God, in their life and they are brought to repentance, a free gift from the Lord Jesus Christ! I thank You, Father, for the salvation of _____. I ask You now to fill them with Your Holy Spirit and let the veils be lifted off of them suddenly so that they shall see the truth, accept the truth, know the truth, speak the truth, and walk in the truth and light of Jesus Christ all the days of their life, fulfilling their divine destiny for Your kingdom and glory, in Jesus' name. Amen.*

- ☐ *"I am in faithful expectation to see the new positive changes in _____ as they give more of their life to Jesus Christ! _____'s heart belongs to You, Father God, their Abba Father!"*

PRODIGAL PRAYERS – BOOK RESOURCES

I highly recommend the teachings and prodigal prayer ministry of Karen Wheaton and her book, *Watching the Road – Praying Your Prodigal Home*. Karen's ministry and her intercession for prodigals is very powerful.

Go into the Courts of Heaven and intercede for your prodigal: See my prayer here or get the Books By Jeanette Strauss/(Book Bundle) From the Courtroom of Heaven & Prayers and Petitions www.glouriouscreations.net

Prayer For Family - How To Pray Protection Over Your Spouse And Children

After hearing me pray over my husband, Mike, and my daughter, Landry, on many occasions on my LIVE broadcasts, many of you have asked for a copy of the prayer to use for your own families.

First, suit yourself and your family up with my "Daily Suit Up Prayer" here in the book.

Then pray this prayer and declaration over them as they go out the door for the day to run errands or to go to work or school.

Identify who you're praying for — your spouse and/or child(ren) — and insert their name(s) in the blanks provided.

- ☐ "I place my (spouse, son, daughter), _____'s, mind, body, soul, spirit, and heart in the blood of Jesus Christ today. I place everywhere _____ puts his/her feet in the blood of Jesus Christ today. I place _____'s car in the blood of Jesus Christ today — bumper to bumper, door to door, from the top of the roof to the bottom of the tires, inside and outside, all in the blood of Jesus Christ. I place everywhere _____ drives his/her car in the blood of Jesus Christ. I ask you, Father, to send your angels to surround _____ and to encamp around him/her and keep him/her in all of his/her ways, in Jesus' name. I say that signs, wonders, miracles, blessings, and favor are _____'s today, in Jesus' name. Thank you, Father God!"

Prayer For The Fruit Of The Womb And The Fruit Of The Loins (Our Children)

As a mother or father, you can pray over your children and command things — even remotely. If you're the mother, they were formed in your body and are the fruit of your womb. If you're the father, they are the fruit of your loins. They have your DNA and RNA, but they also have the DNA and RNA of the Lord Jesus Christ that is coming together in the Spirit, and we can command over that in the name of Jesus.

Pray Out Loud (you can also pray your child's name in here)

- ☐ *"Father, in the name of Jesus, we lift up the fruit of our wombs today. We lift up the fruit of our loins today — our children — and we place them in the blood of Jesus Christ. Lord Jesus, release the power of Your blood over the fruit of our wombs. Lord Jesus, release the power of Your blood over the fruit of our loins for fathers and mothers right now, in the name of Jesus. We command right now, by the authority of Jesus Christ in whom we are seated, that the fruit of our wombs, the fruit of our loins — our children's bodies — be restored to their divine order. We command every cell in their body be restored to their divine order right now, and anything that is not of God be flushed out of our children's bodies right now, in the name of Jesus. We command our children's blood pressure, temperature, hormones, organs, nervous system, endocrine system, and digestive system to be returned totally to normal right now, according to your perfect will, Father, in the name of Jesus. We command their heartbeats, their pulse, their respiratory system, and all of their bodily functions be restored to their divine order right now, in the name of Jesus. We command every bad cell and every toxin to be flushed out of their bodies right now, in the name of Jesus. We command their DNA and their RNA to be restored to its divine order right now, in the name of Jesus, and their minds to be aligned with the mind of Christ! Holy Spirit, we ask you to go now as our helper, and visit our children wherever they are — the fruit of our wombs, the fruit of our loins — and hover over them and do divine miracles in them. We say, in the name of Jesus by the authority of Jesus Christ as the Holy Spirit is hovering over our children right now — created beings made in God's own image — be whole now. We command our children to be whole now, in the name of Jesus, divinely restored even better than before, in Jesus' name. Amen."*

God bless you and our children, in Jesus' name!

Prayer To Remove Un-Godly Relationships And Influences – Ax Of God's Judgment Prayer

This prayer to remove ungodly relationships and influences, "Ax of God's Judgment Prayer," is based on Matthew 3:10, "Even now the ax of God's judgment is poised, ready to sever the roots of the trees. Yes, every tree that does not produce good fruit will be chopped down and thrown into the fire."

What did John the Baptist mean when he said this? In the context of this word, John The Baptist was addressing the Pharisees (the religious leaders of that time). He was letting them have it — calling them a brood of vipers — and he was mad at their judgmental attitude! He was telling them of the Messiah that was coming and how God was leading people to repentance for those who were not bearing the fruit of the Spirit! That is, John was saying that God would be the judge, not the religious leaders, and that God was going to judge them too because they were not perfect! He was warning them that they better get ready because there was One who was coming that was so perfect and sinless that nobody was worthy even to unbuckle His sandals — Jesus Christ!

We know that in Jesus' ministry, He was all about teaching the importance of the fruit we bear in our lives — good fruit, Holy Spirit-filled fruit for the kingdom of God! So I realized that there are a lot of factors that come against this fruit in our lives, such as negative relationships, ungodly influences, demonic strongholds, and old mindsets that no longer should be a part of who you are as a new creation in Christ!

So what needs to be rooted up and chopped out of your life, your family, your marriage, and your ministry?

Even now the ax of God's judgment is poised, ready to sever the roots of the trees. Yes, every tree that does not produce good fruit will be chopped down and thrown into the fire. (Matthew 3:10)

Before You Pray

First, cover yourself and your loved ones in the blood of Jesus Christ and take your Seat of Authority. See my "Daily Suit Up Prayer" here in the book.

When you take your Seat of Authority in Christ Jesus each day, you put all the works of the enemy under your feet. When a loved one is out of the will of God, and their life is not bearing the fruit of the Holy Spirit, YOU TAKE AUTHORITY OVER IT IN THE SPIRIT REALM! The word of God is the WILL of God, so if you or anyone you love is not operating according to the word of God and there are relationships or influences in their life or your life that are coming against the fruit of the Holy Spirit, we are called as believers not to JUDGE them but to INTERCEDE for them in prayer. When we declare the word of God over their lives and even our own, we activate the angelic hosts to bring this to pass expediently. Angels hearken to the word of God.

How do you discern that relationships or influences around a person are coming against the fruit of the Holy Spirit in their lives? First, know and understand what the fruit of the Holy Spirit is according to the word of God: "But the fruit of the Spirit is love, joy, peace, longsuffering, gentleness, goodness, faith, meekness, temperance: against such there is no law." (Galatians 5:22-23)

With the understanding of the gifts of the Holy Spirit, is there a negative relationship or influence hindering the gifts of the Holy Spirit in a loved one's life or your life?

1 Corinthians 12:1-11 Concerning Spiritual Gifts Of The Holy Spirit

"Now about the gifts of the Spirit, brothers and sisters, I do not want you to be uninformed. You know that when you were pagans, somehow or other you were influenced and led astray to mute idols. Therefore I want you to know that no one who is speaking by the Spirit of God says, 'Jesus be cursed,' and no one can say, 'Jesus is Lord,' except by the Holy Spirit. There are different kinds of gifts, but the same Spirit distributes them. There are different kinds of service, but the same Lord. There are different kinds of working, but in all of them and in everyone it is the same God at work. Now to each one the manifestation of the Spirit is given for the common good. To one there is given through the Spirit a message of wisdom, to another a message of knowledge by means of the same Spirit, to another faith by the same Spirit, to another gifts of healing by that one Spirit, to another miraculous powers, to another prophecy, to another distinguishing between spirits, to another speaking in different kinds of tongues, and to still another the interpretation of tongues. All these are the work of one and the same Spirit, and he distributes them to each one, just as he determines."

Note: If there are relationships, habits, or influences around you that are coming against the fruit and gifts of the Holy Spirit in your life, your family, your marriage, your children, or your ministry, you can pray this prayer for God to take His ax of judgment and remove it swiftly out of your life or your loved one's life without too much discomfort or recourse for either party.

In my experience, God is faithful to do this for you, and you won't even have to engage the person. Some of us are not good at confrontation. However, understand that it is not the person or persons who are causing a problem, it's the negative spirit operating behind them. In my experience, I have just prayed this prayer and God has removed people suddenly and peacefully away from my family and we are just no longer friends, as simple as that. God knew what was hidden and that there was an agenda of the enemy operating through that person sometimes when I did not even see it! Of course, I forgave them and moved on! Thank You, Father God, for removing that situation out of my life!

The prayers and decrees below, I have prayed over myself, my family, and my students. We have seen amazing breakthroughs with these prayers! You can also pray this over your loved ones to have God's ax of judgment remove all ungodly relationships and influences out of their lives!

Decree Out Loud

- ☐ *"In the name of Jesus Christ in whom I am seated, I take authority over the ungodly situations, relationships, and activities that _____ is doing in their life! This is NOT the will of God for their life, according to the word of God; therefore, it cannot stay and must cease, in Jesus' name! I put all the works of the enemy in _____ life under my feet, in Jesus' name!*

- ☐ *"Lord, in the name of Jesus, I declare that I WILL NOT ACCEPT OR AGREE WITH ANYTHING THAT IS NOT PRODUCING THE FRUIT OF YOUR HOLY SPIRIT! This is what I see operating in _____'s life that is not according to Your word: _____. I RENOUNCE IT, CANCEL IT, AND COME OUT OF AGREEMENT WITH IT AND COMMAND IT TO LEAVE FOREVER OFF OF _____, in Jesus' name!*

- ☐ *"By the authority of Jesus Christ, I break the power of and sever off ALL the demonic and ungodly strongholds and soul ties off of _____ FOREVER, in Jesus' name. I now wash _____ in the blood of Jesus and invite the Holy Spirit to come and fill those places in _____ where the old soul ties have departed, in Jesus' name.*

- ☐ *"Father God, Your word says in Matthew 3:10, 'And now also the axe is laid unto the root of the trees: therefore, every tree which bringeth not forth good fruit is hewn down and cast into the fire.' I believe Your word, and I want to activate it right now in the spiritual and in the natural!*

- ☐ *"Lord, from my Seat of Authority in Christ Jesus, I command the angelic hosts now on my behalf to assist me for my loved one, _____! I send the hosts on assignment to permanently remove my loved one, _____, from all ungodly relationships, in Jesus' name! Chop these ungodly relationships and influences at the root! Pull the stumps up out of the ground, shake the stumps with no roots remaining in the ground, and cast it all into the fire to burn to ashes, in Jesus' name! I do not have to accept anything that is not the will of God for my life, my marriage, or for my children!*

- ☐ *"I BELIEVE that the word of God is the will of God! I DECREE, as for me and my house we shall honor and obey the word and the will of God and serve the Lord Jesus Christ for all generations thereof!*

- ☐ *"Lord, Your word says in Matthew 3:10 that every tree that does not produce good fruit will be chopped at the root and cast into the fire and that the ax of God's judgment is poised right now and is going to chop down this wrong relationship that is not your will for _____'s life! I believe that You are doing it now, Father, SWIFTLY, in Jesus' name."*

Pray Out Loud

- ☐ *"Father God, Your word says in Matthew 3:10 that Your ax of judgment will chop at the root every tree that does not produce good fruit and cast it into the fire! Father, in Jesus' name, I am asking You to chop at the root all relationships that do not produce good fruit in our lives! I am also decreeing this word and promise over my loved one today! Therefore, take Your ax, Father, and chop this relationship at the root, shake the stump up out of the ground, and pull up all roots!!*

- ☐ *Shake _____ loose, Lord!! Leave nothing in the ground to grow back in _____. Cast it roots and all into the fire, and burn it to ashes, in Jesus' name! Lord, take Your mighty wind and blow the ashes into the dry place forever! This relationship is not bearing good fruit of the Holy Spirit! This is what Your word says!! Do it, Lord, and _____ will never bear or eat fruit from this ungodly relationship again, in Jesus' name! Father God, I ask You to plant godly, Holy Spirit-filled friendships and mentors into my loved one, _____'s life that will bear the fruit of the Holy Spirit in their life! My loved one, _____, shall be like a tree of Lebanon deeply rooted in Your Courts, O God, in Jesus' name.*

- ☐ *I seal this prayer and decree in the blood of Jesus Christ. Thank You, Father, for Your word, my authority in Christ Jesus, and my authority to ask Your angelic hosts for assistance. I am in faithful expectation that I will see Your glory in this situation, and I praise You and thank You, Father and Lord Jesus, for swift action and completion with these prayers and decrees. Amen."*

Prayer To Send The Holy Spirit To Help With Loved Ones

Did you know you can "send" the Holy Spirit to someone or to help with something? Yes! He is your helper, and He knows exactly how to reveal the truth to them! So you may have a loved one who is away from God or not talking to you, dealing with an issue, or maybe they are in deception or even a dangerous lifestyle. Jesus promised us the Helper!

John 14:16 – (Amplified Bible) The Role of the Spirit: And I will ask the Father, and He will give you another Helper (Comforter, Advocate, Intercessor-Counselor, Strengthener, Standby), to be with you forever.

According to the scriptures in John 14:12-13, Jesus said that those who believe in Him, the works He did we shall do also and greater works than those we shall do, and whatever we shall ask in His name that will He do, that the Father may be glorified in the Son. If we ask anything in His name He will do it.

Since Jesus sent the Holy Spirit to his disciples, we can also send the Holy Spirit. In John 15:26 and John 16:7, Jesus promised to send the Holy Spirit to His disciples. In these verses, the Holy Spirit is referred to as the Comforter, Advocate, Helper, or Counselor depending on the Bible translation you are reading. Understand, we do not command the Holy Spirit, we ask Him to help us, in Jesus' name, as our "Helper." However, we can command the angelic from our Seat of Authority as a king through Christ Jesus, our King.

"When the Advocate comes, whom I will send to you from the Father — the Spirit of truth who goes out from the Father — he will testify about me." John 15:26 NIV

"Nevertheless I tell you the truth; It is expedient for you that I go away: for if I go not away, the Comforter will not come unto you; but if I depart, I will send him unto you." John 16:7 KJV

Pray This Prayer Out Loud

- ☐ *"Holy Spirit, my Helper, in the name of Jesus, I send You to hover over _____ to do creative miracles in _____. Open _____'s eyes, mind, heart, soul, and spirit to understanding and receiving truth and God's word and will for their life. Holy Spirit, I ask You to give _____ an encounter with Jesus Christ and reveal to _____ their true identity in Christ Jesus! Holy Spirit, show _____ what You have shown me right now, in Jesus' name. Amen."*

You can ask Him to go and "convict" (meaning give them a truth check in their spirit) that person if they are doing wrong. You can ask Him to bring a loving family memory to the mind of that person if they are hurting or prodigal. The Holy Spirit can help you point that person to Christ and bring that person out of darkness or even find and reveal something that has been hidden to them. That's His job and He loves it when you ask Him to help! The Holy Spirit does the heavy lifting with your loved ones! The Holy Spirit can do in one day what would take you weeks and months to do! A person's heart, mind, and spirit can only be changed by the work of the Holy Spirit! Understand that the more you try sometimes to tell people something, even though you know it to be true and the will of God, they may just ignore you or pull further away from you. But they cannot ignore or run from the Holy Spirit! Keep sending the Holy Spirit every day to that person until you see breakthrough!

I have learned this from experience. I have sent the Holy Spirit many times to help me with my loved ones with huge breakthroughs, especially with my husband! The Holy Spirit is the Spirit of God on the earth. He can go anywhere immediately, and He is your best friend and is eager to help you! He can help you in all things. Remember, Jesus asked the Father as something special for us to have Him! Thank You, Jesus! Thank You, Father God, and thank You, Holy Spirit!

Note: So what do you do in the mean time while you are waiting for the Holy Spirit to work on that person? Just love them and be an example in your own life's walk for Jesus Christ.

I LOVE THIS QUOTE from Evangelist Todd White: "How do you share Jesus with someone who is argumentative and confrontational? Love them the best you can. Pray for them if they will let you. Share your personal testimony. Pray that the eyes of their understanding be opened. Pray for more laborers to cross their path. Just remember that any good seeds that were planted, will not return void." – Todd White

Prayer For Unsaved Loved Ones – Decree To See A Loved One Saved Or To Return To Jesus Christ

Decree Out Loud

☐ *"I put my faith in God and enter His rest!*

☐ *"Father, I come to you, in Jesus' name, praying for _____. I ask You, Father, to bring the perfect divine laborer of Your choosing into _____'s path. Let this laborer speak just the right word to _____ at the right moment, divinely orchestrated by Your Holy Spirit. As I cover _____ with prayer and the blood of Jesus Christ, I thank You, Father, that sin is going to become exceedingly sinful and repugnant to them, and _____ will no longer find pleasure in the sinful things that they have enjoyed in the past! _____ will see that they can only enjoy life when they are in a relationship with you, Father God, and in the Lord Jesus Christ!! I thank You, Father God, that Your Holy Spirit is dealing with _____ right now! Your Holy Spirit is dealing with _____ and dealing with*

_____ and dealing with _____ until _____ gives in and lets You, Father God, in their life and they are brought to repentance, a free gift from the Lord Jesus Christ! I thank You, Father, for the salvation of _____. I ask You now to fill them with Your Holy Spirit and let the veils be lifted off of them suddenly so that they shall see the truth, accept the truth, know the truth, speak the truth, and walk in the truth and light of Jesus Christ all the days of their life, fulfilling their divine destiny for Your kingdom and glory, in Jesus' name. Amen._

- ☐ _"I am in faithful expectation to see the new positive changes in _____ as they give more of their life to Jesus Christ! _____'s heart belongs to You, Father God, their Abba, Father!"_

Part 7
Financial Breakthrough

How To Pray Over Your Offerings To The Lord – Kingdom Finance Prayers And Declarations

Kingdom Giving – Prayers To Name Your Seeds – Claim Your Harvest - And Give In Love And Obedience To God

When giving to the Lord, we have the tithe, which is our obedient 10% that we give in faith believing that He will make good on His promise in Malachi 3:10. There is also the first fruits offering, which is a first offering to the Lord each year or the first of something new that the Lord has done in your life — first paycheck of a new job, first sale of a new book, etc.

An offering is giving to God over and above your tithe or a seed. This is an act of LOVE to the Father for His goodness and to be a part of building His kingdom on earth. Offerings can be made to ministries, missions, or to the poor and needy, in the name of Jesus Christ. You give where He leads you to give and where you feel strongly in your heart to give. Also, you give where you see good works for the kingdom of God happening. You should only give if you feel led by the Lord there, especially to a ministry where you are growing in the Lord and who will pray over your offerings. Do not feel pushed to give offerings. This must come from your heart.

Then there is a seed offering, where you intentionally give into the kingdom of God and name the offering as a "seed." When you plant corn, you don't get daisies, right? You expect a corn harvest. It's all about being specific with your seed. So you write your check or send it via website, and you write the name of the seed and the harvest that you are expecting by faith.

Pray This Prayer Over Your Seed Offering Check Or Online Transaction

- ☐ *"Father, thank You for this $_____. I offer this up to You, Father, and plant this as a seed into Your kingdom, and I name this seed _____. (Example: new car) I believe by faith that this shall produce a harvest for which it is sent, according to Your word, Father, in Isaiah 55:11, 'So My word that proceeds from My mouth will not return to Me empty, but it will accomplish what I please, and it will prosper where I send it.' In Jesus' name, I receive my _____ in faith. Thank You, Father. Amen."*

You can even name your seed, "for the salvation of my loved one, _____" or "for the restoration of my marriage" or "for the returning home of my prodigal, _____." God makes it simple and wants us to understand kingdom finance and giving.

Once your check or offering is decreed by faith into the kingdom of God, it changes realms and is no longer under the earth's curse system, but has been transferred into God's unlimited kingdom where there is no lack, only abundance.

You also want to make sure the ministries where you "plant" your seed are growing and producing much fruit of the Holy Spirit and advancing the kingdom of God. You want to sow into "fertile ground." You can also decree a 1000-fold return on your seed financially.

When you give, do it with faith and say, "I am believing God for a 1000-fold return on my seed, according to Deuteronomy 1:11!!"

Declare Over Your Seed

- ☐ *"Father, I sow this seed of $_____ into Your kingdom and decree by faith over this seed that it will be blessed and multiply a 1000-fold financial return according to Your promise in Deuteronomy 1:11 for me and my household and the ministry I am sowing it into, in Jesus' name. Amen!"*

For A Seed For A Specific Need – Pray This Prayer Over Your Seed/Check

- ☐ *"Father God, Your word says in Mark 11:24, 'Therefore I say unto you, What things soever ye desire, when ye pray, believe that ye receive them, and ye shall have them.' Therefore, Father, I desire _____, and I believe I have received it today, in Jesus' name! Thank You, Father God!"*

First Fruits Offering

There are many teachings out there on kingdom finance and first fruits. These have given me a good understanding of how this works and why God set it up this way. It's all very sacred and all very beautiful when giving to the Father and thinking of Him first and also in understanding God's financial laws of sowing and reaping.

Giving to Israel-based missions is always important for your finances and blessings and connecting yourself to the promises of Abraham. When you give, give with your heart into the kingdom. Give to God in faith!

Tithe

The tithe is the obedient 10% of your income that you give to God regularly. This changed my husband's and my life! When we started tithing 10% of our monthly income to the Lord, within a year we were debt free for the first time in our 20-year marriage!

Read God's promise to the tither in Malachi Chapter 3:10-12, "Bring ye all the tithes into the storehouse, that there may be meat in mine house, and prove me now herewith, saith the LORD of hosts, if I will not open you the windows of heaven, and pour you out a blessing, that there shall not be room enough to receive it. And I will rebuke the devourer for your sakes, and he shall not destroy the fruits of your ground; neither shall your vine cast her fruit before the time in the field, saith the LORD of hosts. And all nations shall call you blessed: for ye shall be a delightsome land, saith the LORD of hosts." I can tell you that God is good on His word. He did this for my husband and I, and He will do it for you!

Tithes must be made to a "storehouse for the Lord." These are ministries who accept tithes and pray over them, according to Malachi 3:10-12, and they are obedient with the tithe themselves.

I have asked the Lord for my ministry to be a storehouse, and He has given me permission to receive and pray over tithes here in agreement with your prayers over them.

Prayer Over Your Tithe - Lay Your Hand On Or Raise Up The Money, Check, Or Transaction To God And Speak This Prayer In Faith

- ☐ *"I acknowledge that YOU, Father God, are my everything and that YOU alone prosper me and my household! I acknowledge Almighty God as my prosperity and the source of all of my needs according to His riches and glory! Father, in the name of Jesus, I'm a believer! I believe what YOU say and that YOU prosper the work of my hands and my faith! My job, my family, and my bank accounts are not my source! You, Father God, are my source! You, Father God, are my prosperity! YOU, Father God, are my Treasure! I am grateful, and I choose to worship You today, Father God! In humble faith and obedience, according to Your word in Malachi Chapter 3 verses 10-12, I ask You, Father God, to receive my tithe, in Jesus' name! Amen!"*

Partnership With A Ministry

Partnering with a ministry for a monthly payment commitment is something you should prayerfully consider before doing. Make sure the ministry is a place that you deeply believe in and you truly feel the Holy Spirit has led you to learn from and be a part of that ministry and the plan God has for it. Make sure you see growth and blessings flowing in that ministry and that it is following God's word and that they teach from the Holy Bible and allow the works of the Holy Spirit.

Partnership is considered a "covenant." Covenants are very important to God, and when you enter into a monthly financial commitment to a ministry, you become of the household of that ministry and the blessings of that ministry pass on to you. We are a prophetic ministry, so we also have the "prophet's reward" spoken of in Matthew 10:41, "He that receiveth a prophet in the name of a prophet shall receive a prophet's reward; and he that receiveth a righteous man in the name of a righteous man shall receive a righteous man's reward." Our TV ministry, Life in The Faith Lane with Annamarie, offers a partnership and we pray these blessings over you.

Kingdom Finance Is For Every Money Transaction

Speak over your money and what you want it to do for Jesus! My husband and I have reaped much fruit from "banking and sowing/reaping in the kingdom," and we want to give to our loving Father who gives so much to us. We want to see our money go to work for the kingdom of God in everything we pay for!

The key I have found is to use your money for the kingdom as much as possible, and if you have to pay into something that is not aligned with the kingdom of God, do like my teaching, "Kingdom Traveler," instructs, and take what you have to pay them and make it a seed unto the Lord for the salvation of the people who own that company and all their employees!

I just love to have all my money put to use for advancing the kingdom! Much love in our Lord Jesus Christ to you and your household and know that God will reward your faith with your finances! We are financing the kingdom of God on earth to grow, expand, and prosper — preparing for Jesus Christ's return. We pray He finds us faithful and we hear the words: "Well done, good and faithful servant."

Pray This Prayer For Finances Out Loud

- ☐ *"Father God, I believe Your word in Deuteronomy 8:18 that says, "And you shall remember the Lord your God, for it is He who gives you power to get wealth, that He may establish His covenant which He swore to your fathers, as it is this day. Father God, show me how to have the power to acquire wealth and access it so I can establish Your covenant in all the earth and teach others to do this also, in Jesus' name!"*

Giving To The Kingdom Of God For Increase And Family Salvation

Speak over your financial seeds to God. The seeds that we sow into the kingdom will break us out of a season lack, sickness, etc!

Decree Out Loud

- ☐ *"Father God, I believe that my seed, planted into your kingdom, breaks me out of a season! Time does not determine my seasons, my seed does. The seeds that I sow today, determine my tomorrow. My seeds will break me out of a season of lack into a season of abundance. Jesus said when I give, I will receive. It takes humility and faith to receive. I will receive what I expect. If I expect a harvest, I will get a harvest. Father God, today, I plant this seed in Your kingdom and name it _____. I ask You to receive my seed in faith, Father God, and for Your Holy Spirit to water it. I receive a swift harvest of _____ on my seed, in Jesus' name. Amen."*

Speak Over Your Offerings To The Poor And Needy

- ☐ *"Father, Your word says that the blessing always stays with the giver. According to Matthew 7:11, God gives good gifts to those who ask. According to Acts Chapter 10, I also give unto the Lord by giving to the poor and needy in the name of Jesus Christ to see salvation of family members and their baptism of the Holy Spirit like You did, Father God, for Cornelius' household in Acts chapter 10. Thank You, Father God. In Jesus' name, I will see Your glory in my household and with my loved ones giving their lives to Jesus Christ and walking with the leading of the Holy Spirit! Amen!"*

Speak Over Your First Fruits Offerings

- ☐ *"Father God, I couple my prayers to You now with a first fruit offering — an offering of the first of a blessing that You have given me — to You, Father, according to Your word in Mark Chapter 10 that says to give what you have first to God, and whatever you give up for God, you will receive 100 times more from God. I give to You first, Father, in love, obedience, and faith, in Jesus' name. Amen."*

Decree Out Loud

- ☐ *If God does not do it, let it remain undone*
- ☐ *I only want what God says I can have*
- ☐ *If God does not give it to me, I don't want it*
- ☐ *If God does not take me there, I don't want to go*
- ☐ *I will not ask for the assistance of man, only of God*
- ☐ *I never need grants or loans*
- ☐ *I am on the kingdom of God's banking system*
- ☐ *I sow seeds into my next season*

- *My seed is for God, the harvest comes for me by faith in my seed*

- *I have a debt-free ministry/business/home, etc*

- *I am the lender, not the borrower*

- *I commit my way to the Lord, and the Lord builds for me*

- *I am the landlord, not the tenant*

- *I am a business owner, not an employee*

- *I own land, buildings, homes, farms, properties, and businesses — all debt free*

- *Everyone God made a covenant with, He gave land to them*

- *I am in covenant with You, God! I want to possess the land You have for me*

- *I am taking the land for God and possessing the good land*

- *I have the builder and restorer anointing*

- *I have fasted and prayed for the promise, and God is faithful to reward my acts of faith*

- *God is my source; everything else is a resource*

- *Father, I ask for a land acquisition anointing, in Jesus' name*

- *Father, I ask for a builder and restorer anointing, in Jesus' name*

- *I have seed to harvest in faith. Every seed I plant will yield an abundant harvest.*

- *God always supplies me with more seeds as I continue to sow into His kingdom, and God shows me where to sow into fertile ministries and into kingdom projects and unto the needs of others as He leads me. I give generously in the name of Jesus Christ! Ephesians 6:8 (KJV) "Knowing that whatsoever good thing any man doeth, the same shall he receive of the Lord, whether he be bond or free."*

- *I know my reward comes from God, not from the people that I have helped*

- [ ] *I do the works of Abraham! The Holy Spirit leads me to be righteous and faithful and a frIend to God as Abraham was! I will be obedient with my 10% tithe as Abraham was! Father, You blessed Abraham for his obedience with his tithe, and I know You will bless me for my obedience! John 8:39 (KJV) "They answered and said unto him, Abraham is our father. Jesus saith unto them, if ye were Abraham's children, ye would do the works of Abraham." I believe my 10% tithe for one week will be more than I have taken in one year*

- [ ] *I ask big; I believe big*

- [ ] *I tap into the anointing by understanding what the Bible says about the work of the Holy Spirit on my life. I ask for fresh anointing and eyes of understanding from the Holy Spirit now to understand God's kingdom financial system*

- [ ] *I give to ministries that have fertile ground. I build God's house, and He will build my house*

- [ ] *I give to God first*

- [ ] *I want to give the best of what I have to God's kingdom*

- [ ] *I want to give God my best first*

- [ ] *I will own and inhabit homes that I did not build and increase them for the Lord. God will also give me homes to build for my own family and others*

- [ ] *Increase is coming bigger and better than I can ever imagine*

- [ ] *Before the need arises, the provision will be there ahead of time*

- [ ] *I seek the kingdom of God first, and He is adding all these things unto me*

- [ ] *When I aqiure land, I am pleasing God as a righteous man/woman who leaves an inheritance to my children*

- [ ] *The Lord is behind His work with me*

- [ ] *What I make happen for God's people, God will make happen for me*

- ☐ *All of my debt is permanently canceled*

- ☐ *I have generational land increase*

- ☐ *My children and descendants will own land, homes, and businesses, and they will do the work of the Lord there and be blessed*

- ☐ *My children and descendants will never be renters, they will only be owners*

- ☐ *All of my debt, my husband's debt, and my children's debt is now permanently canceled*

- ☐ *No debt, no requiring of financing in the future, the last loan I had is paid off, and I will never have to have another loan again*

- ☐ *Just like Joshua, every piece of land that I put my feet/footprints on, God will give it to me. I am possessing it today! My footprints are on: addresses _____*

- ☐ *I got it all from my Father God! My Father God owns everything!*

- ☐ *"I decree this all in the powerful name of Jesus Christ and cover these words in the blood of Jesus! These words will not return void but will prosper for what they are sent, according to Isaiah 55:11, in Jesus' name! I NOW put my faith in God and enter HIS rest in all that He has promised me in His word!"*

Opening The Gates And Doors Of Blessing Into Your Household

Gates And Doors And The One Who Holds The Key

I received another prophetic word about gates and doors. The Holy Spirit has been teaching me about this for some time regarding our country, but now He is teaching me about this for our own households. I did this decree this morning over my household (include home, family, property, business, finances, pets, livestock, and land).

Decree With Me Out Loud

- ☐ "Father, Your word says in Isaiah 22:22 that 'the key of the house of David will I lay upon his shoulder; so he shall open, and none shall shut; and he shall shut, and none shall open.' Lord Jesus, You hold the keys to my household! I repent for any doors or gates that I may have opened to the enemy knowingly and unknowingly. I ask for grace, mercy, and forgiveness and for Your blood to cover these sins. Lord Jesus, I ask You now to close every door and gate of the enemy in and around everything in my household and seal it shut forever with Your blood. You have the KEYS, Lord Jesus, on Your shoulder, and whatever You shut, none can open ever again! Lord Jesus, thank You for shutting those doors of darkness! Thank You for being Lord and King of my household! Lord, I ask You with Your key to now open the doors and gates of blessing, peace, prosperity, and opportunity in my household. I ask You, Lord Jesus, to station sentry angels at these doors and gates for protection. I place Your blood, Lord Jesus, on every door and gate, and I ask that You surround us with a hedge of protection over everything in my household so the enemy can never enter or come near these doors and gates You have opened, Lord! Holy Spirit, I welcome and invite You to come into my household and fill every part of it day and night. Holy Spirit, warn me when the enemy is trying to open a new door or gate and give me wisdom to discern.

- ☐ "I decree and declare on this day, according to the word of God in Isaiah 22:22, that double doors of blessing are being opened right now for me and my household, and I ask that these specific doors _____ be opened, in Jesus' name. I thank You, Father, for Your word and that it is alive and powerful! I thank You for this revelation and declaration today! Thank You, Jesus, for holding the KEYS to my household! As for me and my house we shall serve the Lord, in Jesus' mighty name! AMEN!"

Blessing Impartation

Friends, I bless you and your households today with the complete Shalom of the Lord God of Israel, Jehovah-M'Kaddesh — our Father God who sanctifies us and our lives. I ask the Father to send His Holy Spirit to hover in your homes and do creative miracles today over you! Holy Spirit pour the oil of joy upon all who read this today and flow the living waters straight from the throne room of Heaven to them and through them in the name of Yeshua Hamashiach, Jesus Christ of Nazareth! Amen.

I love you all!! God is GOOD!! I praise HIM for His constant unwavering LOVE for us and the FINISHED work of HIS SON, Jesus!! We are LOVED, REDEEMED, and SET APART for GOD by the ONE who HOLDS THE KEY!

Part 8
Healing & Soul Cleansing

Healing Prayer For Yourself And Loved Ones

Jesus spent His time on earth forgiving people of their sins and healing them of their physical ailments. In Hebrew, rapha means "to heal," so Jehovah Rapha means "the Lord who heals."

There are many scriptures in the Bible that talk about healing. We can read these to build up our faith in God's healing power and also use them as weapons of our warfare by declaring them over ourselves and our loved ones who are struggling with health issues.

Healing Scriptures

Exodus 15:26 (KJV): "And said, If thou wilt diligently hearken to the voice of the Lord thy God, and wilt do that which is right in his sight, and wilt give ear to his commandments, and keep all his statutes, I will put none of these diseases upon thee, which I have brought upon the Egyptians: for I am the Lord that healeth thee." (Jehovah Rapha - the Lord that healeth thee)

Exodus 23:25 (KJV): "And ye shall serve the Lord your God, and he shall bless thy bread, and thy water; and I will take sickness away from the midst of thee."

Isaiah 53:4-5 (NLT): "Yet it was our weaknesses he carried; it was our sorrows that weighed him down. And we thought his troubles were a punishment from God, a punishment for his own sins! (5) But he was pierced for our rebellion, crushed for our sins. He was beaten so we could be whole. He was whipped so we could be healed. Yet it was our weaknesses he carried; it was our sorrows that weighed him down. And we thought his troubles were a punishment from God, a punishment for his own sins!"

Psalm 30:2 (KJV): "O Lord my God, I cried unto thee, and thou hast healed me."

Psalm 107:19-20 (KJV): "Then they cry unto the Lord in their trouble, and he saveth them out of their distresses. (20) He sent his word, and healed them, and delivered them from their destructions."

Matthew 4:23-24 (NLT): "And Jesus went about all Galilee, teaching in their synagogues, preaching the gospel of the kingdom, and healing all kinds of sickness and all kinds of disease among the people. (24) Then His fame went throughout all Syria; and they brought to Him all sick people who were afflicted with various diseases and torments, and those who were demon-possessed, epileptics, and paralytics; and He healed them."

Matthew 8:5-8 (NLT): "Now when Jesus had entered Capernaum, a centurion came to Him, pleading with Him, saying, (6) 'Lord, my servant is lying at home paralyzed, dreadfully tormented.' (7) And Jesus said to him, 'I will come and heal him.' (8) The centurion answered and said, 'Lord, I am not worthy that You should come under my roof. But only speak a word, and my servant will be healed.'"

Mark 16:17-18 (NLT) "And these signs will follow those who believe: In My name they will cast out demons; they will speak with new tongues; they will take up serpents; and if they drink anything deadly, it will by no means hurt them; they will lay hands on the sick, and they will recover."

Luke 4:40 (NLT): "When the sun was setting, all those who had any that were sick with various diseases brought them to Him; and He laid His hands on every one of them and healed them."

Luke 6:18 (NLT): "... as well as those who were tormented with unclean spirits. And they were healed."

Luke 9:11 (NLT): "But when the multitudes knew it, they followed Him; and He received them and spoke to them about the kingdom of God, and healed those who had need of healing."

John 8:36 (NLT): "If the Son therefore shall make you free, ye shall be free indeed."

James 5:13-15 (NLT): "Is anyone among you suffering? Let him pray. Is anyone cheerful? Let him sing psalms. (14) Is anyone among you sick? Let him call for the elders of the church, and let them pray over him, anointing him with oil in the name of the Lord. (15) And the prayer of faith will save the sick, and the Lord will raise him up. And if he has committed sins, he will be forgiven.

Pray over yourself or a loved one: (lay hands on your head or theirs if you are with them)

- ☐ *"Father God, I come to You, in the name of Jesus, and ask You, Jehovah Rapha, to touch _____ today and to give them an encounter with You. I place _____ in the blood of Jesus Christ and ask You to release Your power over them, in Jesus' name. By the authority of Jesus Christ in whom I am seated, I command every cell in _____'s body to be restored to its divine order right now, and anything that is not of God be flushed out of their body, in the name of Jesus. I command _____'s blood pressure, temperature, hormones, organs, nervous system, endocrine system, and digestive system to be returned totally to normal right now, according to Your perfect will, Father, in the name of Jesus. I command their heartbeat, their pulse, their respiratory system, and all of their bodily functions to be restored to their divine order right now, in the name of Jesus. I command every bad cell and every toxin to be flushed out of _____'s body right now, in the name of Jesus. I command all lying symptoms to cease immediately in _____, in Jesus' name. Every cell in _____'s body must bow the knee to the lordship of Jesus Christ.*

- ☐ *"By the Authority of Jesus Christ, I command _____'s DNA and their RNA to be restored to its divine order right now, in the name of Jesus, and their mind to be aligned with the mind of Christ! Holy Spirit, I ask You to go now as my helper to _____, and hover over them and do divine miracles in them. _____'s body is the temple of the Holy Ghost. Sickness, disease, infirmity, and toxins cannot dwell in _____'s temple and must flee from them now. In the name of Jesus, I renounce all sickness, disease, infirmity, toxins, and bad cells off of _____'s body right now! Lord, Your Word says in 1 Peter 2:24 that with the stripes of Jesus _____ was healed. Therefore, I declare that _____ is whole, shalem, complete, nothing missing, nothing lacking, and nothing broken, in JESUS' MIGHTY NAME! Thank You, Lord, for the total and complete healing of _____'s body, in Jesus' name. Amen!"*

Updated: Prayer For Teeth Issues And To Restore And Heal The Mouth - Adapt For All Of The Gates Of The Body

The Holy Spirit showed me that when you have problems with your teeth, it means that you need to repent of the sin of your mouth gate. This includes words that you have spoken — evil words, foul words, cursing, negative words, and gossipy words — that have come out of your mouth, any words against God, and any sinful things that you've put in your mouth — drugs, alcohol, and sexual sins of the mouth. I have to say it. We have to repent for that. The Bible says that God hates gossip. That is a major sin that will come against your mouth gate. It gives the devil a legal right to attack your mouth. So repent for any gossip that you ever spoke. It's time to pray over your mouth gate to cleanse it and sanctify it to God, so He can bring you your new teeth.

I tell you this from experience because I had severe attacks on my mouth over the years, but God fixed my teeth. I've got pictures of what my teeth looked like a couple of years ago, but I repented for all the sins of my mouth. I would not ask you to do something that I haven't done myself.

You see, the enemy was coming against my mouth and against my teeth because he knew I was going to have to be on camera someday. He knew that if he started to do stuff to my teeth, it would come against my confidence of going on camera, but the Holy Spirit is so faithful. Jesus is so faithful that He led me to repentance of the sins of my mouth. Miraculously, the money came to fix my teeth and give me a smile that I was confident enough with to come on this broadcast and be on camera with you all.

I've had to do all of this. I've had to repent for all these things. I would not ask you to do these things if I had not been through it all myself and seen the glory of God in my own life. So take that as a word for yourself, that you shall have a beautiful megawatt white smile that is like the smile of an angel as the Lord sanctifies your mouth for His glory and for His kingdom, in Jesus' name.

Pray This Prayer Out Loud

☐ *"Father, in the name of Jesus, I repent for the sins of my mouth gate. I ask for grace, mercy, and forgiveness. I come out of agreement with all of those sins. I repent for any evil I allowed in my mouth, and I repent for any evil that I allowed out of my mouth. Father God, I repent for any gossip that I spoke out of my mouth. I'm sorry, Father. That's a sin against You to gossip against people or to bear false witness against people, and I repent. I repent for any negative words that I even spoke over myself, and today, I ask for grace, mercy, and forgiveness for all gossip, all negative words, and any cursing words that I spoke over myself or others. I repent for any words of bearing false witness against any other person, and I renounce it. I come out of agreement with it.*

- ☐ *"In Jesus' name, I ask for all these gossipy words, negative words, cursing words that I ever spoke to be washed away by the blood of Jesus Christ from the heavens and the earth and to be remembered no more, Father, for Your sake, in the name of Jesus. If any of my gossiping or negative words or bearing false witness hurt any person, I ask You, Father, to bless them, in the name of Jesus. Lord Jesus, wash my words with Your blood. Wash everything that ever came into my mouth or out of my mouth with Your blood, and, Father God, release me and my mouth from any consequences of those sins by the power of the blood of Jesus Christ that is now on those sins.*

- ☐ *"Thank You, Father God. Thank You, Lord Jesus. Thank You for Your precious blood. I believe by faith that these sins are covered in the blood of Jesus Christ. Now, cleanse my mouth gate with Your blood, Jesus. Sanctify it and make it holy, Father, in the name of Jesus.*

- ☐ *"Lord Jesus, now that my mouth gate has been cleansed by Your blood and sanctified back to God, I ask You, Father God, to restore everything in my mouth to its divine order. I receive my new teeth. I receive the healing of my mouth, in Jesus' name. Amen."*

Note: Now, ask the Holy Spirit to give you fruitful words — the fruit of the Holy Spirit — to speak whatever is lovely and whatever is of good report. If you feel like you want to speak something negative or gossipy, ask the Holy Spirit to help you to keep your mouth in check.

Take This Prayer And Adapt It For All Of The Gates Of The Body

It's important that you also repent for the sins of the other gates of your body — eye gates, ear gates, nose gates, reproductive gates, and skin gates. Take the prayer above and adapt it and pray a prayer of repentance for any and all sins you have committed knowingly or unknowingly of all the gates of your body, and commit to using these gates to bear the good fruit of the Holy Spirit from here on out.

Prayer To Be Delivered And Healed From Rejection

When you are concerned about "being accepted" and worry about your worthiness to receive blessings and abundance, that is connected to a spirit of rejection that needs to be healed off of your soul, off of your past, and released off of you and onto the Cross of Jesus. The works of Jesus Christ make us worthy, and we should have no fear of man, only God.

I am glad you are teachable and want to learn. To get delivered from the spirit of rejection, you must first forgive anyone in your life who rejected you. Then command the rejection wounds and memories to be loosed off of you and onto the Cross of Jesus, and ask the Holy Spirit for the spirit of adoption from Abba, Father.

Pray Out Loud

- *"Father, I thank You that I am not rejected. Your word says in Ephesians 1:6 that I am accepted in the beloved. I come out of agreement with rejection, in the name of Jesus. I no longer take ownership of rejection in my life. You said in Galatians 4:7 that I am Your child. I say that I am no longer a slave. I am free from the pain of rejection. I am free from the pain of isolation. I am free from every spirit that has tormented me in the area of rejection. I decree and declare that my mind is free! I command the spirit of rejection to go from me, in Jesus' name! I break your power off of my life. I say that I am not easily offended or moved by the opinions of man. I declare that the love of God is washing over me and bringing deliverance to my life. I boldly confess that I am free and Your word says that he whom the Son sets free is free indeed, in the name of Jesus! Amen."*

Proclaim Out Loud

- *"FATHER, I CALL FORTH YOUR SPIRIT OF ADOPTION UPON ME TO CAUSE ME TO CRY OUT ABBA, FATHER, IN JESUS' NAME!"*

LISTEN TO ME! You are not rejected. You are rescued, accepted, adopted, and chosen by Father God. He calls you by name! "Do not fear, for I have redeemed you [from captivity]; I have called you by name; you are Mine! (Isaiah 43:1)

"To the praise of the glory of His grace, by which He made us accepted in the Beloved." (Ephesians 1:6 KJV) You are the beautiful and intentional creation of a loving God. Your sins have been totally paid for through the blood of His Son, Jesus. If you accept the Son, the Father accepts you. And If God accepts you, then it doesn't matter what anyone else says or thinks.

Remind yourself daily and declare, Lord Jesus, give me grace to walk in truth today. I reject every lie of the enemy. I know I am a beloved and accepted child of God!

Be encouraged in the love of Jesus Christ with thanksgiving and praise being filled with the Holy Spirit.

Meditate On These Scriptures And, By Faith, Believe And Receive What God Says About You

- ☐ *"For we are God's masterpiece. He has created us anew in Christ Jesus, so we can do the good things he planned for us long ago." Ephesians 2:10 NLT*

- ☐ *"Even if my father and mother abandon me, the Lord will hold me close." Psalm 27:10 NLT*

- ☐ *"The fear of man brings a snare, but whoever trusts in the Lord shall be safe." Proverbs 29:25 NLT*

- ☐ *"But when you are praying, first forgive anyone you are holding a grudge against, so that your Father in Heaven will forgive you your sins too." Mark 11:25 NLT*

- ☐ *"For you have not received the spirit of bondage again to fear; but you have received the Spirit of adoption, whereby we cry, Abba, Father." Romans 8:15 KJV*

- ☐ *"If the Son therefore shall make you free, ye shall be free indeed." John 8:36 KJV*

- ☐ *"To the praise of the glory of His grace, by which He made us accepted in the Beloved." Ephesians 1:6 KJV*

- ☐ *"Wherefore thou art no more a servant, but a son; and if a son, then an heir of God through Christ." Galatians 4:7 KJV*

- ☐ *"For I know the thoughts that I think toward you, saith the Lord, thoughts of peace, and not of evil, to give you an expected end." Jeremiah 29:11 KJV*

- ☐ *"Beloved, we wish above all things that you may prosper and be in health, even as your soul prospers." 3 John 1:2*

Updated: Soul Cleansing and Healing Prayer

Loose And Bind Soul Cleanse Prayer - Pray Out Loud

- ☐ *"Father God, in the name of Jesus Christ, I humbly ask to come before You, and I confess and repent for all of my sins and the sins of my bloodline. I ask You, Father, for grace, mercy, and forgiveness, in the name of Jesus Christ, my Lord, King, and Savior. Father God, I am truly sorry for my sins! I have sinned against You, Father God, and I am sorry! I am also sorry for the sins of my bloodline, and I ask the Lord Jesus Christ to wash clean and cover all of my sins and the sins of my bloodline with Your precious blood! Cleanse me of all sin, Lord Jesus! (Take a moment to envision the blood of Jesus cleansing your sins.)*

- ☐ *I now repent of any and all unforgiveness and bitterness I have been holding against any person or even myself. I now forgive that person and myself right now. Father God I ask you to bless those who have hurt me in my past, I release them back to you Father God and bless them.*

- ☐ *"I ask You, Father God, to remember these sins no more for Your sake and wipe them clean from my soul, wipe them clean from Heaven and earth, and wipe these sins clean by the blood of Jesus Christ from any and all record books in the Heavens and in the spiritual and natural realms forever, in Jesus' name!*

- ☐ *"Father, I ask, in the name of Jesus Christ and by the power of His blood that speaks for me on the Mercy Seat, that all consequences and accusations from these sins be removed from me and from my bloodline forever, in Jesus' name.*

- ☐ *"By faith, I believe that I am now cleansed from my sin and that my bloodline is now cleansed from sin. My bloodline and I now walk in complete innocence from these sins only by the cleansing blood of Jesus Christ that has spoken for us in the Heavens and in the earth! Thank You, Father God, for Your grace, mercy, and forgiveness! I am redeemed! My bloodline is redeemed! Thank You, Jesus!!*

- ☐ *"Now, Father God, I thank You for Your gracious word. I do now take my seat (be seated) of authority at Your right hand in Christ Jesus where I rule and reign as a king and a priest of the order of Melchizedek in Christ Jesus and through Christ Jesus.*

- ☐ *"I place myself — mind, body, soul and spirit — in the blood of Jesus Christ. Lord Jesus, release the power of your blood over me and in me. Your blood, Lord, destroys all darkness and sanctifies me! I am marked in the spirit by the blood of Jesus Christ, therefore no evil can mark me! All evil must go! I belong to the kingdom of God through the finished work of the Cross and by the blood of Christ that has purchased me and set me apart for the plans and purposes of God. I am seated now in the Name above all names — King of kings, Lord of lords, Jesus Christ — and I put the kingdom of darkness under my feet! I enforce the finished work of the Cross and the blood of Jesus Christ right now in my life!*

- ☐ *"In the name of Jesus Christ, I do now take authority over my mind, body, soul, and spirit, and I command my mind, body, soul, and spirit to yield to the authority of Jesus Christ, the blood of Jesus Christ, and the the power of the Holy Spirit! Father God, according to Your word in Matthew 16:19, I have been given the keys to the kingdom of Heaven, and whatsoever I bind on earth shall be bound in Heaven, and whatever I loose on earth shall be loosed in Heaven."*

Put Your Hands On Your Stomach And Make The Motion Of Pulling Off Of Your Soul And Onto The Cross Of Jesus As You Decree Out Loud

Therefore, in the name of Jesus Christ:
- ☐ *I command all fear to be loosed off of my soul now and onto the Cross of Jesus Christ, in Jesus' name*

- ☐ *I command all trauma to be loosed off of my soul now and onto the Cross of Jesus Christ, in Jesus' name*

- ☐ *I command all negative memories to be loosed off of my soul now and onto the Cross of Jesus Christ, in Jesus' name*

- [ ] *I command all false beliefs to be loosed off of my soul now and onto the Cross of Jesus Christ, in Jesus' name*

- [ ] *I command all curses to be loosed off of my soul now and onto the Cross of Jesus Christ, in Jesus' name*

- [ ] *I command all hateful words, words of gossip, and all negative words from any source, including family members, friends, bullies, teachers, bosses, doctors (diagnoses), and even negative words I've spoken over myself to be loosed off of my soul now and onto the Cross of Jesus Christ, in Jesus' name*

- [ ] *I command all rejection to be loosed off of my soul now and onto the Cross of Jesus Christ, in Jesus' name*

- [ ] *I command all wounds from repented sin to be loosed off of my soul now and onto the Cross of Jesus Christ, in Jesus' name*

- [ ] *I command all pain to be loosed off of my soul now and onto the Cross of Jesus Christ, in Jesus' name*

- [ ] *I command all false responsibility to be loosed off of my soul now and onto the Cross of Jesus Christ, in Jesus' name*

- [ ] *I command all pride and false humility to be loosed off of my soul now and onto the Cross of Jesus Christ, in Jesus' name*

- [ ] *I command all fear of man to be loosed off of my soul now and onto the Cross of Jesus Christ, in Jesus' name*

- [ ] *I command all religious spirits to be loosed off of my soul now and onto the Cross of Jesus Christ, in Jesus' name*

- [ ] *I command all familiar spirits to be loosed off of my soul now and onto the Cross of Jesus Christ, in Jesus' name*

Put Your Hands On Your Head And Decree

- ☐ *"By faith and in the name and by the authority of Jesus Christ, I command every traumatic event that ever happened in my life, even when I was bullied or abused — the words, the actions the accusations — to be loosed right now off of my soul, off my mind, off my heart, off all my organs, off of my bones and bodily tissues, and off of all cell memories and onto the Cross of Jesus Christ, in Jesus' name."* (Make the motion with your hands of grabbing off of your body and onto the Cross!)

Put Your Hands On Your Stomach And Decree

- ☐ *"By faith and authority in Jesus Christ, I now bind forever to my soul the love of God, the life of God, the healing of God, the peace of God, the presence of God, and the joy of the Lord, in Jesus' name! In Jesus' name, I bind to my soul the divine restoration and resurrection power of the Holy Spirit! In the name of Jesus Christ, I command my mind, body, soul, spirit, and all of the cells, organs, bones, and tissues in my body to now align to the divine order of the kingdom of Almighty God, in Jesus' name!*

- ☐ *"I am excellent of soul. I now prosper because my soul is prospering, and I am SHALEM. I AM WHOLE, complete, nothing missing, nothing lacking, nothing broken, in Jesus' name! I welcome the Holy Spirit inside me to fully fill and take over every part of me! I am a temple for the presence of the LIVING GOD! I am a GLORY carrier! I COMMAND MY SOUL, MIND, BODY, AND SPIRIT TO YEILD DAILY TO THE WONDER MIRACLE-WORKING POWER, GUIDANCE, AND WISDOM OF THE HOLY SPIRIT!*

- ☐ *"I am cleansed and renewed in the blood of Jesus Christ. I reflect the glory light of Jesus, and the glory of God is my covering forever and ever! Amen. Thank You, Father God! Thank You, Lord Jesus! Thank You, Holy Spirit!"*

Now, praise Him! HALLELUJAH!!

Declare These Heart Scriptures Over Yourself Or A Loved One Out Loud

- ☐ *"In Jesus' name, I proclaim that _____ has a heart after God's own Heart!"*

- ☐ *"In Jesus' name, I declare Ezekiel 36:26-27 over _____. The Lord will give _____ a new heart and put a new spirit within _____. The Lord will take the heart of stone out of _____'s flesh and give _____ a heart of flesh. And the Lord will put HIS spirit within _____ and cause _____ to walk in HIS statutes, and _____ shall keep all the Lord's judgments, and do them, IN JESUS' NAME!"*

- ☐ *"In Jesus' name, I declare Jeremiah 32:39 over _____. The Lord will give _____ one heart and one way, so that _____ will fear THE LORD always, for _____'s own good and for the good of _____'s children after them, IN JESUS' NAME!"*

- ☐ *"In Jesus' name, I declare Jeremiah 24:7 over _____. The Lord will also give _____ a heart to know Me, for I am the Lord; and _____'s household and descendants will be My people, and I will be their God, for they will return to Me wholeheartedly, IN JESUS' NAME!"*

SO BE IT! SO IT IS! AMEN!

Part 9
Repentance & Salvation

The Power Of Repentance – How To Pray A Prayer Of Repentance To Remove Any Consequences Against You

Repentance is a free gift from God. We GET to repent. It's a treasure! True prophets will always tell you to repent and turn from your wicked ways in order to get ready for the next amazing thing God is doing. It's a time to prepare the way of the coming miracle, to prepare the way of the Lord, and to prepare the way of God's glory.

When praying prayers of repentance, it's important to pray targeted prayers such as, "I repent for the sin of gossiping about so and so. I'm sorry about doing or saying such and such." Once your sins are under the blood of Jesus Christ, the Bible says they're remembered no more for God's sake, not yours, His, because He doesn't want to look at your sin anymore, and He wants to bring you into Heaven with Him. So when you repent of your sins, you ask Jesus to get His blood on your sin and wash it away and erase it forever and then to release you from all consequences of your sin.

Prayer Of Repentance

- ☐ *"Father, in the name of Jesus, I repent for the sin of _____. I come before You, Father God, in Jesus' name, and I'm sorry for sinning against You by doing/saying _____. I ask the Lord Jesus to put His blood on my sin of _____ and wash it away and erase it forever. Father God, I ask for Your grace, mercy, and forgiveness. I ask You, Father, that now that the blood of Jesus is on my sin that it will be remembered no more for Your sake and that it be wiped away from the Heavens and the earth forever. I ask You, Father God, to release me from all consequences of my sin because the blood of Jesus Christ is on it. I ask You, Father God, that anything that the devil has been using against me because of my sin of _____, that You would silence him, by the blood of Jesus, and strip him of any legal right. I receive the blood of Jesus right now to speak for me so that the devil can never use this sin against me ever again, and, even if he tries, I will remind him that it's under the blood of Jesus. Amen."*

Salvation Prayers – Give Your Life To Jesus Christ
Invite The Baptism of The Holy Spirit

Salvation Prayers

Jesus said to him, "I am the way, and the truth, and the life. No one comes to the Father except through me." (John 14:6) The greatest miracle of all is the salvation of a person's soul to Jesus Christ. Maybe you've never prayed a prayer of repentance or a prayer of salvation before. If you would like to give your heart and soul to the Lord Jesus Christ and invite Him and the Holy Spirit to come into your life, join me in these prayers of salvation.

Pray Out Loud

> ☐ *"O Father God, be merciful to me, a sinner. I've missed the mark and path with my life, and I'm sorry. I need You, Father God, and I want the greatest miracle — the salvation of my soul. I repent of every sin in my life. I turn my back on the past. I renounce the devil. I receive Your Son, the Lord Jesus Christ, as Savior of my life and my soul. Come into my heart, mind, soul, and spirit, Lord Jesus, and save me right now. I receive Your salvation power, Lord Jesus. Wash me with Your blood, Lord Jesus, and cleanse me of my sins. Create in me a clean heart, and make me a new creation in YOU, Jesus. I believe that You are the Son of the living God, Lord Jesus, and that You died for my sins on the Cross and rose again three days later — alive, out of the tomb! I believe You ascended into Heaven and are seated at the right hand of Father God. I believe in the power of Your Holy Spirit, Lord, and I invite the Holy Spirit into my life right now. I belong to You now, Lord Jesus, and to Your Kingdom forever! I have now become of the family of Almighty God because of You, Lord Jesus! I proclaim this all, in Jesus' name. Amen."*

Jesus said, "I came that they may have life and have it abundantly." (John 10:10) This means a complete life full of purpose and victory! Before you can prosper your soul and in your life, Jesus must live in you and work through you, and you must invite the Holy Spirit to come and work in you and with you! It's good to also pray this to reconfirm your commitment to Jesus Christ and the Holy Spirit.

"Beloved, I wish that thou be prospered in all things and be sound, even as thy soul prospers." - 3 John 2

Jesus said: "And I will ask the Father, and he will give you another Helper, to be with you forever, even the Spirit of truth, whom the world (worldly — those in deception and away from God) cannot receive, because it neither sees him nor knows him. You know him, for he dwells with you and will be in you." - John 14:16-17

Pray Out Loud

☐ *"Lord Jesus, for too long I've kept You out of my life. I know that I am a sinner and that I cannot save myself. I repent of all my sins. No longer will I close the door when I hear You knocking. By faith, I gratefully receive Your gift of salvation. I am ready to trust You, Jesus, as my Lord and Savior. I believe Your words are true, Lord. I repent for my sins, and I ask You, Jesus, to wash away and cover all my sins and iniquities with Your blood. Come into my heart and my life, Lord Jesus, and be my Savior and my King. Thank You, Lord Jesus, for coming to earth to redeem us. I believe You are the Son of God who died on the Cross for my sins, took the keys of hell and the grave, then rose from the dead on the third day. I believe that You, Jesus, then walked the earth in your glorified body and ascended into heaven. I believe You, Lord Jesus, are seated at the right hand of the Father right now ruling and reigning over all! Thank You, Jesus, that You paid the price so I could be seated with You next to the Father and become a son/daughter of God, too. I am truly sorry for my sins against God the Father and His word and grateful that they are now all covered by Your blood, Jesus. I will not look back! I renounce everything of the kingdom of darkness. I renounce Satan, and I come out of any agreements with sin or evil! I have been redeemed by the blood of Jesus Christ out of the hand of the devil and set apart for the plans and purposes of God! Thank You, Lord Jesus, for taking on all my sins and giving me the gift of eternal life with You and access to Your Kingdom. Thank You, Father God, for Your grace, mercy, and love. Because of Your Son, Jesus, my sins are forgiven, cleansed, and remembered no more for Your sake. Father God, I ask for You to remove any consequences of my sins from me and my life. Father God, I now invite Your Holy Spirit to come and baptize me in Your Spirit! Heal my life, my body, my mind, and my soul. Heal all of my soul wounds and live inside of me and beside me and be my helper and guide me, Holy Spirit, as I move forward doing exactly what You have called me to do for the kingdom and Your glory, in Jesus' name. Amen."*

Now, Let's Start On Getting Your Soul Healed And Prospering Because Jesus Made It Possible

1. Repent for any known sins and unknown sins, and ask God for forgiveness.
2. Forgive anyone who has hurt you, and forgive yourself.
3. Ask Jesus to wash all these sins, hurts, and bitterness with His blood.
4. Thank God for His grace, mercy, and forgiveness.
5. Ask God to remember your sins no more (wipe them out).
6. Ask God to erase the sins and bitterness from your memory (wipe them out).
7. Ask the Holy Spirit, with His resurrection power, to heal your soul wounds and prosper your soul.
8. Do the "Soul Cleansing Prayer" for a deep clean here in my book.

Part 10
Spiritual Warfare

Cancel Any "Soulish" Prayers, Negative Words And Curses Off Your Life!

Excerpt From My Book: *Faith At Full Speed* **– Chapter 2**

Sometimes there are people around you who love you and want the best for you, but they may be praying their own will, opinions, or religious beliefs over your life, causing major entanglements with your progress. These are called "soulish" prayers. These are prayers and words being spoken over you, but, whatever the intention, can be coming against your prayers and worse, against God's word and will for your life. The spirit realm responds to what is being spoken over you, good or bad!

These "soulish" prayers, negative words, and curses spoken about you or over you — even the ones you have spoken yourself — can be working against what you are praying for now. It's like a "spider's web." These negative words and prayers are in the atmosphere and are trying to entangle our prayers and decrees. We need to break down any webs or entanglements in the spirit realm now. We need to cancel any negative words or soulish prayers anyone has prayed for us that are not in alignment with our prayers and decrees and forgive the people who did it. Then, ask the angelic hosts of Heaven to come and get our prayers and decrees out of any entanglements and expedite them to our Father God to be fulfilled, in Jesus' name, and ask God to release His holy fire to burn up the webs so your prayers never get entangled again!

For about a year, I found myself making progress with my prayer life and my breakthroughs. Then, there would be times of great stalling. I kept rebuking the enemy, but there was still much stalling. I asked the Holy Spirit to show me what was going on.

One morning, I saw a praying mantis caught in a web outside my bedroom window right near my place of prayer! I heard the Holy Spirit say to me that I was asking the wrong people to pray for me and that my prayers were caught up in a web — getting entangled — and not going anywhere. There were well meaning people in my life praying "soulish prayers." They were praying for their own will, opinions, and religious beliefs on me! These people meant well and some were in my own family! However, it was totally coming against and throwing confusion into the spirit realm against my own prayers.

Now, I don't ask certain people to pray for me anymore, or I tell them how to specifically pray for me! I realized in a conversation with my Mom that she had been inadvertently praying something completely different for me than I had been praying! She meant well — BUT NO — it was stalling me.

I asked her to pray like this: "Mom, just say, 'Lord, I come into agreement with what my daughter is praying for at this time.'" She happily agreed to do that.
I also realized that prayers prayed on the rosary to Mary (and Catholic saints) were actually religious prayers and UNBIBLICAL. We are supposed to pray directly to the Father in the name of Jesus, as Jesus instructed us. Soulish prayers that I had prayed in the past when I was "religious," were still in the spirit and causing entanglements with my new prayer life as a born-again believer. Those old soulish prayers were holding things back!!

I was alarmed at the fact that all these soulish and religious prayers needed to be canceled and renounced immediately. If not canceled, you could be stalled and stalled and stalled. I know you are here to learn about the acceleration of blessing and breakthroughs in your life, and this could be a major thing coming against it!

I want to be clear, I honor Mary and her faith and all the faithful ones who went before me. However, we are all saints as believers and followers of Christ. We are all kings and priests. I do not need the intercession of a saint in Heaven with God when Jesus clearly said He is the only one between us and the Father! We do have a "cloud of witnesses" that the Bible states in Hebrews 12. They are witnessing Jesus Christ's intercession for us. They are cheering for us to fulfill our assignments on the earth for Jesus to receive His reward and us to receive our rewards in Heaven. We do not need them to go to the Father for us — only Jesus Christ. He is our High Priest. We agree with what Jesus prays about us to the Father.

I might offend some of you with deep set religious beliefs. I had to overcome these old beliefs myself. I will tell you, I love all believers in Christ. I love all people. I know many Holy Spirit-filled Catholics. No matter what church or denomination you attend, I pray for the guidance of the Holy Spirit and for you to fulfill what God has called you to do. I believe Jesus is dealing with all the religious denominations right now and getting His Church back as "one" like it was in the Book of Acts. I want each person to hear from Jesus themselves on this matter, as I have.

Jesus said we will know everything by its fruit. Jesus also did not like "religious law." He was all about the kingdom and revealing who He was and is for us. I want to tell you, as soon as I canceled these soulish and religious prayers off my life, I had a huge breakthrough, great fruit, and acceleration. Confirmation! Thank You, Jesus!

Pray This Prayer To Get These Soulish Prayers Canceled ASAP

- ☐ *"Father, in the name of Your Son, Jesus, I thank You for Your grace and mercy and for hearing my prayers. Right now, I cancel and mark null and void any soulish, superstitious, or religious prayers that have been prayed by me or others over me and my life! I repent for these types of prayers because they are not in accordance with Your word and Your will. Lord Jesus, cover these sins and soulish prayers with Your blood. I ask that all these soulish, superstitious, opinionated, judgmental, religious, and false prayers be washed now from the atmosphere, blotted out of the record books, and wiped away forever by Your blood, Lord Jesus! I forgive those who have been praying these soulish, religious, and opinionated prayers. I ask Your Holy Spirit to guide me in my prayer life. I ask that all soulish, religious, and opinionated prayers coming against my breakthrough be completely removed, canceled, and marked null and void forever! I decree today that my true prayer is this _____. I ask that this prayer come directly to You, Father, in the name of Jesus, and I ask for my own prayers and decrees according to Your will, Father, that have been held up in the spirit realm to be released now directly to Your throne, Father God. I ask for restoration of any time that was held back or stalled. Thank You, Holy Spirit, for revealing this to me! I ask for Your angels to be assigned, Father God, to block any soulish, religious, or opinionated prayers being prayed against me and God's will for me, so they will never entangle or come against my prayers or decrees again, in Jesus' name! Father, in the name of Jesus, send Your holy fire to burn up all webs and anything entangling my own prayers, in Jesus' name!*

- ☐ *"I decree I am no longer in agreement with the prayers of _____. I cancel them, in the name of Jesus! Holy Spirit, please go to these people and give them guidance in their prayer life with the truth. Also, alert me any time a soulish prayer is coming against me and who I need to not ask for prayer from. I believe in the power of agreement in Your word, Father, and I will now ask for my advocate, the Holy Spirit, to come into agreement with my prayers today. I also ask for Holy Spirit-filled prayer intercessors to come into my life who pray according to Your will, Father, and in agreement with my personal prayers and decrees and I with theirs. I also come into agreement with your intercession for me, Lord Jesus! Thank You for Your mercy and grace, Father, I am excited to see Your glory at work in my life, in Jesus' name! Amen."*

If the Holy Spirit shows you a specific person in your life who is praying soulish, opinionated, or religious prayers over you, ask that their prayers be canceled, in Jesus' name!

Canceling Curses And Negative Words Decree

- ☐ *"In the name of Jesus, I rebuke and renounce every assignment of the enemy and cancel every curse or negative word ever spoken over me or my family right now! I cover every negative word in the blood of Jesus Christ, including every negative word I have ever spoken over myself. I repent for speaking any negative words over myself or anyone else. I decree that every negative word and every curse spoken against me is now null and void, in Jesus' name! I decree I am blessed, redeemed, and covered in the blood of Jesus! I have been set apart for the plans and purposes of Almighty God as a blood-bought believer in Jesus Christ! I decree the favor of God surrounds me as a shield! I decree the glory of God is my covering! I also keep up my shield of faith and extinguish every fiery dart coming against me. No weapon formed against me shall prosper, and I command every curse of witchcraft sent to harm me be returned back to the place from which it was sent, in Jesus' mighty name and by the power of His blood that covers me and protects me! Amen, and so be it!"*

Get Laser Targeted

Recently, I had another conversation about prayer with my mom, and she said, "Annamarie, you are my daughter, and I want to pray for you." Then I asked her, "What do you want to pray for me?" She told me very basic prayers like health, safety, etc. I told her; "Mom, right now, I need a breakthrough on a very specific thing." I then gave her my direction and strategy, and she was very excited to be able to pray that specifically for me! Now, she can celebrate with me when the breakthrough comes! It's awesome having my mom asking me to send her specific prayers, and it's a beautiful thing we share together! She knows now to pray directly to the Father, in Jesus' name. We have seen great breakthroughs together!

If you have a specific prayer strategy and then multiply it with more people praying for you in unity with laser targeting on a detailed specific prayer, it's going to add power to your request to God like high octane rocket fuel! This is the power of agreement. "Pray for us, that the word of the Lord may speed ahead and be honored, as happened among you." (2 Thessalonians 3:1)

LET US ALL COME INTO AGREEMENT TO EXPEDITE OUR PRAYERS TO FULFILLMENT IN OUR LIVES!

Discerning, Removing, And Avoiding The Spirit Of Divination/Python Spirit

Excerpt From My Book – *Faith At Full Speed* – Chapter 11

Discerning, Removing And Avoiding The Spirit Of Divination
(Also Known As The Python Spirit)

Now, I am not trying to scare you, I am trying to prepare you for the public life with your ministry or calling. You must have this understanding so you know how to properly and effectively deal with it. It's called a spirit of divination or "python" spirit.

I would not include it in this chapter if I did not think it was crucially important. I want you to be properly equipped. Jesus warned His disciples to be wise to these things. As soon as you launch out into the public for the kingdom, there is a sneaky evil spirit that will try to mess with you.

You may even be dealing with it right now, so let me teach you how to discern it and get rid of it. This spirit is very rampant in our society, and we as leaders must be aware. In 2 Corinthians 2:11 Paul said; "Lest satan should get an advantage of us: for we are not ignorant of his devices."

I want you to be welcoming of people who want to help you when you launch out in public, BUT you must also be wise that the enemy looks for a way in to stop you or hinder you through wrong relationships. He will try to send a person who is operating in this demonic spirit to infiltrate your inner circle, and you must know how to discern this. The bigger the impact you will have for the kingdom, the more this evil spirit tries to sneak in!

I want you to love people, and I don't want you to be paranoid at every person you meet thinking that they might be operating with a spirit of divination. That's why you must be careful to discern properly. I have had this spirit try to infiltrate my business and ministry at least three times! The more my ministry and name grew publicly, the more it seemed this spirit was trying to attack. Two were women and one was a man. It is not gender specific!

Now please don't be saying, "Gee, Annamarie if there is a chance I might get an attack from the enemy when I launch out in public with my ministry or purpose for the kingdom, then I'm not going to do it." Listen to me! You can get attacks and open a door to the enemy just sitting at home and watching the wrong shows on TV!

Your desire to be obedient to God and your calling for the kingdom should be so passionate that you will not worry about this at all and I am going to equip you right now to discern it, destroy it and keep it away for good!

First, Let's Get Discernment On The Evil Spirit Of Divination

There is a very deceptive spirit that has been operating in the world, especially at this time, and it's an antichrist spirit. A lot of people who you may know, and many around us in society, are under the deception of this spirit. It's based in witchcraft and the occult and stems from idolatry. It's been operating in all the Seven Mountains of Influence.

One of the sneaky evil spirits that operate under the antichrist spirit is the spirit of divination. It's like a python and it targets those who are powerfully and boldly representing the kingdom of God in these seven mountains. The spirit of divination tends to target ministry leaders and those in ministry with a prophetic gifting. It sneaks in looking like it's harmless and even flattering OR acts like a "copycat" and then slowly works to squeeze you into shutting down and quitting.

Now, Let's Reveal The Spirit Of Divination Also Known As The Python Spirit

The Apostle Paul dealt with this spirit early on in his ministry when he entered the Greek city of Philippi: Acts 16:16-20 (KJV), "And it came to pass, as we went to prayer, a certain young woman possessed with a spirit of divination met us, which brought her masters much gain by soothsaying; The same followed Paul and us, and cried, saying, These men are the servants of the most high God, which shew unto us the way of salvation. And this did she many days. But Paul, being grieved, turned and said to the spirit, I command thee in the name of Jesus Christ to come out of her. And he came out the same hour. And when her masters saw that the hope of their gains was gone, they caught Paul and Silas, and drew them into the marketplace unto the rulers, And brought them to the magistrates, saying, These men, being Jews, do exceedingly trouble our city,"

The SPIRIT OF DIVINATION is someone who will placate you when they think things go their way and try to destroy you when it doesn't. You would never know that they are if you were giving them everything they wanted. They expose themselves in different ways.

You have a mission to complete — a mission from God. You cannot let anyone hinder that or try to distract that no matter who they are! This spirit has to be exposed early before it does too much damage. You take authority over that spirit operating through them, and you set boundaries with them even if they are "friends." Some may even say they are "Christians." These are people with wicked spirits operating through them. Understand, it's not the person, it's the spirit operating through them!

These Are The Signs Of The Spirit Of Divination Or "Python" Spirit Operating In A Person Who Wants To Be Around You And Your Ministry Or Your Kingdom Purpose

- Gives you flattery in the beginning to pull you in, almost like a groupie — "I am your biggest fan"
- Wants what you have but is not willing to learn or work for it
- "Acts" like they have the same gifting you have and begins to mimic you to pull your followers to them
- Hogs up your time away from others
- Begins to constantly pull attention to themselves in your public setting and away from your message for the Lord
- Constantly tells you what you should do in your ministry and pushes you away from pursuing God's guidance and wants to be your only "guide"
- Squeezed feeling of pressure that comes on you after you have started listening to them or agreeing with them; you may even begin to experience shortness of breath, and difficulty swallowing
- Wants you to do everything their way; gets easily hurt or offended
- Works behind the scenes to pull people to "their side" to put pressure on you to do what they want
- They focus on dividing you away from your people and your people away from you
- May have been involved in witchcraft or New Age practices and never got fully delivered (you will see the signs on their social media – take the time to check them out and what they post)
- In group settings, they are not eager to pray for anyone else's issues; they want most of the prayer for themselves
- Tries to prophesy over your followers and counter what God has spoken to you over them without your consent (if you have a prophetic ministry)
- Usually avoids Communion time and any type of worship of Jesus; more drawn to the supernatural stuff
- Tries to compare you and your ministry to what everyone else is doing; tells you that you should do that
- Cries and weeps alot and uses guilt to manipulate you; wants to have access to you even at night to pull you away from family
- Usually a "loner-type" person; has trouble with relationships; has been through many churches
- Focused on getting constant prophetic words and squeezing/pressuring you to give them every day to them; gets overly needy
- Never carries out what you advise them to do; you see no fruit, just more drama
- When they tire you out, they try to act in your place and influence your people and followers
- Sometimes they act like a "prophet" and give false prophetic words that are coming from familiar spirits instead of the Holy Spirit
- Tells you they have "angels" talking to them all the time, but they do not have a relationship with the Holy Spirit
- Thrives in constant drama and strife
- Brags how they told off church leaders, pastors, or people of authority
- Usually shows up at a time you are close to a breakthrough

- When you try to use boundaries with them they get offended and accuse you of not being a loving Christian
- They profess love for you but are always questioning your message and your strategies (a person truly sent by God would resonate and support your message and respect you and your strategies.)

Understand that the spirit of divination partners with the religious spirit, and it will find others operating with a religious spirit to try and gang up on you and accuse you of ruining things for them and not being a caring or loving Christian if you call out their behavior. You must be careful to keep your emotions in check.

Observe all this wisely, stay calm, and prepare to strike this down behind the scenes. Do not get caught up in the drama around this person.

So what do you do about this situation? What if this person has embedded themselves in your life, business, and ministry? How can you deal with this spirit and still love them? How do you discern this before it takes over and squeezes you until you are so distracted that you cannot fully function for the Lord and your calling and your faith starts struggling?

PLEASE LISTEN TO ME! When you have faith even as small as a mustard seed, you don't have to compromise or "put up with" anything or anybody that comes against your faith! Jesus Christ is the author and finisher of your faith only! What you do with your faith and calling in this life, nobody has any right to try and change, attack, question, force their will, squeeze, or twist it in any way!

- GUARD AND PROTECT YOUR FAITH AND MISSION AT ALL COSTS!
- KNOW NO WILL BUT THE FATHER'S FOR YOUR LIFE!
- HIS WILL IS FOR YOU TO HAVE ALL THE PROMISES OF HIS WORD!
- DO NOT LET THE ENEMY TOUCH YOUR PROMISES!
- CRUSH THE ENEMY UNDER YOUR FEET!

Jesus gave you AUTHORITY to destroy and crush anything that would come against you! "Listen carefully: I have given you authority [that you now possess] to tread on serpents and scorpions, and [the ability to exercise authority] over all the power of the enemy (satan); and nothing will [in any way] harm you." – Luke 10:19 (AMP)

What did the Apostle Paul do? He took authority over the spirit of divination/python operating through the girl and commanded it to leave! He did not rebuke the girl, he rebuked the evil spirit. Paul discerned it quickly and nipped it in the bud! How did Paul discern it? Read the scripture — the girl kept on pressuring him and even drawing attention to herself while Paul was trying to preach the Gospel, something Paul did to bring "Good News" to a new town. He was usually filled with the joy of the Lord doing this. However, when this girl was around, it says, "But Paul, being grieved …." That's the opposite of joy! Paul began to feel grieved in the spirit. That means this evil spirit was coming against the work of the HOLY SPIRIT operating through Paul!

This is exactly what I went through when I had this happen to me, and let me tell you, you will feel this too if you have this situation. The python/divination spirit will cause you to feel grieved, frustrated, and distracted, even stressed and depressed. Pressure comes around your throat and heaviness on your chest. You begin to feel weary and do not feel like moving forward. If this persists, it could cause you to question what you are doing and to start thinking that maybe that person could do it better, blah blah blah …. This gets worse the more you agree with this evil lying spirit.

I want you to understand something. People can try to copy you, try to steal your ideas, try to do what you do, but they can never do what God gifted you to do just like you. Never. People will try to steal your special "recipe," but it will not taste the same when they try to use it without your anointing! Stay focused even when an attack like this comes. The best thing you can do is stand and not be shaken one bit.

Stay focused on the words of Jesus Christ when discerning relationships. Is it building up and creating abundance or tearing down? Jesus made it clear how to discern what was from Him and what was not in John 10:10, "The thief comes only in order to steal and kill and destroy. I [Jesus] came that they may have and enjoy life, and have it in abundance (to the full, till it overflows)."

The spirit of divination will try to play with your emotions, make you feel unsettled and unfocused, try to trip up your work in public, and pressure you to make you quit. They will try to shadow your light. It wants to tear down what you are building. You cannot allow it!! You have to take authority over it ASAP and here are the steps below.

How To Take Authority Against The Spirit Of Divination

If the person is being overly difficult you do not have to confront them. You can take care of this all in the spirit realm in prayer. Remember, it's not the person, it's the evil spirit operating through them.

1. Suit Up

Get on your armor of God, take your Seat of Authority, and apply the blood of Jesus to yourself, your family, your ministry, and your business.

2. Forgive And Repent

Forgive the person who is doing this, and repent for any bitterness or offense you have toward them. Ask Jesus to wash your sins in His blood and put all offense and bitterness on the Cross. Ask God to bless the person you are forgiving and for the Holy Spirit to go to them and lead them fully to Christ and to remove all veils of deception from their eyes of understanding and bring them to deliverance. If we do not forgive them, the accuser can use our unforgiveness against us, and the evil spirit will still have a legal right to operate.

3. Ask God To Remove The Person And All Their Influence Out Of Your Business And Ministry With His "Ax Of Judgment"

Do this prayer after you have forgiven the person. If you can clearly see that this individual is not there to produce good fruit for you or anyone else, you can stand on the word of God in this situation. Jesus said we would know them by their fruit, and the bad fruit is to be removed. Relationships in the Bible are mentioned in comparison to trees that either produce good fruit or bad fruit. Fruit coming from a relationship should always bear the fruit of the Holy Spirit. If not, that relationship will be removed by God. You must be able to bear good fruit in all of your relationships for the kingdom. If any relationship is clearly coming against that, such as those operating in divination, you can pray this prayer powerfully. The Ax of God's Judgment Prayer is based on Matthew 3:10, "Even now the ax of God's judgment is poised, ready to sever the roots of the trees. Yes, every tree that does not produce good fruit will be chopped down and thrown into the fire."

Pray Out Loud

- ☐ *"Father God, Your word says in Matthew 3:10, 'Now also the axe is laid unto the root of the trees: therefore every tree which bringeth not forth good fruit is hewn down, and cast into the fire.' Father, I believe Your word, and I want to activate it right now in the spiritual and in the natural in my life and in all my relationships! I do not have to accept anything that is not the will of God for my life, my family, my ministry, or my business. I BELIEVE that the word of God is the will of God! I DECREE as for me and my house we shall honor and obey the word and the will of God and serve the Lord Jesus Christ for all generations thereof! Father, in the name of Jesus Christ, I ask You to take Your ax of judgment and permanently remove any ungodly relationships around me swiftly, particularly _____, in Jesus' name! Chop these ungodly relationships and influences at the root. Pull the stumps up out of the ground, shake the stumps with no roots remaining in the ground, and cast this relationship and any influence it had into the fire to burn to ashes, in Jesus' name! I will never eat fruit from this ungodly relationship again! Father, let all remaining influence from this relationship be burned up forever by Your holy fire, in Jesus' name. Let this be swift and calm, with no recourse or backlash. Let Your holy fire burn up any bad seed left from this ungodly relationship. We know that it's the relationship that is removed and burned to ashes and all their influence, not the person. I have prayed for the person to move on and into what You have for them Lord, but far away from me and my _____, in Jesus' name!*

- ☐ *"Thank You, Father, for Your word and Your promises and the ability to discern good and bad fruit! Father, replace any bad, ungodly relationships with Holy Spirit-filled relationships to bear good fruit together for Your kingdom and glory, in Jesus' name! Amen."*

4. Declare This Out Loud To Sever All Soul Ties With That Person

- ☐ *"By the authority of Jesus Christ, I break the power of and sever off ALL the demonic and ungodly strongholds and soul ties off of myself and _____ FOREVER, in Jesus' name. I now wash myself and _____ in the blood of Jesus and invite the Holy Spirit to come and fill those places in myself and _____ where the old soul ties have departed, in Jesus' name."*

5. Get The Python Removed

Get the python removed off of you if you have been getting a "smothering or choking feeling". I would still do this prayer either way.

Stand And Pray Out Loud

- ☐ *"In the name and authority of Jesus Christ, I command the python spirit to drop off of my body and onto the floor, in Jesus' mighty name! Python spirit, I renounce you and all of your evil, and I command you off of me and under my feet right now, in Jesus' name! Drop off of me NOW, python! I take authority over you in the Name above all names, Jesus Christ! Drop NOW to the ground, in Jesus' name! (Take a breath, raise your sword of the Spirit, and continue on.) In the name of Jesus Christ, I crush the head of the python spirit (stomp your foot on its head in the spirit), and I take my sword of the Spirit and chop this python to pieces! (make a chopping motion on the floor below you) I chop you up python! Your head was crushed by the Cross of Jesus Christ, and I crush you! You have been cursed by God, you vile python spirit, and I curse you and destroy you to pieces! You will never touch me again, python! I scrape your chopped carcass into the fire of God to be burned to ashes (do a scraping motion with your sword of the Spirit). Let the breath of the Holy Spirit of the living God blow what is left of you, python, into the dry, uninhabited place where you will stay forever, in Jesus' name!*

☐ *"I raise up my sword of the Spirit and let the fire of the Holy Spirit cleanse my sword! Let the fresh breath of the Holy Spirit fill my lungs! I breathe You in, Holy Spirit, in Jesus' name. I am free and delivered from python forever! Holy Spirit, I ask You to pour fresh oil on me, so much oil that no python can ever attach to me again. It will slide off of me because of the abundance of anointing, in Jesus' name! I declare that I move freely and breathe freely, in the natural and in the spiritual. Those whom Christ has set free are free indeed! I am fully free in Christ Jesus! I place myself — mind, body, soul, and spirit — in the blood of Jesus Christ forever! Through the blood of Jesus Christ, I am redeemed from all evil and set apart for the plans and purposes of the kingdom of God, and nothing shall come against it, in Jesus' mighty name!"*

6. Ask God For Sentry Angels

Ask Father God, in Jesus' name, to assign and station "sentry angels" at the gates of your home, business, ministry, and all around you personally to block these evil spirits.

Decree Out Loud

☐ *"In the name and authority of Jesus Christ in whom I am seated, I thank You, Father, that You send Your angels to keep me in all my ways. I ask You, Father God, to release to me sentry angels that will protect all of my gateways. Thank You, Father God. Therefore, in Jesus' name and authority, I command and post my divinely assigned sentry angels of the Lord to these gateway areas to my _____, both the natural gates and the spiritual gates to my _____, including all gates to all the gates of communication, phones, computers, internet, social media, email, and websites that I have. I command the sentry angels of the Lord that I have just posted to these specific areas to stand and protect these areas from all evil with fiery swords and shields 24 hours a day, seven days a week from this day forward, in Jesus' name! I command my sentry angels of the Lord to not allow anything that is not of God to enter or come near any of my gates, in Jesus' name. I apply the blood of Jesus Christ to all of the gateways to my _____, in the natural and in the spiritual. All of my gates belong to Jesus Christ! I ask my sentry angels of the Lord to also go and locate, arrest, bind, and remove any evil spirits that may have come in my gates and block those evil spirits from coming in or coming near my gates or near me ever again! I renounce those evil spirits, and especially the spirit of divination is strictly prohibited from entering or coming near me, my _____, or my gates from this day forward, in Jesus' name!*

- ☐ *"Thank you, sentry angels of the Lord, for your obedience and faithfulness to God, and thank You, Father, for my authority in Christ Jesus to receive and command my assigned angels of Your kingdom, for Your glory forever and ever! Amen!"*

DO THESE STEPS UNTIL YOU SEE THE BREAKTHROUGH!

It's crucial that you do not waiver or let this spirit of divination/python manipulate you for too long! It comes against the good fruit that you are meant to produce for the kingdom of God!

Pray This Out Loud To Ask God To Release His Holy Fire Into You

- ☐ *"In the name and authority of Jesus Christ, I renounce and come out of agreement with all religious spirits and words and out of agreement with all spirits of divination and words and command them off of my mind, body, soul, and spirit right now, in Jesus' name! LEAVE ME NOW, YOU VILE SPIRITS! I send the fire of the Holy Spirit against you! Get out and go to the uninhabited dry place and stay there until Jesus Christ comes and tells you where to go, and never come near me again! I close the door to these evil, vile spirits and seal it with the blood of Jesus Christ forever!*

- ☐ *"I invite the fire of the Holy Spirit of Almighty God to come in me now and burn in every place in me and around me to destroy any remnant of these evil spirits and to refine me and make me excellent of soul with your DUNAMIS power, Holy Spirit, in Jesus' name. Holy Spirit, I ask You to fill every place in me and stand hold there forever! I declare a divine wall of Holy Spirit fire is now around me protecting me, and if any evil spirit tries to pass through this wall of holy fire, they will be burned up to ashes, in Jesus' mighty name! Amen."*

You will begin to feel a huge positive difference. I am telling you, you'll feel lighter and that heaviness and guilt will be gone! You will begin to accelerate in your public life and message like never before! My students and I have had incredible results from doing this. The growth and increase will come almost immediately. It's like burning off the dead grass in a pasture, driving out the snakes to have new green, beautiful pastures with nothing harmful hiding that can trip you up! FREEDOM!

The people in question also need deliverance from these evil spirits! Pray that the Holy Spirit will go to them and lead them to full deliverance. You can also pray those deliverance prayers over that person in the natural or in the spirit. In the meantime, don't let one or two deceived people that are trying to upset your mission ruin it for so many more who really need you and are truly sent by God.

Get mad at the devil, not the person. Be solution-oriented in the spirit realm! These evil spirits are more afraid of us when we come in the name of Jesus Christ. We are their worst fear! Remember that!

The devil can't stop you through any person or situation. You have authority over all of it. You are a representative of the King of glory who crushed the kingdom of darkness! All you have to do is enforce the finished work of the CROSS and the BLOOD of Christ in the name of Jesus! You have all access credentials to everything the kingdom of God has!

The Cross and the blood of Jesus is your KEY, but you must use it and enforce it in your Seat of Authority. The fire of the Holy Spirit can be called forth by faith to burn up and chase out any remnant operating in and around you that is hidden.

Flash your badge of the blood and the Cross and blind the enemy! Make the enemy bow the knee to Jesus Christ! You carry the authority through Christ! The devil has no teeth!
Jesus already gave YOU victory over all the works of the enemy! You must put ON the blood of Christ every day in the spirit and wear it like an official credential to get you through every gate and door of influence you want to get into! Keep going. Do not stop for any distractions, even people who try to distract you! Do not allow it. Deal with it swiftly!

RESOURCE

Get my book: Faith At Full Speed – Your High Horsepower Manual To Success
www.annamariestrawhand.com

Discerning The Spirit Of Discord In Your Life And Removing It: Revelation And Prayers

MAKE SURE YOU READ THIS FULL TEACHING BEFORE YOU TRY TO CAST OUT THIS SPIRIT!!!

1. Revelation

Last week, while doing a spiritual walk-through of a student's house, the Holy Spirit kept showing me shoelaces without shoes. I saw it over and over in the spirit. Then, even after that session, I was seeing it. I kept asking the Holy Spirit what it meant. I saw the shoelaces again in the spirit throughout the week. They were the kind that are more like a cord.

This morning, I was praying for my daughter and had a vision. I saw a dark figure with a bunch of messy hair on top of its head. I asked, "Who are you?" He said, "I am DISCORD!!!" I was like, "What? That's it! The shoelaces without shoes! Dis-cord!" I thought, "Well, It was first revealed at the student's house then again through the week here and then again this morning with my own prayer and family. So this must be for many of us here, not just her. It's come out of the closet!" It's interesting that I discerned it during a spiritual house walk-through when she was in her closet. That's when it started to show me the shoelaces. This is a very sneaky spirit! The student had been dealing with much strife and discord coming against her, so this was confirmation. I have researched this "discord spirit," and with the revelation of the Holy Spirit, this is how we pray against it and kick it out!!!

THE SPIRIT OF DISCORD COMES TO LOOSEN AND DISRUPT YOUR SHOES OF PEACE!

2. More Revelation On The Spirit Of Discord

It comes in through a "sower." In other words, someone had to have access to you and your family at some point to "sow" the seeds of this spirit to take root and operate. This is connected to Proverbs 6:12-19, "A naughty person, a wicked man, walketh with a froward mouth. He winketh with his eyes, he speaketh with his feet, he teacheth with his fingers; Frowardness is in his heart, he deviseth mischief continually; he soweth discord. Therefore shall his calamity come suddenly; suddenly shall he be broken without remedy. These six things doth the LORD hate: yea, seven are an abomination unto him: A proud look, a lying tongue, and hands that shed innocent blood, An heart that deviseth wicked imaginations, feet that be swift in running to mischief, A false witness that speaketh lies, and he that soweth discord among brethren."

GOD ACTUALLY SENT A SPIRIT OF DISCORD ON PURPOSE TO THE ENEMIES OF ISRAEL!! He caused division and emnity in the enemies' house/camp to avenge and judge what they did against His people. (Judges 9:23-25)

After God sent the discord into the enemies' camp, they ended up having strife among themselves. This was similar to God hardening Pharaoh's heart in order to get His people delivered across the Red Sea and to render judgment on Pharaoh's army.

Similarly, God will also cause your enemies to fall into the pit they dug for you. Can you ask God to render judgment on those who have caused or sowed discord in your life? I believe so, YES, according to this word!

Judges 9:23-25 Complete Jewish Bible (CJB): "23 But God sent a spirit of discord between Avimelekh and the men of Sh'khem, so that the men of Sh'khem dealt treacherously with Avimelekh. 24 This came about so that the crime against the seventy sons of Yeruba'al might be avenged and the responsibility for their bloody death be placed on Avimelekh their brother, who murdered them, and on the men of Sh'khem, who helped him kill his brothers. 25 So the men of Sh'khem sent out men to ambush him on the mountaintops. They robbed everyone who went past them, and Avimelekh was told about it."

WOW!! God will avenge your enemies by sending discord — the thing they did to you and even worse! I believe this connects to the ax of God's judgment that Matthew 3:10 spoke of too — that God will remove every bad tree that does not produce good fruit, and you can ask Him to judge anything according to His word!

See my "Ax of God's Judgment Prayer" here in the book.

Remember, these prayers are not going to hurt "people." It's the spirit operating through them and its effects, powers, and influences that God will remove. Why should we not repay evil for evil? (Romans 12:19) Because we are told, "Never avenge yourselves, but leave it to the wrath of God, for it is written, 'Vengeance is mine, I will repay, says the Lord.'"

Decree Out Loud

> ☐ *"Father, I ask You, in the name of Jesus, to render judgment on the spirit of discord coming against my life and expose those who are the seed sowers of discord! I ask You, Father, to send Your judgment of discord to those who have caused discord against Your people, including my family and me, in Jesus' name! Father, I ask according to Your word in Judges 9:23-25, that by Your judgment, You will send a spirit of discord to those who have come against me and have sent discord into my life. Father, You said that You will repay those who have done evil to me. I believe Your word is true, and You are fighting for me right now and coming against all who are sowing discord in my life, in Jesus' name! Thank You, Father God, for being my Defender and Righteous Judge in all things! Amen."*

3. More Revelation On The Spirit Of Discord

It comes in as a seed and grows as a weed to sow more seeds into your family and against your good harvest! This is the season of REVEALING and destroying these weeds (tares). They are being revealed! These tares must be bundled, removed, and cast into the fire of God!!

THIS WAS REVEALED TO ME ON AUGUST 29, 2019, THE FIRST DAY OF THE HEBREW MONTH OF ELUL — "THE KING IS IN THE FIELD"

The apostle Paul wrote, "You are God's field, you are God's building" (1Corinthians 3:9). Throughout this passage, Paul makes it very clear that though he or another minister may have sown seed or tended and watered, it was God who gave the increase. God controls His field and what it produces for harvest (1Corinthians 3:5-9).

HE COMES TO CHECK ON THAT FIELD AT THE TIME OF HARVEST

Check Your Households – Check Your Hearts! Is There Discord?

- Enmity (putting another person against the other)
- Quarreling
- Strife
- Jealousy
- Prolonged anger
- Fits of anger
- Hostility
- Rivalries
- Slander
- Dissensions
- Gossip
- Divisions
- Conceit
- Envy
- Disorder
- Chaos

Galatians 5:19-21 (ESV): "Now the works of the flesh are evident: sexual immorality, impurity, sensuality, 20 idolatry, sorcery, enmity, strife, jealousy, fits of anger, rivalries, dissensions, divisions, 21 envy, drunkenness, orgies, and things like these. I warn you, as I warned you before, that those who do such things will not inherit the kingdom of God."

2 Corinthians 12:20 (ESV): "For I fear that perhaps when I come I may find you not as I wish, and that you may find me not as you wish — that perhaps there may be quarreling, jealousy, anger, hostility, slander, gossip, conceit, and disorder."

DISCORD COMES AGAINST THE FRUIT OF THE HOLY SPIRIT IN YOUR LIFE. JESUS WANTS TO SEE GOOD FRUIT AND ABUNDANT HARVEST IN HIS PEOPLE.

The Lord Jesus Christ gave this parable immediately following the parable of the sower. Notice what He said: "The kingdom of heaven is like a man who sowed good seed in his field; but while men slept, his enemy came and sowed tares among the wheat and went his way. But when the grain had sprouted and produced a crop, then the tares also appeared.

"'So the servants of the owner came and said to him, 'Sir, did you not sow good seed in your field? How then does it have tares?' He said to them, 'An enemy has done this.' The servants said to him, 'Do you want us then to go and gather them up?'

"'But he said, 'No, lest while you gather up the tares you also uproot the wheat with them. Let both grow together until the harvest, and at the time of harvest I will say to the reapers, 'First gather together the tares and bind them in bundles to burn them, but gather the wheat into my barn.'" (Matthew13:24-30)

Prayer Of Repentance - Pray Out Loud

- ☐ *"Father, in the name of Jesus, I repent for any seeds of discord that I have ever knowingly or unknowingly sowed into my life, my family, or anyone else's life. I repent for ever coming into agreement with discord. Lord Jesus, cover my sins with Your blood and wash me clean. Cover all acts of discord that I have done in my life with Your blood, Jesus, and render them all null and void. I am sorry, Father God, for disobeying Your word and coming against the fruit of the Holy Spirit. I ask, Father, that You remember these sins no more, and wipe them from the record books of Heaven, in Jesus' name. Father, I ask now for grace, mercy, and forgiveness by the blood of Jesus Christ. If anyone has been hurt or affected by my sins of sowing discord, I ask now for them to be blessed and restored, in Jesus' name. I no longer want to sow seeds of discord! I rebuke discord and every evil spirit connected with it! Holy Spirit, give me guidance and check me and correct me so I only sow seeds that will grow the fruit of Your Holy Spirit from this day forward! Thank You, Father. Thank You, Jesus! Amen."*

Decree Out Loud

- ☐ *"Father, in the name of Jesus and through the Holy Spirit, expose the seed sowers of discord in my life and remove them far, far away from me. I command every seed of discord ever sowed into my life by me or anyone else to shrivel and die at the root now and all fruit of discord and its seeds be plucked up now and cast into the fire of God, burned to ashes, never to come back, in Jesus' name!! I renounce the spirit of discord and command it to leave, in Jesus' name!!! Holy Spirit, I invite You to come and fill every place the spirit of discord has vacated and stand hold here forever to bear Your good fruits, in Jesus' name!"*

Note: Before you do any prayers asking for angels on assignment or prayers of deliverance where you are binding demonic powers, make sure you are suited up!

What this means is you have put on your FULL ARMOR OF GOD, AND YOU HAVE TAKEN YOUR SEAT OF AUTHORITY NEXT TO THE FATHER IN CHRIST JESUS. Also make sure you have applied the blood of Jesus to yourself, your family, and your household before you speak these prayers.

See my "Daily Suit Up Prayer" here in the book.

MY PRAYER TO REMOVE THE TARES – WEEDS/SEEDS OF DISCORD

Pray This Prayer Out Loud To Ask For Harvest Angels

- ☐ *"Father, I thank You for the blessings and abundance You have promised for my life and the life of my loved ones — my family, marriage, household, and children, _____. Father, Your word is true and good, and I praise You for Your faithfulness in our lives. Today, Father, I am calling in Harvest Angels into my life and family now, in Jesus' name. In Your word, Jesus teaches us in Matthew 13:24 that the enemy comes in when we are not looking and sows tares and weeds into our harvest fields. I decree that my family, _____, are ripe for the harvest for Jesus Christ right now.*

- ☐ *"In the name of Jesus, I ask You, Father, to release Your Harvest Angels into my life, my family, and my household's field of harvest. I ask, in the name of Jesus, for the Harvest Angels to go right now and pull up at the root every weed and tare that the kingdom of darkness has sowed in our family's harvest field. Pull up at the root every ungodly relationship and evil influence that has sowed the seeds of discord at the roots and bundle them and cast them into Your holy fire to be burned to ashes! Destroy every seed and weed of discord ever planted in my life and family and cast those seeds and weeds into the fire of God! I decree that every single seed of discord ever planted in my life, family, and household is now removed, burned up, and can never return or grow again, in Jesus' name!*

- ☐ *"I decree that my family, my household, these specific loved ones, _____, and I are ripe for the harvest for the Lord Jesus Christ. I also ask, Father, that my family, my household, and I be harvested right now like good wheat by Your Harvest Angels, and that we would be bundled and put safely into the barn of our Master, Jesus Christ, and that the harvest fields of my household would now be covered in the blood of Jesus, fully protected from any seeds of discord from this day forward, in Jesus' mighty name! As for me and my house, we shall serve the Lord! Amen."*

A POWERFUL Act Of Faith

Sow a seed offering to a fertile ministry in the name of your loved one as a seed to come to harvest for the LORD.

PRAYER TO PLANT GOOD SEEDS

Pray This Prayer, "Sowing Of Good Seed," Out Loud

- ☐ *"Father, I thank You for who You are and all that You do for us. Today, I lift up my life and my loved ones, _____, to You in prayer. I thank You, Father, for our lives and the plans and purposes You have for me and my family. Father, in the name of Jesus, I decree over myself and my loved ones, _____, that we become the fertile ground that our Lord Jesus speaks about in Matthew 13:18, 'Still other seed fell on good soil, where it produced a crop — a hundred, sixty, or thirty times what was sown.' Father, I ask in the name of Jesus, that You would release Your Sower Angels to sow good seeds into _____. I ask that these seeds would actually be Holy Spirit-filled and godly mentors, friendships, and influences to come into our lives and that we can also be this to each other. I ask that, through the help of Your Holy Spirit working with the Sower Angels, these "good seeds" be ushered into my life, my home, and my family right now. I ask that the Sower Angels go and gather these Holy Spirit-ordained influences and bring them into the path of _____ as soon as possible. Father God, I am declaring your word in Genesis 1:11, 'And God said, Let the earth bring forth grass, the herb yielding seed, and the fruit tree yielding fruit after his kind, whose seed is in itself, upon the earth: and it was so.' Show me and instruct me and my loved ones how to plant good seeds that yield good fruit of the Holy Spirit! Help us Lord to desire and have understanding of sowing and reaping in the way You, Father God, intended for us, that we are a family after Your own heart, Father God!*

- ☐ *"I am also asking, Father, for Your divinely inspired books, videos, music, events, and teachings to come as an opportunity to us in an unexpected way. Usher this in through Your angelic assistance to plant a good seed in our hearts and minds, that we'll be fully walking with Jesus Christ. I am asking for these new Holy Spirit-filled relationships and influences that You have for our lives to take root and grow to help _____ have a closer and deeper relationship with You, Father, and begin to walk in their divine calling and purpose. I pray that all these seeds of faith, peace, love, holiness, unity, prosperity, joy, and patience come to an abundant harvest in our lives with abundant fruit of the Holy Spirit being produced in my family and household forever, for Your glory, in Jesus' name. Amen."*

Decree Out Loud

- ☐ *"As for me and my household, we serve the Lord God of Israel, the God of Abraham, Isaac, and Jacob! Yahweh is my Father God, my Creator! The Holy One of Israel and His only Son, Jesus Christ of Nazareth, Yeshua Messiah is my Lord and King forever. I invite You, Lord Jesus, Yeshua, into my home. I surrender every room to You, Lord. I surrender my marriage and children to You, Lord Jesus! I also invite You, Holy Spirit, to come now and fill my home and family with Your presence! You are welcome here, Lord Jesus and Holy Spirit!! Have Your way, Lord, in this home and family! I decree the shalem and shalom of the Lord is upon my household and family. We are whole, complete, nothing missing, nothing lacking, nothing broken! Therefore, nothing from the kingdom of darkness can dwell here! We will never serve the kingdom of darkness! Get out, Satan!! We only serve the kingdom of Almighty God in this house! As for me and my family, we are covered in the blood of the Lamb of God, the blood of the Lord Jesus Christ, Yeshua. We have been redeemed out of the hand of the devil and set apart for God by the blood of the Lord Jesus Christ!! I decree that my family and household are filled with the peace of Almighty God, and we also have the supernatural protection of the blood of Christ and the kingdom of Almighty God. I put the shoes of peace on myself and my family members. These shoes of peace are bound to us by the Gospel of the Lord Jesus Christ and can never be loosened or removed, in Jesus, Yeshua's mighty name!"*

PRAYER TO DEDICATE AND ANOINT YOUR HOME

Learn How To Anoint Your Home - See my teaching, "How To Pray Over And Apply Anointing Oil," here in the book or on my website, to learn how to anoint your home as you pray this prayer below.

Room By Room Prayer - (Can be done while you anoint the doors, windows and items in the room.)

- ☐ *"Father, because of the blood of Jesus and His FINISHED work on the cross, the devil has been defeated. I take ahold of this right now as my restraining order against all evil. According to Ephesians 2, I am seated next to You, Father, in Christ. I thank You, Father God, for my new authority in Christ given to me. Because of this authority, I now rule and reign in Christ Jesus and put everything of the kingdom of darkness under my feet because it is all under the feet of King Jesus. Therefore, I enforce the blood of Jesus and the finished work of the cross over and in every room of my home. I invite you, King Jesus, to be Lord over every room and every space in this home. I declare, through the blood of Jesus, that my home has now been redeemed out of the hand of the devil and back in the hand of Almighty God! Now, each room is set aside for the plans and purposes of God. I consecrate and dedicate this home and everything in it to You, Almighty God! King Jesus, I invite You to stay with us here in our home! Let the blessings and protection of the kingdom of God come forth in and through every room of my home, in Jesus' name!*

- ☐ *"According to Psalm 91:1, I declare that this _____ (room), Father God, has been transformed in the spirit into Your secret place and that it abides now under Your shadow. I repent for and renounce every sin that was ever committed in this _____ (room) of my house, including but not limited to all sins listed in I Corinthians 6:9-10 — indulgence of sexual sins, idolatry, adultery, prostitution, homosexuality, theft, greed, drunkenness, abuse of any kind, and cheating or extortion of any kind."*

Go To The Center Of Your Home And Pray This Out Loud Over Your Entire Home

- ☐ *"I place this home and all of its residents in the mighty blood of Jesus. In the name of Jesus Christ, I take authority over every evil spirit, evil influence, discord, and even hidden evil things that have inhabited this home or affected it in any way and command them all to leave this house now and go to the uninhabited dry place and stay there! Get out and never come back, in Jesus' name! I now ask the Holy Spirit to come and fill every place those evil spirits and influences vacated and stand hold there. I close any and all doors to the kingdom of darkness and seal them with the blood of Jesus!!"*

- ☐ *"I place everything below this house, in this house, and above this house in the blood of Jesus! Lord Jesus, release the power of your blood! Your blood, Jesus, destroys all curses and demonic assignments right now, in Jesus' name! I proclaim this house — every room, every item, every space, every molecule of air — everything in this house is now cleansed and sanctified by the blood of Jesus!"*

- ☐ *"Father God, in the name of Jesus Christ, I ask for You to post Your sentry angels to all of the gateway areas of my home — natural, spiritual, and digital — to keep watch and guard around the clock and protect these gates from all evil! I ask for the sentry angels of Almighty God to stop and destroy any evil or demonic assignments that would attempt to go in or out through any and all gateways of my home with their supernatural fiery swords and shields from this day forward, in Jesus' name!*

- ☐ *"Holy Spirit, I ask You now to come in and breathe Your fresh breath of life into every room in my home and the surrounding property at _____ (address). Fill every space with Your love, joy, happiness, peace, and truth, in Jesus' name. Thank You, Holy Spirit, that my home and property are now filled with Your holy presence from this day forward! Amen."*

Finishing Up

After you pray over and anoint every room of your home (I do all the doorways and windows), stand in the middle of your home and play the recording of the shofar (loud) in your home. This is the sound of the trumpet in Zion to take out any spiritual enemies and call forth the hosts of Heaven to fight for you, according to Nehemiah 4:20. Here is a recording that I use: "12min Of Non-Stop Shofar" on YouTube.

Then, decree the Aaronic Blessing, found in Numbers 6:22-27, or play the recording in Hebrew in your home.

You can refer to the anointing prayers here in this book, and prayers for spiritual housecleaning for more.

Fourth Watch Prayer For Deliverance

If the Holy Spirit wakes you up at a certain time, particularly 3am, that is the beginning of the FOURTH WATCH. Biblically, and according to God's timing in the Hebrew calendar, the Fourth Watch is from 3am - 6am. It is a time of DELIVERANCE.

The Fourth Watch time is when the Red Sea parted and the children of Israel were delivered from their enemies and captivity and into freedom and the promise of God.

The Fourth Watch is when Jesus calmed the storm and also walked on the water. The Fourth Watch is when Jesus was being pressed in the Garden of Gethsemane and took on the cup of our sin.

The Fourth Watch is when the STONE rolled away from the tomb and when Jesus Christ was resurrected.

You are being awakened at that time to get out of bed and pray for deliverance for yourself, your family, and your loved ones.

Get Up and Pray During The Fourth Watch Time (3am - 6am)

DELIVERANCE PRAYERS SHOULD BE PRAYED DURING THE 4th WATCH! It's the time of day (early morning watch 3am - 6am) known as a time of deliverance in the Bible with many mighty miracles happening at that time. If you need deliverance from something or you know a loved one who needs deliverance, set your clock to awaken at this time, and pray this powerful prayer, speaking their name out loud.

- ☐ *"Father GOD, YOU are the great and mighty DELIVERER! Today is the day of _____'s deliverance! In the name of Jesus, I decree Your word in Exodus 13:3 over _____. This is the day to remember forever! Today is the day of _____ leaving Egypt and slavery; for the Lord has brought _____ out with mighty miracles, in JESUS' MIGHTY NAME!! AMEN. PRAISE BE TO GOD!"*

Prayers And Decrees Against Witchcraft

This is an edited transcript - as spoken by Annamarie during her broadcast

First: Make sure you are suited up in the morning with the armor of God and have taken your Seat of Authority in Christ and that you, your family members, and your home are covered in the blood of Jesus.

See my "Daily Suit Up Prayer" here in the book.

Speak Out Loud For Your Own Prayer - This Is Even More Powerful To Speak While Taking Communion

- ☐ "By the authority of Jesus Christ and the power of the blood of Jesus, I speak against every curse of witchcraft that has been sent to harm me, my household, or my children. In the name of Jesus Christ and by the power of the blood of Jesus, I renounce all witchcraft curses. I take authority over them in the name of Jesus. I break the power of all witchcraft and all witchcraft curses in the name of Jesus. I command all witchcraft and all witchcraft curses to be null and void, in Jesus' name. I enforce the blood of Jesus Christ against all witchcraft. I enforce the blood of Jesus Christ against all witchcraft curses, and I command all witchcraft to go under the blood of Jesus Christ right now. I proclaim the word of God that a curse causeless cannot light! Therefore, all witchcraft curses have been made causeless by the blood of Jesus right now, in Jesus' name!

- ☐ "Bow the knee to Jesus Christ, all you witches, all you warlocks, all you witchcraft curses, all you witchcraft incantations! I enforce the blood of Jesus Christ against you! Bow the knee unto the Lord Jesus Christ! Kingdom of darkness, I take authority over you in the name of Jesus in whom I am seated in — the Name above all names, King of kings, Jesus Christ! I remind you now, kingdom of darkness, that you were defeated at Calvary by the finished work of the Cross of Jesus Christ. I enforce the blood of Jesus Christ against you right now, kingdom of darkness! Be now helpless against the blood of Jesus Christ. Bow the knee to the Lord Jesus Christ NOW, in Jesus' name. Witchcraft curses canceled null and void, causeless, in Jesus' name, by the power of the blood of Jesus. Thank you, Jesus. Thank you, Lord.

☐ "I proclaim right now, in the name of Jesus, that in place of witchcraft, everywhere in place of witchcraft, shall come the fire of the Holy Ghost. Holy Ghost fire, Holy Ghost fire, Holy Ghost fire be released against all witchcraft and anywhere that witchcraft is operating, in the name of Jesus! Thank you, Lord. Thank you, Jesus.

☐ "Let the power of the fire of the Holy Ghost come upon every one that's practicing witchcraft. Oh, Holy Ghost fire, come upon every one that's practicing witchcraft — so hot, so hot, so hot. Bring them to their knees. Put them on their faces before Jesus Christ. Release repentance into "them — a free gift — in Jesus' name! Holy Ghost, reveal their Savior to them — Jesus Christ! They shall cry out to Jesus to save them, and He will hear their cries and bring them out of sin into salvation, in Jesus' name!

☐ "In the name of Jesus, I proclaim that everyone who has been practicing witchcraft on any level, that the fire of the Holy Ghost is upon them right now burning up every remnant of witchcraft and driving that individual to their knees and on their face into repentance to the Lord Jesus Christ, crying out to Jesus, right now. So be it, in Jesus' name.

☐ "In the name of Jesus Christ of Nazareth and by the power of HIS blood, I speak to every curse of witchcraft that's coming against _____ right now — any curses of witchcraft that are coming against the life, blessings, and divine purpose and plans for _____ must go right back to the place from where they were sent, right now, in Jesus' name! I close the door to any and all witchcraft curses coming against _____. They must never come near them again, and I seal those doors with the blood of Jesus and cover _____ in the blood of Jesus Christ!

☐ "I speak to every curse of witchcraft that's been sent to harm God's prophets, leaders, and teachers. Go right back to the place from where you were sent, right now, in the name of Jesus and by the power of the blood of Jesus Christ. I close the door to every curse of witchcraft and seal it in the blood of Jesus. Holy Spirit, come and fill every prophet of God with a greater anointing, in Jesus' name.

- ☐ *"I speak to every curse of witchcraft that's come to harm God's people and our children, every curse of witchcraft that's coming against the intercessors of God, to go right back to the place from where it was sent, right now, in the name of Jesus. I close the door to all witchcraft curses and seal it in the blood of Jesus Christ.*

- ☐ *"Holy Spirit, I ask You to come upon every person that is interceding and praying to God — every intercessor — Lord, let your Holy Spirit come upon them and give them a greater anointing, favor, and answered prayers, in Jesus' name.*

- ☐ *"Father, in the name of Jesus, I ask You to release more angel armies on the earth and around Your people. In the name of Jesus, I ask for more heavenly hosts and more of Your angels and more special forces armies of God to come right now into the earth and destroy every unholy, ungodly power and principality that's been operating in the earth. Bash it; trash it; kick it out; drag it all out to the uninhabited dry place. Bind it; shackle it, and imprison every unholy, ungodly principality for it no longer has power to remain, in Jesus' name.*

- ☐ *"Father, I ask You, by the power of the blood of Jesus Christ, to send Your special forces angels, Your arresting angels, Father God, to go and arrest any remaining demonic principalities that are operating in the earth. Bind them; shackle them; cage them up; drag them to the uninhabited dry places where they will stay until Jesus Christ comes and tells them where to go, in Jesus' name. Close the door to them and seal it forever like Joshua did with the evil kings, with the despots. You had Joshua take the despots out of the promised land and seal them in a cave and burn them. We stand upon that right now, in the name of Jesus, that You, Father God, are doing the same right now for us, in the name of Jesus.*

- ☐ *"Father, raise up Your holy, godly, anointed leaders. Give them favor, favor, favor. Give them more angel armies to fight for them. O defender of Israel, Archangel Michael, raise up an even mightier army. More, God; more, God; more angels to fight alongside Archangel Michael for Israel, for Israel is forever. God's plans and purposes shall prevail in the land of Israel. Jerusalem is God's darling — God's jewel. Let the plans and purposes of Almighty God go forth for Israel and Jerusalem. O Archangel Michael, defender of Israel, destroy the enemies in your wake. Destroy them beneath your feet!*

Trample them with your angel armies. Nothing shall come against God's people. Nothing shall come against Israel, in the name of Jesus. Thank You, Lord.

- *"Father God, You had us study the book of Zechariah. You've told us what You're doing with the spirit of wickedness. You're taking that vile spirit of wickedness and putting it into a basket and sealing it with a heavy talent of lead and making the demons take it out to a special place You have for it where it will stay in exile forever. Wickedness shall never bother Your people again. This is what we want, Father, and we want it right now. We ask for it, in the name of Jesus, Father God, for You to take that vile spirit of wickedness that has been operating in the earth, according to the book of Zechariah, stuff that spirit of wickedness in that basket that You have and put that heavy talent of lead on it. We ask You to crush the mouth of wickedness and seal it in that basket with that heavy talent of lead and, just like it says in the book of Zechariah, you will have the demons take out their own trash and put them all in that special place You have for them where they will stay until Jesus Christ comes and tells them where to go, and that wickedness will never bother us or Your children again because this is the time of Your glory, God.*

- *"This is the time of the outpouring of Your Holy Spirit upon all flesh. Your sons and daughters shall prophesy. This is the time of the Billion Soul Harvest for Jesus Christ. This is the time for the preparation of the bride of Christ without spot or wrinkle. Raise up Your teachers, Your prophets, Your leaders, O God. Raise up Your evangelists. Revival, revival, revival, restoration, and renewal — let the fire of the Holy Ghost ignite over the United States of America and over every nation thereof, in the name of Jesus. Blow the victory trumpet of the Lord. Yahweh has fought for us. Yahweh is victorious. Jesus Christ is Lord and King of all the Nations. So be it, in Jesus' name!"*

Prayers For Calming The Storm In Your Mind

The Storm In Your Mind Can Rise Up When You Are Getting Close To Your Promise

If you are in the process of crossing over the other side into the next level of your promise, the enemy may try to bring storms against you. Many times the storm is in your own mind. The devil tells you lies about yourself and tries to make you feel like a failure, fearful, and even keeps your head spinning in confusion about the course you are on, but you have the authority of Jesus. You speak to that storm! Command it to be still now!

Decree Out Loud

- ☐ *"I am on a path to my DIVINE promise and nothing can come against it. I am filled with the Holy Spirit, and I have the authority of the King of kings, my Lord Jesus Christ. I take authority over every storm in my mind of fear, lies, chaos, and confusion, and in the name of Jesus, I command all fear, lies, chaos, and confusion to cease now and be still, in Jesus' name! I invite You, Holy Spirit, to be the only spirit operating in my mind, soul, and spirit, and I declare that I have the mind of Christ! I live in the complete power, peace, and shalom of the kingdom of God because I am seated with Christ right now next to the throne of the Father! Thank You, Jesus!!"*

Whooo hooo!!! Get to the other side because Jesus is with you on this journey! Use the authority He gave you! Every time any little storm starts to swirl up in your mind, say this command: Peace Be Still!

Prayer For A Clean Heart - New Heart For God

Declare These Heart Scriptures Over Your Yourself Or Loved One

- ☐ "In Jesus' name, I proclaim _____ has a heart after God's own Heart!"

- ☐ "In Jesus' name, I declare Ezekiel 36:26 -27 over _____. The Lord will give you, _____, a new heart and put a new spirit within you, _____. The Lord will take the heart of stone out of your flesh, _____, and give you a heart of flesh. And the Lord will put HIS spirit within you, _____, and cause you to walk in HIS statutes, and _____ shall keep all the Lord's judgments, and do them, IN JESUS' NAME!"

- ☐ "In Jesus' name, I declare Jeremiah 32:39 over _____ and the Lord will give _____ one heart and one way, so that _____ will fear THE LORD always, for _____'s own good and for the good of _____'s children after _____, IN JESUS' NAME!"

- ☐ "In Jesus' name, I declare Jeremiah 24:7 over _____. The Lord will also give _____ a heart to know Me, for I am the Lord; and _____'s household and descendants will be My people, and I will be their God, for they will return to Me wholeheartedly, IN JESUS' NAME! SO BE IT! SO IT IS! AMEN!"

Updated: Prayer To Remove Spiritual Arrows and Daggers

My friends, this is a huge revelation that the Holy Spirit has given me to share with you! He has shown me that many of us are walking around with spiritual arrows, daggers, knives, and darts that have been thrown at us by wicked words spoken over us or even from the works of the enemy against our assignments for God's Kingdom. When we have not asked the Lord to remove them, we continue to allow the weapons of the enemy to take away all of our energy, zest, and clarity for what God has called us to do. These spiritual arrows can even cause physical weakness.

Stand Up And Pray This Prayer Out Loud To Call On The Ministering Angels Of The Lord To Remove These Arrows, Knives, And Darts Out Of You And To Receive Your Healing And Breakthrough!

- ☐ *"Father God, I come to You in the name of Your Son, Jesus Christ. I humbly ask You, Father God, to send Your ministering angels to me (or loved one's name) right now to pull out every spiritual knife, dagger, arrow, spike, and flaming dart that the enemy has thrown or stabbed in me over the years. I also ask that the angels of the Lord assigned to minister to me remove and uproot anything that You, Father God, have not planted in me or my life!*

- ☐ *"This is according to Your word in Matthew 15:13-14 where Jesus said, 'Every plant which my heavenly Father hath not planted, shall be rooted up.' I ask now that any demonic seeds be uprooted from me and my life and cast into the fire, in Jesus' name! I also ask that any spiritual chains, ropes, bands, tethers, yokes, weights, vices, or any devices of the demonic be removed from me and my life, in Jesus' name!*

- ☐ *"In Jesus' name, let the angels of the Lord now assigned to me, remove in the spiritual and the natural, any demonic marks, tattoos, piercings, scars, clothing, soul wounds, or cell wound memories. I pray for healing from those wounds and cell memories and for all cursed items to be removed, such as clothing or jewelry. I sever off all unholy, ungodly soul ties and renounce all ungodly covenants, in Jesus' name! I come out of agreement with these lying spirits now! Let the angels of the Lord pull all of these evil weapons and demonic devices out of me so that they will be loosed off of me, removed from my possession, and cast into the fire of God to be burned to ashes, in Jesus' name. I invite the Holy Spirit to come and fill all these places in me forever!*

- ☐ *"I also ask the Angels of the Lord now assigned to me to flush all toxins and parasites out of my body safely and quickly! I renounce and cancel any curses and demonic assignments or any negative words, even the things I've said over myself, and renounce any Jezebel spirit or spirit of betrayal!*

- ☐ *"Now, I speak to the ministering angels that are here with me right now. Thank you for coming and for your obedience to God to minister to me. I command you by the authority of Jesus Christ to pull out and remove from me any and all remaining weapons of the enemy right now, in the name of Jesus. Pull out and remove forever every arrow, dart, dagger, knife, spike, sword, rope, chain, or any other weapon or device that you see on me or in me that is not of God! Remove all razor marks, needle marks, ink markings, pin marks, thorns, or slivers! Remove any and all demonic blocks, blinders, scales, or veils from the eyes, ears, and mouth. Clear all my gateways in the natural and spiritual! These weapons, blocks, and devices of the enemy are no longer allowed to remain, in Jesus' name! I am a child of God, redeemed by the blood of Jesus!*

- ☐ *"I ask the angels of the Lord now assigned to me to remove every dagger of Jezebel and every dagger of betrayal out of my heart and back now, in Jesus' name!*

- ☐ *"Father God, I thank You for sending Your ministering angels to come to my aid at this very moment and pull these evil weapons and devices all out of me and my life! I praise you, Father God, and worship You and Your Son, Jesus Christ. I thank You, Father God, for the authority You have given me as a believer in Jesus Christ and for all the benefits of Your Kingdom — including Your angelic assistance!*

- ☐ *"Now, I speak to the ministering angels that are here with me right now. Thank you for coming, and I command you by the authority of Jesus Christ to pull out and remove from me all weapons of the enemy right now, in the name of Jesus. Pull out and remove forever every arrow, dart, dagger, knife, spike, sword, rope, chain, or any other weapon or device that you see on me or in me. Remove all razors, needles, ink, markings, pins, thorns, or stakes, and any demonic blocks, blinders, scales, or veils from the eyes. These weapons or marks of the enemy are no longer allowed to remain, in Jesus' name!*

- ☐ *"Lord Jesus, come and pour Your blood on my wounds from where those darts, arrows, and daggers were and any other wounds where any weapons of the enemy were removed. I ask You, Lord Jesus, to wash my wounds with Your blood. I ask Your ministering angels to apply the healing balms of Gilead on those wounds and pour the oil of the Holy Spirit upon them and to then refresh me with fresh oil. I ask these ministering angels to strengthen me to go into battle again. This time, as the Lord is my shield and buckler and I have my shield of faith, no more weapons formed against me will prosper, and every tongue that rises up against me, You shall condemn, O Lord. And I'm not afraid of the terror by night nor by the arrow that travels by day because You are my shield and buckler, Father God, according to Your word in Psalm 91.*

- ☐ *"I now put on my full Armor of God daily as described in Your word, Father God, in Ephesians 6:10-20 and put up my shield of faith and quench all the fiery darts of the wicked, in Jesus' name!*

- ☐ *"Father, I ask that You remove the scales off my eyes, and lift any veils — I want to see into the spirit realm. Give me eyes of understanding in Your wisdom and truth. Send your warrior angels to go before me and scatter my enemies and flank me day and night with Your sentry angels covering me with their fiery swords and shields. I ask this all in the name of my Lord Jesus Christ. Amen."*

Now, thank and praise God the Father! Thank the Lord Jesus for giving His authority to ask for this help, and thank the angels for their assistance!

For your daily "Suiting Up" strategy for taking your Seat of Authority in Christ and to fully cover yourself, your family, and your home, see my "Daily Suit Up Prayer" strategy here in the book.

Stay strong in the Lord, my friends!

Renouncing And Breaking Unholy Covenants – Prayer And Decree To Renounce Freemasonry

Why should we come before God and repent for any unholy covenants? Because our God is all about covenants. They are very important to Him, and He even sacrificed His only Son to have a way, through the blood of Jesus, that we can all fully return to one holy covenant with Him, the one true God — the God of Abraham, Isaac, and Jacob. God will bless those who are in covenant with Him alone like He did Abraham (Genesis 15). When you are in covenant with other things besides God, especially unholy things, many of your blessings can be held back. Why? Because the accuser (Revelation 12:10) is in the Courts of Heaven accusing us — the brethren, the people of God — night and day of sin and any covenants that we or our ancestors entered into that are against God. How do we know what an unholy covenant is? Can some agreements (both written and verbal) that we were in with business, religion, groups, and personal relationships in our past still be used to hold us back in life? The answer is YES!

Unholy covenants can include Freemasonry (the most evil) on you or your family's bloodline, secret societies and fraternities and sororities, past relationships and engagements other than your current spouse, written agreements with a past employer, witchcraft covenants, finger prick blood brothers or blood sisters as a child, or any covenant promise to any person, club or organization that swears allegiance to instead of God.

We should only be in one holy covenant with Almighty God through Jesus Christ. Even your covenants with your spouse or your church or allegiance to your nation should be made in the name of Jesus unto God and under God. God first, then your marriage, then your family, then your country. All should be through God and unto God for His glory and hand to be upon it. If not, you are held captive to those unholy covenants and even your ancestors and children until they are verbally repented for and broken off in the name of Jesus! LET'S GET FREE NOW!

Renouncing Unholy Covenants - Decree And Pray Out Loud
(This Can Also Be Done In A Courts Of Heaven Appearance)

> ☐ *"Father God, I come before You to confirm by faith that I stand on and agree fully with YOUR word now, according to Galatians 2:20, that 'I am crucified with Christ: nevertheless I live; yet not I, but Christ liveth in me: and the life which I now live in the flesh I live by the faith of the Son of God, who loved me, and gave himself for me.' Therefore, Father God, my testimony is this: Through the blood of Jesus Christ, I am redeemed out of the hand of the devil — spirit, soul, and body. I belong to Jesus Christ. I am sanctified and set apart to You, Father God, by the blood of Jesus.*

- ☐ *"Thank You, Jesus, that Your blood speaks for me before our Father God night and day on the Mercy Seat! Thank You, Father, for grace and mercy! Father God, I come before You, and I renounce, rebuke, revoke, and cancel all unholy covenants that I have ever made in my life and those that my ancestors made in their lives, including freemasonry and any other society; witch coven; luciferian organization, fraternity, or sorority; employer; or other person or cult going all the way back to Adam and Eve, in Jesus' name!*

- ☐ *I repent, Father God, for these unholy covenants in my life and my ancestors' lives, and I ask for Your grace, mercy, and forgiveness! Lord Jesus, wash away my sins with Your blood and wash my ancestral bloodline clean with Your precious blood, Lord Jesus! I decree today that the only Covenant I am in from this day forward is one HOLY COVENANT with Almighty God through the blood of Jesus Christ! I also decree this over my bloodline, in Jesus' name!*

- ☐ *Father God, I ask that all records of unholy covenants be wiped off my record books and the record books of my ancestors in the Courts of Heaven by the blood of Jesus and remembered no more for Your Sake and mine! Father God, I also ask that my entire bloodline — my children and all my generations thereof — and I be released and set free from all consequences of these sins and unholy covenants, in Jesus' name! I ask that the NEW HOLY COVENANT that I have with You, Father God, through Jesus Christ be written and decreed now in my record books in Heaven, and that this record of repentance will be made available for all of my future court appearances in Your holy Courts, Father God, from this day forward, in Jesus' name. Thank You, Father God, for Your grace and mercy and forgiveness! Amen, and so be it!"*

See my teaching and prayer on "How To Appear in the Courts of Heaven to Cleanse Your Family Bloodline and Remove Generational Curses" here in the book.

It's time for you to get FREE of all entanglements that would try to hold back your destiny! It's time for great blessings and breakthroughs to come forth in your life, family, household, finances, ministry, and business! Whooo hooooo!!!

MAKE SURE YOU REMOVE AND BURN OR THROW AWAY ANYTHING TO DO WITH FREEMASONRY OR ANY UNHOLY, UNGODLY COVENANTS THAT MAY BE IN YOUR HOME! DO NOT SELL THESE ITEMS!

Steps To Remove Demonic Frequencies Out Of Your Home And Bring In The Frequency Of God

Are you having a hard time praying or even dealing with distraction, discord, and strife in your home? It's time to deal with these demonic frequencies and get them moved out and usher in the frequency of God!

DO THE STEPS IN THE TEACHING FIRST AND THEN USE MY PRAYER BELOW

Steps

1. Suit up with armor and take authority in Christ (See my Suit Up Prayer here in the book.)
2. Repent for sins on home, land, and family (Repent in the Courts of Heaven. See "How to Appear in the Courts of Heaven" here in the book.)
3. Dedicate home, land, and family to God (Do a land assignment. See "How To Do A Land Assignment" here in the book.)
4. Invite the Holy Spirit and anoint your home (See "How To Pray Over And Apply Anointing Oil" here in the book.)
5. Do spiritual housecleaning (Clean demonic clutter with this "How To Remove Demons From Your Home - Spiritual Housecleaning Prayer" here in the book.)
6. Partner with Heaven and the angel armies of God (See prayer below)
7. Bring in the frequencies of God daily into your home (See below)

Pray Out Loud

☐ *"Father God, I ask, in Jesus' name, for You to send Your warrior angels and heavenly hosts over me and my household to take us off of the frequency of the demonic. Scatter Your enemies, O God, far, far away from me and block them and smite them down with Your fiery swords and shields so the demonic cannot see, hear, perceive, or touch me, my family, or my household at all today, in Jesus' name! I invite the HOLY SPIRIT to come and hover over me and FILL my household so the ONLY frequency we operate on is YOUR FREQUENCY and YOUR KINGDOM, Almighty God! Amen!"*

Bring The Frequencies Of God Into Your Home

If you don't have a shofar, you can play a recording of the shofar to usher in the angelic of God and bring the frequency of God into your home. I try to blow my own shofar as much as I can at my front door and even in my home and studio.

UNDERSTAND, there is a "frequency" that is a sound and vibration that is of the demonic just as there is also a sound and vibration that is of God. This is not "New Age." They stole that term and twisted it! It always belonged to God! God created the world with a sound, a word. He spoke it into existence, and HIS sound is what is holding creation together. This is in the Bible.

The demonic tries to come against this with their sounds, particularly in music. God's frequency is 444 MEGAHERTZ. This is the KEY OF KING DAVID. Young King David played his harp in this key and demons fled! Read about David playing his harp for Saul! The sound of the shofar — the ram's horn — is the sound of the voice of God in battle and summons the angel armies and releases a heavenly vibration and frequency that destroys demonic strongholds. This is what took down the walls of Jericho!

This is all being re-discovered now. Our music used to be tuned to godly frequencies, such as 444, 396, 528, and 432. During the Nazi era, they changed it to 440 which is demonic! Look at the Holy Spirit-based teachings and music of Michael Tyrrell of Wholetones. He has a list of GODLY FREQUENCIES. Johnny Cash and old gospel musicians knew to tune their instruments to 528, which is a godly frequency! Study up on this, and fill your home and atmosphere with GODLY FREQUENCIES.

RESOURCES FOR GODLY FREQUENCIES AND MUSIC

Shofar Sounding and Recordings

Wholetones by Michael Tyrrell

John E Kelly Music 444hz

Healing Sounds By John Tussey

David's Harp By Peregrinnatti

This is a very good practice in your home to bring peace. If you are dealing with major discord in your home and family, look into my "Removing Discord Prayers" here in the book.

How To Pray The Prayer of Jabez Over Yourself and Your Loved Ones

Edited Transcript Of Biblical Teaching And Prayer Based On 1 Chronicles 4:10

This is the most powerful prayer that you can pray over yourself and your loved ones in the word of God! You will see the hand of God move swiftly in them because the word of God is the will of God for your life and the life of your loved ones.

1 Chronicles 4:10 (KJV): "And Jabez called on the God of Israel, saying, Oh that thou wouldest bless me indeed, and enlarge my coast, and that thine hand might be with me, and that thou wouldest keep me from evil, that it may not grieve me! And God granted him that which he requested."

We see in 1 Chronicles 4:9, that Jabez's mother named him after the pain of childbirth. Jabez means, "I bore him in pain." He was going around his whole life thinking he was terrible, but as he got older, he was like, "No, this isn't who I am!" So he went before God and said, "Lord God, take this evil away from me that it'll never touch me again, and expand my territory. Bring me out." He wanted to be brought out of it, and he wanted to go out and expand his territory.

You see, the enemy tries to put labels on our children — Jabez labels. For example, "Your child is autistic. Your child is bi-polar. Your child is ADHD, etc." The enemy tries to put all of these labels on our children. But Jabez said, "Wait a minute, I'm not going to take that label! I'm going to go before God because I want my territory expanded. I'm not just going to sit around here and be stuck with a label. That's not who I am. I am who God says I am!"

Look at your children or your spouse today and say to them, "You are who God says you are. Don't believe any negative word that any teacher, any adult, any bully, or any doctor ever put on you. Those negative words are canceled off of you, in the name of Jesus. You are who God says you are. I pray this prayer of Jabez over you that your territory is now expanded. Go out to all the world and share the Good News." Ask the Holy Spirit to use you (your child, spouse, etc) to meet people right where they are for Jesus, and for Jesus to meet them right where they are!

If anyone ever put a negative label on you or your children, you repent, renounce, cancel, and come out of agreement with those labels and negative words in the name of Jesus, and pray the prayer of Jabez over you or them right now!

Pray Out Loud Over Yourself

- ☐ *"Father, I believe in what You did for Jabez. I believe this word is for me today, and it's for my child (or spouse, grandchild, etc). I believe right now that you did it for Jabez, and I ask now that you do it for me (my child, my spouse, etc), in Jesus' name. Father, I believe this, and I want it! Father God, according to Your word in 1 Chronicles 4:10, Jabez called upon You, O Lord, God of Israel, that You would bless him indeed and enlarge his coast, enlarge his territory, and that Your hand would be with him and that You would keep him from all evil, that it would never grieve him again, and that You granted it for him. I want this. I want the same thing. So Father, in the name of Jesus, I call upon You right now, O Lord, God of Israel, that You would bless me indeed and enlarge my coast, enlarge my territory, and that Your hand would be with me and You would keep me from all evil that it will not ever grieve me, and that You grant my request right now, in Jesus' name."*

Pray Out Loud Over Your Loved Ones

- ☐ "Father God, according to Your word in 1 Chronicles 4:10, I call upon You, O Lord, God of Israel, that You would bless my loved one, _____, indeed, and enlarge their territory, that Your hand will be with them, that You would keep them from all evil, that no evil will ever greive them, and that You grant this request right now on behalf of my loved one, _____, in Jesus' name."

Declare Out Loud

- ☐ "My loved ones, _____, and I are blessed. We are doing the work of the kingdom of God!"

RESOURCES

Do you have a child that you are struggling with in understanding how they're "wired by God" and how to parent them? Visit the following website for some Holy Spirit-filled, Christian based Godly parenting strategies:

Kirk Martin - Celebrate Calm - Calm Christian Parenting
celebratecalm.com

Bonus!!
Faithful Decrees

SPEAK These Faithful Decrees

- [ ] *Thank you, God, for causing me to see _____ coming to full fruition in the spirit and in the natural for my life, in Jesus' name!*
- [ ] *I decree that I am designed by God for a heavenly purpose.*
- [ ] *I decree that this is a year of purpose and divine alignments.*
- [ ] *I decree that I am fulfilling those things that are written in my destiny scroll.*
- [ ] *I decree that God is accelerating me and redeeming the time and good things that were lost.*
- [ ] *I decree that I was sent to Earth for such a time as this!*
- [ ] *I decree I am coming into a new season of increase and multiplication.*
- [ ] *I decree that every good seed I have planted into God's Kingdom is coming to full harvest for me and my household.*
- [ ] *I decree that I have 20/20 vision in the natural and supernatural.*
- [ ] *I decree my discernment is getting stronger and God is showing me the hidden things.*
- [ ] *I decree that I speak what I see by faith and God will perform it according to His word in Jer.1:11.*
- [ ] *I decree that my loved ones around me who were spiritually blind are now being given eyes of understanding.*
- [ ] *I decree I will see all God's promises manifest in my life, in Jesus' name!*

MORE POWERFUL DECREES

- ☐ *THE GLORY OF GOD IS MY COVERING!*
- ☐ *THE FAVOR OF GOD SURROUNDS ME AS A SHIELD!*
- ☐ *THE ANGELS OF THE LORD ENCAMP AROUND ME AND PROTECT ME!*
- ☐ *THE LORD GOD GOES BEFORE ME. HIS HORNETS DESTROY THE ENEMIES OUT OF MY PROMISED LAND!*
- ☐ *THE LION OF JUDAH ROARS OVER ME AND BEFORE ME!*
- ☐ *MY HOUSEHOLD AND I SERVE THE LORD. THEREFORE, WE ARE CHOSEN AND HIGHLY FAVORED!*
- ☐ *I HAVE GODLY WISDOM OF THE HOLY GHOST. HE IS MY GUIDE AND CONFIDENCE!*
- ☐ *I AM SEATED WITH THE LORD JESUS CHRIST — THE NAME ABOVE ALL NAMES!*
- ☐ *I RULE AND REIGN THROUGH CHRIST! I PUT ALL DARKNESS UNDER MY FEET!*
- ☐ *THE BLOOD OF JESUS COVERS ME, AND I WALK IN THE GLORY LIGHT OF JESUS CHRIST!*
- ☐ *I AM A CHILD OF THE MOST HIGH GOD!*
- ☐ *THE ENEMY SCATTERS AT THE SOUND OF MY VOICE BECAUSE OF THE AUTHORITY IN CHRIST I CARRY!!*

IN JESUS' MIGHTY NAME!

INDEX

Anointing:
Pages
20, 32, 45, 47, 48, 50, 52, 53, 54

Blessings:
Pages
20, 32, 45, 47, 60, 66, 167, 175, 186, 193, 250

Breaking Covenants, Soul Ties:
Pages
32, 45, 86, 111, 137, 177, 221, 250

Children:
Pages:
20, 60, 66, 86, 111, 167, 175, 176, 177, 181
197, 205, 255

Curses:
Pages
20, 32, 45, 48, 60, 66, 70, 82, 86, 111, 137
205, 217, 231, 241, 247, 250, 253

Deliverance:
Pages
16, 20, 32, 45, 47, 48, 50, 66, 70, 82, 86, 111
137, 203, 221, 231, 240, 241, 247, 250

Discernment:
Pages
32, 60, 162, 221, 231

Discord:
Pages
20, 32, 48, 231, 253

Divination, Witchcraft:
Pages
9, 32, 60, 70, 82, 86, 111, 137, 221, 241, 250

Dreams:
Pages
20, 60, 167

Grace / Favor :
Pages
9, 20, 66, 164

Government:
Pages
70, 86, 111, 137

Healing:
Pages
20, 66, 70, 197, 200, 203, 205

Heart, Mind and Soul:
Pages
45, 205, 217, 245, 246

Holy Spirit:
Pages
20, 47, 48, 53, 181, 197, 200, 203, 205, 212

House / Rooms:
Pages
20, 32, 45, 47, 48, 50, 52, 53, 54

Land / Property:
Pages
20, 66, 70, 82

Marriage / Spouse:
Pages
167, 175, 177, 181, 197, 205, 255

Money / Finances / Inheritance
Pages:
66, 111, 186, 193

Prodigals:
Pages

66, 167, 177, 181, 205

Purchases:
Pages
20, 54

Teeth / Mouth:
Pages
200

Repentance / Sins:
Pages
66, 70, 82, 86, 111, 137, 211, 212

About Annamarie Strawhand - Faith Lane Ministries

Christian Faith Leader, Coach, Author, and Prophetic Intercessor

Annamarie Strawhand is passionate about helping people discover their gifts and fully come into their true calling and divine purpose for the Kingdom of God.

Her highly anticipated book and dynamic teaching, *Faith At Full Speed,* is a step-by-step guide for those who want to reach their life, career, and business goals at full speed while powerfully building their faith.

During the last several years of ministry, and while praying for others during Annamarie's broadcasts, many prayers and prayer strategies have been written, collected, and organized into a book of "Faith and Victory Prayers." This is the first volume of the collection of prayers.

Annamarie was called by God to promote His goodness and point and direct people to His amazing promises for their lives. After years of coaching professional race car drivers, God called Annamarie to coach and teach HIS people how to be victorious in their lives and purpose for the Kingdom of God. She has mentored many individuals on how to receive divine breakthroughs and blessings beyond their wildest expectations! God wants you running your race strong!

Join Annamarie and her ministry team on Monday, Wednesday, and Friday mornings at 11am Eastern for *Faith Lane Live* online faith teaching, encouragement, and strategies on how to activate your gifts and reach your goals — to truly walk in your divine purpose.

You can also join Annamarie as a prayer intercessor to pray over the Nation. An American Patriot at heart, she believes strongly in the American dream, and that America was founded for the Gospel of Jesus Christ. She has led "boots on the ground" intercessory prayer groups to pray for our country, our children, and our leaders and to bring our Nation back to God.

Enjoy Annamarie's encouraging videos, prophetic words, and biblical success teachings by subscribing to her broadcasts. Visit her website for more prayer strategies, prophetic words and bible teachings at www.annamariestrawhand.com.

"All of Heaven Is Cheering You On!" Hebrews 12

"All things work together for good to them that love God, to them who are the called according to his purpose." Romans 8:28

www.ingramcontent.com/pod-product-compliance
Lightning Source LLC
Chambersburg PA
CBHW080535170426
43195CB00016B/2569